Lee George

Our Lady of America

Liturgically Known as Holy Mary of Guadalupe

Lee George

Our Lady of America
Liturgically Known as Holy Mary of Guadalupe

ISBN/EAN: 9783337242879

Printed in Europe, USA, Canada, Australia, Japan

Cover: Foto ©Lupo / pixelio.de

More available books at **www.hansebooks.com**

HOLY MARY OF GUADALUPE.

OUR LADY OF AMERICA

LITURGICALLY KNOWN AS

HOLY MARY OF GUADALUPE.

BY

Rev. G. LEE, C. S. Sp.

"Hail, Mother, clad in light,
the light that sets not."
Eph. Fr.

JOHN MURPHY & CO., Publishers,
Printers to the Holy See and to the Cardinal Archbishop of Baltimore.
BALTIMORE and NEW YORK.
1897.

CONTENTS.

	PAGE.
PREFATORY NOTE	v
CHAPTER I. PRELIMINARY	1
II. ROME AND GUADALUPE	16
III. LEO XIII. AND GUADALUPE	31
IV. GUADALUPE AND THE MEXICAN HIERARCHY	43
V. GUADALUPE AND THE MEXICAN NATION	59
VI. HISTORICAL GROUNDS OF THE DEVOTION	73
VII. THE INDIAN NARRATIVE	96
VIII. THE PICTURE	114
IX. THE SHRINE	133
X. THE MIRACLES	151
XI. OTHER REPORTED MIRACLES	175
XII. THE FRUITS	191
XIII. THE FRUITS (CONTINUED)	208
XIV. THE PATRONAGE	232
XV. THE CORONATION	251
XVI. CONCLUSION	271
INDEX	287

PREFATORY NOTE.

A HUNDRED years ago the author of the *Pensil Americano* ventured the assertion that the Miracle of Holy Mary of Guadalupe (Gwa-da-loó-pay) was "a prodigy which, in all its circumstances, will ever be heard of with transports of admiration." I wish the prediction may prove as true for my readers as it has for many others. The Guadalupan story is unmixedly admirable: it needs but fair telling to win every Catholic heart. Though I have studied, both at the Shrine and through the country, all that concerns this first of American devotions, I shall, as far as convenient, make Mexican authors speak; for in this matter no one else can think and feel as they do.

Among early writings I find best guidance in the *Felicidad de México* (1667) of the Oratorian, and University Professor, Father Becerra Tanco; and in the *Estrella del Norte* (1686) of the Jesuit theologian and historian, Father Francisco Florencia. Of living authors the works to which I am most indebted are those of the learned Canon Vera, now Bishop of Cuernavaca; and of Father Antícoli, who seems to merit an eulogium passed on his Order, and to be indeed "the sound, calm, discriminating Jesuit, who, above all others, has learned how to exercise the constant caution of criticism without injuring his spiritual-mindedness." To this Father's book, *La Virgen del Tepeyac: Compendio Historico-Critico*, I have repeatedly to refer, and shall do so under the abbreviation—Hist. Comp.

Many other works consulted I may mention incidentally. I must also state that different Mexican periodicals, especially the excellent Catholic Daily, *El Tiempo*, with various publications issuing from its office, have furnished me important facts.

But when all ordinary Guadalupan authorities have been acknowledged and thanked, it remains to add that the best inspiration on this American subject is found in Roman and papal documents; and that, beyond all doubt, the most effective preachers of devotion to Holy Mary of Guadalupe are Benedict XIV. and Leo XIII.

Catholics can hardly take full interest in a religious question until they know, in some degree, what the Church of God thinks and says of it. For this reason I shall try to indicate the ecclesiastical standing of Guadalupe, before I enter on the details of its history. It may be fitting, also,— if worth while—to add that all here written is unreservedly submitted to the judgment of the Church; and that the qualifying of facts as supernatural or miraculous—where she has not so qualified them—is merely on the strength of human testimony and human appreciation.

HOLY GHOST COLLEGE,
    PITTSBURG, PA. *Easter*, 1897.

OUR LADY OF AMERICA.

CHAPTER I.

PRELIMINARY.

I BELIEVE that the Mother of God appeared on this continent, and spoke to its people, and left them a wondrous memorial of her visit. The main facts connected with the Guadalupan Apparitions and Picture are morally and historically certain. We may, as we advance, find them theologically and ecclesiastically certain: at least, we shall understand how authors of distinction can speak of theological and infallible certainty in a matter that, objectively, lies outside the domain of dogma and definition.

Holy Mary of Guadalupe has grown into the Catholic life and the sacred liturgy of a whole nation. An entire episcopate has, for more than three centuries and a half, authoritatively corroborated the Guadalupan tradition. The Holy See has repeatedly sanctioned and blessed and, practically, enjoined observances and usages which suppose or imply the certainty of the facts on which this great American devotion is founded. The history of the Church offers few cases of similar authority and authentication in a similar matter.

Catholics are convinced that heavenly apparitions sometimes occur. They see no reason for limiting Divine manifestations to the Old Testament period, or to the age of the Apostles; while they have irresistible motives for accepting some more recent revelations, technically called private or special. Evidently, there is here no question of Catholic Faith; for, the matter on which the Church's faith is exercised was all delivered, either orally or in writing, before the death of St. John. "Our faith," says St. Thomas, "rests on the revelation made to the Apostles and Prophets who wrote the canonical books; but not on any revelation made to other doctors."[1] It is rather an affair of Christian reasonableness, of common sense and consistency. If we are told that somewhere in the Church Our Lord, or His Mother, or an Angel, or a Saint, has appeared, we are not determined to contradict, though we are often far from ready to believe. They may have shown themselves, may have deigned to visit us; in itself the occurrence is neither impossible nor improbable. But the favor is too great, too exceptional, either to be accorded easily or to be easily credited. We want proof and we wait for it.

In some cases the proofs are so strong and abundant—accompanying proofs, and more still consequent ones—that our reserve melts and we deliberately accept the supernatural event. There is doubtless an instinct of faith and faith's graceful sincerity in our assent. There may even be the merit of faith, for great theologians[2] teach that we can, and sometimes should, exercise the Divine virtue on sufficiently accredited private revelations. Yet,

---

[1] I. I., 1. 8.   [2] Suarez, De Lugo, Benedict XIV., Franzlin, etc.

in most cases, it seems rather that we are convinced than that we believe. In fact, we are not asked to believe; we are asked to accept evidence and to be piously consistent.

As most Catholics are slow to admit, in each particular case, that anything so wonderful as a heavenly apparition has really occurred, so when the great event is proved do they generally make much of it. They naturally think that, if the Lord has come or sent to visit them, He does not approve of indifference to such a favor.

It is then somewhat strange and, I think, regrettable, that English-speaking American Catholics pay so little attention to Guadalupe. Supernatural events that concern us all are proved to have occurred there. About Our Lady's Apparition where now is her Shrine, about her orders and promises to the first neophytes of this country—orders and promises which have had a marvellous and most visibly providential effect—about the Picture she left and the miracles that have accompanied its veneration, an intelligent Catholic, who is acquainted with the facts, can hardly allow himself to doubt. Recently the devout Bishop Vargas of Puebla could write from Rome: "My firm and very sincere assent to the admirable Apparition of the Most Holy Virgin Mary of Guadalupe . . . has been or was until lately pious and rational; but now I believe and unshakenly hold it on the teaching and infallible declaration of our holy mother the Catholic Church."[1] Others may state the actual case differently; the practical conclusion is, however, the same: there remains no room for doubt about these Guadalupan, that is, these American wonders.

[1] Pensam. Obisp. sobre Guad., Mex., '94.

That Catholics in this country are so little occupied with Our Lady under the title of Guadalupe may, perhaps, be explained by the fact that they know little about the origin of that title, or about the world of devotion of which it is the centre. Then, too, it has been said that these special revelations have a local when they have not a merely personal significance; and hence that Guadalupe may be left to the Mexicans. True it is that the hill of Tepeyac, sanctified by the Apparitions, belongs to what is now politically the Republic of Mexico; but it is also to be remembered that when Our Lady came American boundaries were unknown: it was one country from the isthmus to the lakes. The new Christians to whom she spoke were Americans; and the ecclesiastic to whom her message was addressed was then the representative of the Church on this continent. She came, as in past centuries it was well understood and freely expressed, for America and for Americans.

In the older Guadalupan panegyrics and other publications we meet frequent indications of the belief that the Apparitions and the Picture were for the whole continent and all its people. The preachers as well as the poets were constantly exclaiming: "Happy America! . . . Favored Americans! . . . America, loved of Mary! . . . O Americans! whence was this to you that the Mother of your Lord should come to you?" Historians and canonists spoke similarly. They style Guadalupe "America's glory and crest."[1] The Picture, in the great Cabrera's treatise on it, is entitled "The American Marvel;"[2] and the author expresses the belief that Our Lady wished for

[1] Opusc. Guad., Madrid, 1785.
[2] Maravilla Americana, Mexico, 1756.

a temple at Guadalupe in which she would be served "by the whole New World." The ecclesiastical censor of the same work asserts that the oath of Guadalupan patronage was emitted in the name of "all North America;" and though this is not literally correct—as we may see farther on—it still indicates the sentiment of the time. Carrillo y Perez called Guadalupe the "American Bouquet," and dedicated his work on it to "The Most Special Mother of the Americans."[1] Similarly the censor of Guiridi y Alcocer's Guadalupan treatise writes: "The Apparition of Our Lady of Guadalupe forms the religious coat of arms of North America."[2] Dr. Campos had earlier declared that "the heavenly Picture illuminates and illustrates the whole of this our hemisphere."[3]

Expressions and titles like those I have quoted—of which examples abound—are a clear indication that the special domain of Holy Mary of Guadalupe in the New World was formerly not supposed to be confined to Mexico or to Spanish America. Indeed the title was and is both known and loved in the Old World likewise. And happily at present Guadalupe seems again to be gently but effectually asserting its claims on all of us. The surge and resurge of devotion to and from the Tepeyac sanctuary is felt far and wide; and piety as well as reverent curiosity is drawing the eyes of many to the Hill of the Apparitions and to the miraculous Picture. We can see a grounded prevision—which we pray may prove a prophecy—in the confident words of one of Mexico's most lately consecrated prelates. "The

[1] Pensil Americano, Mexico, 1793.
[2] Contestacion á Muñoz, Mexico, 1820.
[3] Parecer al *Manifiesto Satisfactorio*, Mex., 1790.

day is near," writes the scholarly Bishop of the new diocese of Cuernavaca, " when the celestial splendors of the most august Virgin of Tepeyac will illumine every temple in the Catholic world."[1] May it prove so, at least in this land of the Apparitions! For the graceful, unworldly, chivalrous ardor, that characterises devotion to Holy Mary of Guadalupe, is of something like need in many humdrum and hurried Catholic lives.

However, Catholics may not all echo our wish. Some do not welcome devotions that rise out of private revelations—hardly, perhaps, welcome the revelations themselves. There may be a trace of the St. Louis spirit in the bearing of such persons : they want no extraordinary proofs of the Faith which they already hold absolutely. But it is possible that there is some misapprehension in regarding special revelations as proofs of religion. These favors seem rather loving importunities to practise what we already believe than arguments for a first acceptance of the Truth. In fact they have mostly been granted to the faithful, or not, at least, to complete unbelievers.

Then, there are those who fight shy of whatever is too manifestly supernatural, especially of asserted modern miracles. Such things they consider aggressively Catholic, knowing them to be in particular disfavor with their non-Catholic friends. The practical remark here is, that there can be little wisdom in consulting those outside the household of the Faith about our likings or dislikings in a matter so exclusive as supernatural religion. It is, indeed, sometimes said that we need not trouble ourselves or others about what is not of faith or strictly obligatory.

---

[1] Pensam. Obisp. sobre Guad., Mex., '94.

But the statement is misleading. Professed indifference to what is possibly or probably or certainly Divine cannot serve any Christian purpose. Experience shows that this worldly-wise moderation never effectually disarms anti-religious prejudice; and careful reading informs us of the fact that our best guides never followed so dubious a path. For, as it has been well said, "to judge from the works of our greatest Catholic divines, it would appear that the deeper theologian a man is the less does he give away to this studious desire of making difficulties easy at any cost short of denying what is positively *de fide*."[1]

Some reference to the direct opponents of the Guadalupan devotion may, perhaps, be expected. It will, however, suffice to speak of them very summarily here, and incidentally elsewhere. They concern an English-speaking Catholic comparatively little. In the first place, I find them, for such a subject and such a length of time, extraordinarily few. Then, too, the whole of their opposition is plainly reducible to crotchet or impiety: this I feel bound to affirm, after a laborious examination of their earlier and later pretences, and of all that is now to be found in the Mexican press and the Mexican libraries. They are either critics who make a fetich of so-called history, and endlessly ask for written records in matters in which authorised traditions and practices are the best and sometimes the only guides; or they are quibblers who demand categorical definitions of a Church in which they themselves most manifestly do not believe.

Guadalupan authors, with great learning and research, have, for centuries and particularly these later years,

[1] Orat. Lives, pref.

refuted point by point every objection advanced. In Mexico this may be useful and even necessary; for the insidious and satanically pertinacious attacks that have long been made on the people's faith, are almost all just now directed against Holy Mary of Guadalupe. Elsewhere Catholics may not see the need of paying attention to every odd reviler of what is so sacred and so fully authorised. In this as in all Christian questions, when we understand the real state of the case objections fall flat. In presence of an "ancient, unvarying, constant tradition," of an unanimous national episcopate, of repeated approvals of the Holy See, and of many proven miracles, what matters to us the sour and illogical carping of a few discontented unbelievers or misbelievers? Real Catholics have never wittingly opposed the Guadalupan teaching or practice—a fact worthy of special notice, considering the freedom ordinarily allowed and always presumed in such affairs. Passion or perversity or ignorance may have momentarily led one or other sincere Catholic to find fault with the common belief of his brethren; but studied attacks have been made only by those who really admit no Divine Revelation, or at least no present teaching Church.

It has been observed that men who go out of their way to resist special manifestations of piety, have invariably about them something that we may call—in no bitter or invidious sense—'the mark of the beast.' They inevitably show in character or conduct the ground and origin of their prejudiced opposition. Hence, knowing them we are at no pains to refute their opinions or assertions: it is enough to know that they are theirs. This manifestation of tainted source is strikingly noticeable in what little opposition there has been to the Guadalupan devotion.

Unfortunately the first to trouble pious Mexicans was a refractory preacher, who, in 1556, just twenty-five years after the Apparitions, publicly arraigned his bishop (Montufar, the second Archbishop of Mexico) for sending the faithful to the Shrine. But the unhappy man hardly knew what he was doing. Such was his jealous rage—apparently because his Order did not get charge of the very Shrine he was attacking—that he wantonly exposed himself to excommunication. He appealed to the secular power in a matter so purely religious and insisted that the King's ministers had sufficient jurisdiction temporal and *spiritual* to coerce the Guadalupan Archbishop and his flock.

This erratic proceeding had no adverse effect on the new devotion. The misled preacher was temporarily secluded, and the people forgot the scandal in redoubling their recourse to the Shrine.[1]

Then for more than two hundred years, while the name and the image of Holy Mary of Guadalupe were spreading over all Spanish America and into many European countries, nothing was heard but praise and thanksgiving. In 1794, however, John Baptist Muñoz, when trying to gain admittance to the liberalised Madrid Academy of History, presented a *Memorial* which aimed at casting doubt on the received account of the memorable events at Tepeyac. His argument was the often discredited negative one of the silence of certain authors. As Muñoz was a man of erudition—though accused of

[1] Informacion sobre un Sermon de Francisco de Bustamente . . ., Sept. 8, 1556, . . . Mex., 1891.

plagiarism—his opposition might seem of some weight. But we easily discount it when we find him elsewhere resisting the spread of devotion to the Sacred Heart, and constituting himself the advocate of the Pistoian revolters against Pius VI.[1] Indeed he plainly took his cue from the Jansenistic synod, among whose 'grievances' were 'devotion to particular images,' 'excessive devotion to the Blessed Virgin,' and 'indulgenced prayers.' Coming from such a school he certainly could not approve of what was done in Mexico.

A friend of Muñoz, Dr. S. T. Mier, is commonly mentioned among the opponents of the Guadalupan devotion. A sermon which he preached on the 12th of December, 1794, gave such scandal that he had to make a retractation. He indeed protested his complete belief in the Miracle of the Apparitions and the Picture; but he so hedged and higgled afterwards that his real mind is problematical. Similar was the case with the eccentric Dr. Bartolache, who set out to prove scientifically the truth of the tradition and the supernatural origin of the Picture. Yet his posthumous work,[2] published by his widow, renders his good faith rather questionable. He and the shifty Dr. Mier had the folly to prefer their own views and proofs to the belief of the common faithful and the authentic teaching of the hierarchy.

Of opposition to the reign of Holy Mary of Guadalupe in Mexico, there was little during the greater part of this century. In the troubled years of civil upheaval most people were glad to follow her banner and wear her insignia. Then with the triumph of a party there came

---

[1] Hist. Comp., p. 333.   [2] Manifiesto Satisfactorio, 1790.

persecution. Latterly there has been a breathing spell, the first consequence of which is that the wonderful recuperation of the plundered Church is enraging all the powers of evil. And as Guadalupe is known to be the well-head of Catholic piety in the country, it is the object of the most fiendish attacks. There is, at present, formed against it a combination of the sacrilegious spoilers of God's house and acre, of the more arrogant atheists, and of a colony of mercenary *Evangelicals*.

But all these plotters are peculiarly unsuccessful 'advocates of the devil.' They have nothing to offer except a nauseating rehash of the old objections, their stock in trade being the silence argument. They certainly annoy Catholics in various ways, especially with injurious pamphlets and press communications which are either anonymous or spuriously attributed to deceased persons and distant places. Possibly also they furnish a passing excuse to one or other boy or man, who has just reached the downward point at which he looks round for a pretext to give up the practice of religion. But unintentionally they do some good.

Occasionally they call forth the ripe ecclesiastical knowledge and keen dialectics of different Guadalupan defenders. The refutations with which they are then honored form pleasant and instructive reading, particularly when they come from the vigorous pen of Bishop Vera or of Father Antícoli, S. J.

The more, also, they oppose the Guadalupan devotion the more the people attach themselves to it. Indeed, the recorded effect of the first overt opposition to the Shrine seems to have proved prophetically figurative. For, immediately after the scandalous pulpit onslaught in 1556, a canonical Information was taken; and the fact was naïvely attested, that "the devotion did not cease, but was rather increasing." On the same occasion a venerable Spanish priest swore to the following significant statement: "He (the preacher) is understood to be annoyed because Spaniards go there (to the Shrine); but for once that we went hitherto we will now go four times."[1]

The same happens to-day. If the faithful Mexicans hear that any one has uttered a word against Holy Mary of Guadalupe, they hasten to prostrate themselves before their Queen and Mother and condole with her, and, perhaps, pray for the blinded sinner. Then pilgrimages grow in frequency and magnitude, while new practices of honor and reparation are lovingly conceived and zealously propagated. If her enemies murmur because her crown is of gold, her children will add to it one of diamonds.

As it is with the simple faithful so is it also with the learned and the studious: an attack on Guadalupe at once occasions an increase in their knowledge of the tradition, and in the strength of their adherence to it. Age by age they put on record the same strong affirmation. Of many instances a few may be mentioned:—

In 1688 the Jesuit historian, Father Florencia, could write: "Let the incredulous and the suspicious, who want not constant tradition but evident certitude, opine as they will; let the Castillos and Torquemadas be silent on what they omitted through caution or inadvertence; what weighs more with me than all the assertions and views which we might wish our authors had left in writing, is the testimony of all the miracles that God has worked

---

[1] Inform., 1556, . . . Test. del P. Salazar.

and is every day working through the most holy Picture of Guadalupe, and in confirmation of the pious belief which the faithful hold concerning it and its accredited origin."[1]

Again Dr. Sartorio in 1820 writes: "That the august Queen of Heaven, with admirable condescension, came to honor and bless America by her Apparitions on the revered hill of Tepeyac, is a truth which for nearly three centuries has held possession of our credence; and we have had the happiness of having even the foreign nations with us in this belief."[2]

And still, in these last years of the nineteenth century, the present distinguished Metropolitan of Mexico can say of the tradition: "A truth so ardently believed by Mexicans is happily too deep-rooted in our hearts to allow us to debase it by submitting it to sterile discussion. And if there was never any call to discuss it—except on the rare occasions when we grieved to see it impugned—much less is there to-day when the Holy See has thought opportune to authorise it in so explicit a manner."[3]

The explicit authorisation to which the Archbishop refers will find its place in the third chapter. Another slightly less recent and, perhaps, less direct one has here to be introduced incidentally. In saying that no real Catholics ever opposed the Guadalupan devotion, I qualified the statement. An absolute exception has also to be mentioned—and one, in the circumstances, that may well be called honorable.

[1] La Estrella del Norte, cap. XII.
[2] Parec. de la Contest. á Muñoz.
[3] Carta Pastoral, 12 de Abril de 1894.

Eight years ago the editor of a Mexican provincial paper put himself in evidence as an opponent of Guadalupe. The Sacred Congregation of the Holy Office judged the matter sufficiently serious to call for its interference; and the Cardinal Secretary in his own name and the name of the other Cardinal Inquisitors General severely reprehended (*summopere reprehenderunt*) the editor's proceeding. That gentleman at once showed himself a sincere, if a momentarily mistaken, Catholic. He published a retractation that may distantly recall Fenelon's. His noble words were: "As we never intended to depart one hair's breath from the doctrine and judgment of the Holy See, or of its high Tribunals and Congregations, we say to all who have read our writings: that we also *most severely reprehend* our way of acting and speaking against the Miracle or Apparitions of the Most Holy Virgin of Guadalupe, and that we revoke, annul, and destroy all our writings in which was conveyed, expressed, understood, or capable of being understood, anything against the Miracle or Apparitions of Our Lady of Guadalupe."[1]

The action of the Holy Office, in the case stated, will, presumably, surprise some readers. All those who knew little or thought little about Guadalupe, might well wonder that Rome should be so quickly aroused by opposition to this far-off American devotion. The surprise is a healthful one: we the better remember that Guadalupe is a great reality. Indeed, to the elements of Catholic life that resemble those connected with the Tepeyac shrine, most of us are liable to pay too little

---

[1] *La Verdad*. Victoria, Tam., 17 de Agosto de 1888.

attention. There is so much that is wonderful in our religion, ordinarily and extraordinarily wonderful, that we grow stolidly familiar with facts of awful import. How many take lightly and indifferently the announcement of Visions and Apparitions in the Church's life past or present! Yet think what such events are and what they imply. That any one from God's presence should come out to us ought surely be enough to shake our Earth to its centre. And what words have we to express the wonder that God's Mother, from her throne above all Saints and Angels, from her seat near her Son, should show herself to poor wayfarers, and ask something of them and give her promises in return?

Undoubtedly the Church's great treasure is *the* Revelation once for all entrusted to her. And yet she is wise to make much of the passing or partial heavenly gleams accorded to her children; and it becomes her to be jealous about their true record and remembrance. All Manning's keenness of insight and thoroughness of Catholicity are reflected in that magisterial saying of his: "Visions, if true, are at all times acts of omnipotence, and no human intelligence can prescribe limits to their effect."[1]

---

[1] Letter to *The Times*, Sept. 8, '73.

CHAPTER II.

ROME AND GUADALUPE.

THE Holy See, it may be boldly but reverently affirmed, believes that the Blessed Virgin appeared at Guadalupe, and that her Picture there venerated is miraculous.

The grounds for this statement are not far to seek. Within these three centuries not less than fifteen Popes have had occasion directly or indirectly to approve of the devotions founded on the Apparitions. I venture to use the word 'directly,' because, as we shall presently see, the acts of several of these pontiffs, notably of Benedict XIV. and Leo XIII., constitute something more than an indirect approval. It may be remarked also that it has been the Popes specially distinguished by liturgical, doctrinal, and historical research and decisiveness, who have most favored the devotion to Holy Mary of Guadalupe. And among these the reigning Pontiff is prominent. He more, perhaps, than any of his predecessors has officially stamped authenticity on the living American tradition, and more effectually sanctioned and encouraged the veneration of the Picture.

Very soon after 1531, the year of the Apparitions, public devotions and pious associations in honor of the Guadalupan Virgin begin to be mentioned. Within the first half century of its existence the Shrine was served by Confraternities of hundreds of members. Whether these earliest practices had any other than episcopal approval it is not possible to say; though some of the Associations seem to have enjoyed privileges and indulgences that neither bishops nor archbishops could ordinarily grant. It is rather unlikely, too, that they, with their Spanish direction and Spanish leanings, would be satisfied with anything less than Rome's approval and blessing. However, no documents on that point are found earlier than 1660.

Since that time at least half the Sovereign Pontiffs have, as occasion offered, affixed their signatures to favorable Guadalupan decrees. In 1663 Alexander VII. sanctioned the formal introduction of the cause for the approval of the existing devotion, and for the granting of a special Office. In 1667 Clement IX. granted a jubilee for the 12th of December—the day of the last Apparition and of the formation of the Picture. The two following Popes approved the Guadalupan Congregations in Mexico, and granted indulgences for their prescribed devotions and for the annual celebration of the 12th of December. Benedict XIII., in 1725, made the Guadalupan sanctuary a Collegiate Church, granting it the rare privilege of a special Chapter of Canons. His immediate successors confirmed that privilege and added others. Under Benedict XIV. the Church of Our Lady was made a Lateran Basilica; Congregations of Holy Mary of Guadalupe were authorised outside Mexico; the Guadalupan Patronage was canonically erected; a special Mass and Office was accorded to New Spain, and soon after extended to all the Spanish dominions. A similar extension of the privilege of the Guadalupan

Mass was made to several religious houses in Italy by Pius VI., about 1785. Pius IX. in 1869 had a chapel dedicated to Holy Mary of Guadalupe in the Church of St. Nicolas at Rome, the immediate object being the better collocation of a miraculous copy of the sacred Picture. Finally Leo XIII., besides commending the devotion, and ordering the Picture crowned in his name and inscribed with verses composed by himself, has accorded most important additions to the special Office.

This list of pontifical favors, though brief and incomplete, is strikingly significant. It surely makes a strong array in favor of Guadalupe and in proof of its claims. If Rome so favored this American devotion it was because she considered its motive demonstrated: that much is plain, even before we enter into details about the nature of some of these concessions.

We must be aware that in these matters the cautious reserve of the Holy See is extreme. Anything new or extraordinary in religion, if noticed at all at Rome, is rigidly scrutinised. And if, after long and calm deliberation, any sanction or encouragement is given, it is usually in very measured terms. Rarely is their direct recommendation and advocacy; most rarely the imposition of anything like obligation, whether canonical, liturgical or devotional. This restrictive attitude of the Church in presence of new special devotions, an attitude little suspected by many, is graphically described by Father Dalgairns. "Let an outburst of feeling," he writes, in his book on the Sacred Heart, "arise in any part of Christendom, the Holy See at once puts itself into a posture of jealousy toward it; if it be accompanied with alleged visions or miracles, so much the worse; the features of the vigilant guardian of the faith instantly wear a look of suspicion. The devotion spreads, and the whole world rings with its triumph; still there is cold, dead silence on the part of Rome. At last some of its zealous friends apply for an authorisation; then all the official gravity of solemn tribunals is exercised upon the question; unenthusiastic theologians coldly weigh it; canonists plead for and against the evidence of its supernaturalness, with the acuteness and the dryness of lawyers; and judges sit upon it like a criminal. Let us not wish it were otherwise; this wariness of the Holy See is a drag, if you will, upon the devotion, but at the same time, it is its guarantee."[1]

This unimpeachable Roman guarantee is held in exceptional fulness by Guadalupe. Rome was asked to authorise and enrich this American devotion, not for vague, uncertain, or general reasons, but categorically because the Blessed Virgin had appeared at a determined place in this New World, and had spoken to the first neophytes; because, too, the wishes and promises of that august Mother were being admirably fulfilled. There was demand, inquiry, opposition, and concession—concession even surpassing the demand. The conclusion is rigorous: the Sovereign Pontiffs—so many of them!—knew what they were doing when, *according to the petition*, they granted extraordinary privileges in honor of Holy Mary of Guadalupe; and knowing how their acts would confirm the Guadalupan belief, they clearly must have held it themselves and wished to confirm it. For, as Bishop Ricards prudently and moderately observes, "if the Holy Father will give his sanction to devotions that

[1] Ch. 1, Hist. of the devotion.

have their origin in the supposed event, or encourages the building of churches and sanctuaries on the spot where the Apparition showed itself, then it is almost certain that the Holy Father himself believes what has been circulated through the Church."[1]

The personal belief of the Vicar of Christ is certainly a strong support for any tradition and a strong motive of credibility, especially the personal belief of a whole series of Pontiffs. But it has to be said that Guadalupe enjoys something more explicit than that. In its favor there has been a public exercise of the Apostolic Authority in deciding and commanding, in prescribing duties and imposing obligations. And this to such a degree, that, however wonderful the Catholic student finds many things connected with the Apparitions and the Picture, what may most agreeably surprise him is Rome's treatment of the whole question. An analysis of certain facts and documents will make this more evident.

About the middle of the seventeenth century, the love and gratitude of the people of New Spain made the civil and religious authorities wish for a higher approval of the national devotion than they themselves could give. They had in fact exhausted their powers. Their great annual feast was well established; but it needed Rome's authority to raise it to a higher rank, and to dignify it with a special and appropriate liturgy. It was desired, too, that the abundant and juridically signed proofs of the Apparitions and of the miraculous origin of the Picture, should finally come under the eyes of the Head of the Church, and be safely laid up in the pontifical archives.

[1] Aletheia, p. 123.

The wishes of these good Guadalupans were, for the time, but partially accomplished. Their envoys who bore to Rome voluminous sworn and most unimpeachable testimonies in support of the miraculous facts at Tepeyac, were well received in the Eternal City. There was however some opposition. Alexander VII. and his successor, Clement IX., showed themselves most favorable to Guadalupe; but the papal court seemed at the moment fixedly determined to oppose what was called the 'canonization of miraculous images.' There appeared also some traces of national jealousy. Italian ecclesiastics complained of not being yet able, after four centuries and with all manner of proofs and petitions, to obtain for Loretto what these Mexicans seemed to think so readily obtainable for their distant Guadalupe. These strangers, too, it was murmured, if pious were arrogant; for they applied to themselves and the Blessed Virgin's favors to them the words of the Psalmist: "Non fecit taliter omni nationi: He hath not done in like manner to every nation."

These minor difficulties might have been smoothed over, had not more serious ones supervened. Clement IX. died in 1670, as did also several other powerful friends of Guadalupe; and the cause seemed thrown back indefinitely. Indeed the delay was long, as the honor of glorifying the American Virgin was reserved for Benedict XIV.

In the pontificate of that great Pope, the people and clergy of New Spain, who had never ceased their demand for a papal approval, were urged to new efforts by the manifest influence of devotion to the sacred Picture in suddenly stopping the ravages of a fearful plague. To the petition long since forwarded for an obligatory Feast with its proper Office and Mass, they now added the supplication for a general canonical Patronage. Holy Mary of Guadalupe, or, as they more definitely put it, Holy Mary in her miraculous Picture of Guadalupe, was to be solemnly declared Principal Patroness of all New Spain. The special envoy chosen was Father Francis Lopez, S. J., and by him the complete documentary processes of the nation's demand were carried to Rome. In Mexico there had preceded most impressive civil and religious ceremonies, to which we may later refer.

The people of New Spain must have been intimately persuaded of the strength of their case, since they confidently sought a decision at the hands of Benedict XIV. That the pontiff was a most thorough and searching canonist and liturgist was matter of common notoriety; and that in questions bearing on his favorite studies he was a strict, if not a severe judge, was proved by experience. To his influence, when he was Promoter of the Faith, is attributed, among other refusals, the rejection of a petition for a Mass of the Sacred Heart—though among the petitioners was the last Catholic Queen of England, a queen, too, who had lost her throne for the Faith, the wife of James II. As pope he made many concessions, but always on clearly established grounds and with much reserve.

To him however the Guadalupans went confidently. Father Lopez obtained an audience; and the scene that followed is lovingly dwelt on by Mexican authors and artists, both because the interview was touching and because it had momentous results. The Procurator had wisely brought to Rome an excellent copy of the Tepeyac

Virgin. It was the work of the best painter then, perhaps, living, Miguel Cabrera, and was considered—at a distance from the original—incomparably beautiful. "The Father Procurator," says the historian Dávila, "holding a rolled canvas in his hand, came before Benedict XIV., and having obtained permission to speak, gave briefly but eloquently the narrative of the Miracle of the Guadalupan Apparition. And while the Pope was listening attentively and wonderingly, the speaker suddenly stopped and cried out: 'Holy Father, behold the Mother of God who deigned to be also the mother of the Mexicans!' Thereupon taking the canvas in both hands, as did once the happy Juan Diego before the venerable Bishop Zumárraga, he unrolled it on the platform occupied by His Holiness. Benedict, who was already moved by the narration, at this unexpected action and at sight of the beauty of the figure, cast himself down before it with the exclamation that has since been the distinctive motto of our amiable and venerable Patroness: *Non fecit taliter omni nationi.* These words of the 107th psalm, applied by the Holy Father to our people, were afterwards introduced into the Office and stamped on the first medals."[1]

It certainly did seem providential that the very text, whose application to themselves was considered arrogant in the Mexicans when first heard at Rome, should, ninety years later, be spontaneously appropriated to them and their Picture by the Sovereign Pontiff himself.

The incident is commemorated in many works of art, very specially so in a magnificent painting which now adorns the renovated Sanctuary.

---

[1] Hist. de la Compañia. . . . T. I., C. 5.

The impression made on Benedict XIV. by the story and the figure of Holy Mary of Guadalupe, must have been great, for eye-witnesses recount that he wept. There is also a Jesuit tradition which reports the Pontiff's saying in substance to Father Lopez, that were he in this country he would go on pilgrimage to the Tepeyac Virgin, not only barefoot but walking on his knees.

This very favorable disposition of the Pope gave promise of the speedy success of the Guadalupan cause. Yet things had to follow their regular course. The proceedings were even interrupted by an unexpected and, for the time, apparently irremovable obstacle. Documents were lost, whose recovery was truly extraordinary —but the details are not for this place. Keeping our thoughts on Benedict XIV., the force of whose pontifical sanction we want to understand, we learn that he sent the proposed Mass and Office to the Congregation of Rites, while he studied the general question of the devotion and the Patronage himself. And when the liturgical documents were returned to him with a favorable vote, he issued his famous letters approving what was asked, and adding spontaneous favors. He embodied in his Brief[1] *Non est Equidem*, the Mexican petition, with a summary history of the Apparitions and Miracles, and the evidences of the popular devotion and generosity. He, also, inserted the new Mass and Office, together with the decree of approval issued by the Congregation of Rites. Then he promulgates his own decision and order in these unmistakable terms :—

---

[1] Mexican writers commonly call it a *Bull;* in form and seal it appears to be a *Brief.* Of course the authority is the same.

"For the greater glory of Almighty God and the
"furtherance of His worship, and for the honor of the
"Virgin Mary, We by these letters approve and confirm
"with apostolical authority the election of the Most Holy
"Virgin Mary under the invocation of Guadalupe, her
"whose sacred image is venerated in the splendid col-
"legiate and parochial church outside the city of Mexico,
"as Patroness and Protectress of New Spain, with all and
"every one of the prerogatives due to principal patrons
"and protectors according to the rubrics of the Roman
"Breviary; an election which was made by the desire, as
"well of Our Venerable Brothers, the Bishops of that
"Kingdom, as of the Clergy secular and regular, and by
"the suffrages of the people of those States. In the next
"place We approve and confirm the preinserted Office and
"Mass with the Octave; and We declare, decree and com-
"mand that the Mother of God called Holy Mary of
"Guadalupe be recognised, invoked, and venerated as
"Patroness and Protectress of New Spain. Likewise, in
"order that henceforth the solemn commemoration of so
"great a Patroness and Protectress may be celebrated with
"the more reverence and devotion, and with due worship
"of prayer by the faithful of both sexes who are bound to
"the Canonical Hours, by the same apostolic authority We
"grant and command that the annual feast of the 12th of
"December in honor of the Most Holy Virgin Mary of
"Guadalupe, be perpetually celebrated as a day of precept
"and as a double of the first class with Octave; and that
"the preinserted Office be recited and the preinserted Mass
"be celebrated."—Then follow lists of indulgences and
special favors, such as that of the privileged altar, with
the accustomed conclusion: "Given at Rome, in St. Mary

"Major, under the Fisherman's Ring, 25th of May, 1754, "in the fourteenth year of Our Pontificate."

This Brief of Benedict XIV. is one of Guadalupe's best charters. It is authoritative and decisive. No wonder that a learned and fervent defender of the Holy Mother, after quoting the Pontiff's words, is led to remark: "When we read what precedes we find it hardly explicable that a man who falsifies history and deals in sophism, in order to controvert the Marvellous Apparition, should still pretend to call himself a Catholic."[1]

Opposition, certainly, from a Catholic standpoint, seems utterly unjustifiable; and whatever of it has been offered is characterized neither by exactness of knowledge nor by logic of argument. The hackneyed recourse to the word *dicitur* (it is related) in the Office has not been forgotten; but the attempted reasoning is ineffectual and inconclusive. While the Pope who approved the Office was still Promoter of the Faith—and many times before as well as since—the same objection, in similar cases, was vainly raised to be duly demolished.

A very slight acquaintance with ecclesiastical procedure will enable us to understand that the Church, in using expressions like *dicitur*, *fertur*, *pie creditur*, etc., has no intention of casting doubt on evidence which she herself finds sufficient to motive important legislation or concession. She merely indicates that she is not defining, as she never does in those matters, but rather is making the facts narrated rest on their proper foundation, that is on testimony religiously considered trustworthy. But

---

[1] Contestacion . . . al Libro de Sensacion, p. 504.

who would pretend that she acts on mere report, or on allegations of which she has not tested the truth?

In any case the Guadalupe *dicitur* objection can no longer serve its purpose; for in the new Lessons of the Office the expression is not 'it is related' but 'as it is handed down by a long-standing and constant tradition.'

Feeble attempts have also been made to show that the papal approval might bear on devotion to Our Lady, more or less independently of Guadalupan facts and titles. To this the obvious answer is that a whole century's negotiation, with countless expensive and laborious proceedings both in Mexico and Rome and on the relatively long road between them, was scarcely required in order to obtain the ordinary votive Office and Patronage of the Blessed Virgin. Besides, the categorical demands and concessions bear on them their literal and irrefragable evidence. Indeed the learned Pontiff himself seems to have carefully forestalled all cavilling on the distinctive import of his decrees, for he impressively dwells on the specialty of the case. He inserts bodily the Guadalupan petition and the Guadalupan Office; and then calls attention to the fact that it is only after he has considered the whole contents of these documents that he declares, approves and commands: "all that is contained" he writes "in the preinserted petition (of the Mexicans) and decree (of the Congregation of Rites) having been taken into account: *attentis iis omnibus quae in supplici praeinserto libello et decreto continentur*."

Moreover he strikingly insists on the very name of Guadalupe. I find by actual count that, in the Brief, he repeats it as many as nine times. Once he copies it from the petition and once from the decree, while he introduces it seven times himself. In the earlier paragraphs he refers to the Mother of God 'under the invocation of Guadalupe' or 'named of Guadalupe;' but as he advances he freely says: 'the Blessed Virgin Mary of Guadalupe' or 'the Immaculate Virgin of Guadalupe.' He was quite conscious, too, of the reiteration, for toward the end he styles Guadalupe 'the oft-mentioned' (saepe-memorata), as undoubtedly it is in this most important document.

It has been asked also, as well it may, why the Holy Father issued a Brief at all; since an affirmative rescript of the Congregation of Rites would have satisfied the Mexican demand. Neither was it necessary, nor very usual, to make such special reference to the Apparitions; for in other similar cases, though apparitions and miracles are mentioned in the local petition, they are passed over in silence in the Roman reply—even when that reply is most favorable. It is true that the Pontiff had a precedent to follow, for, thirty years earlier Benedict XIII. made explicit mention of the Miracle, when he granted indulgences for "the feast day of *the Apparition of Holy Mary Virgin of Guadalupe*." Nevertheless it is strongly evidenced that the great Pope-Liturgist was determined to set his own personal seal on the very title of the New World Sanctuary and Patronage.

More even than the form and wording of the Brief, *Non est Equidem*, its drift and foreseen effect are unanswerably corroborative of the Guadalupan traditions. For here we have the Pontiff, who of his age knew best the implied force of ecclesiastical legislation and concession, enshrining, by apostolic authority, in the liturgy of several great nations a new title for the Mother of God, and new obligations for the clergy and the people. He quotes the history of the Apparitions and the Picture, and then solemnly grants what, on the strength of that history, is confidently demanded. He therefore holds it and represents it as true. He himself had taught that in similar cases Apparitions were the foundation for granting special Offices. Surely he did not grant the Guadalupan one without foundation, much less did he without reason impose it on thousands of Priests and Religious.

The imposition of another obligation is startling: it not only corroborates the Guadalupan story but overwhelmingly establishes its undeniableness. It is admittedly most rare to find the Apostolic Authority called in to decree a Feast of Precept, for several ecclesiastical provinces and many millions of Christians, in commemoration of a special revelation and a special devotion. Yet that is what Benedict XIV. did for Guadalupe when he decreed rite of first class and obligatory solemnization, in all New Spain, for the 12th of December, the anniversary of the final Apparitions and the formation of the Picture.

Again, it is to be distinctly noted that the Pontiff confirmed and imposed the Guadalupan Patronage in New Spain, according to the strict decrees of his predecessor, Urban VIII. Now one of those decrees, which Benedict XIV. must repeatedly have had occasion to expound and enforce, absolutely forbade the establishment of patronage over kingdoms or provinces under any lower title than that of Canonization. In giving New Spain this patronage he, therefore, implicitly canonized the title of Guadalupe: and canonization is inerrant. I say, implicitly, for there is no need to force the argument. The plain facts of the case abundantly demonstrate that, in the Church's opinion, Guadalupe is a title worthy of the Mother of God, therefore a true one; therefore, as it claims, heavenly and supernatural. Hence we may fairly conclude that the Apparitions which originated that title are as ecclesiastically undeniable as the Picture which perpetuates it is lovably venerable.

FAÇADE OF THE COLLEGIATE CHURCH.

CHAPTER III.

LEO XIII. AND GUADALUPE.

PRACTICAL greatness is felt to be characteristic of Leo XIII. He has displayed a complete assemblage of extraordinary qualities, of gifts most varied yet never discordant. Between his immense learning and his most tender piety there seems no strife, no encroachment. If in some Encyclicals he appears so doctrinal that one might think he could be nothing else, in others he is all devotion. The most elevated and boundless views, which the complex philosophy of human destiny can suggest or require, are familiar to him; and at the same time he is a marvel of order and detail. Aspirations, vast, untrammelled, and rather abstract, are manifestly to his liking. Nevertheless, a certain polished exactitude in particulars —be they of piety or diplomacy or literature—very strongly marks his action.

The confidence which the aged Pontiff inspires is extraordinarily far-reaching. Many, who are untouched even by his world-wide authority, are under the sway of his personality. In fact the impression that where he has passed it is at least safe to follow has become practically universal. His intellectual sureness and his transparent rectitude are accepted guarantees for good guidance. Catholics, of course, have other reasons for confiding in him; but they too must naturally lean much on his tried wisdom and noble character.

A peculiarity of an audience with him is that he seems to read his visitors thoroughly and yet leaves them at their ease. His great lustrous eyes pierce one through and through; but their ardent yet soft glance excites no mistrust. Some similar peculiarity belongs to his teaching. His letters and administrative acts, while deeply searching, have about them a placid, well-wishing authoritativeness which conveys the utmost confidence.

It is interesting to see such a Pope brought into contact with a many-sided, delicately venerable question like that of Guadalupe. Here was authorised doctrine, but not so general and well-defined as to bear all treatment; and devotion enthusiastic but jealously sensitive; and considerations of public and private fitness, as well as of racial and national partiality. It was never easy to legislate for Guadalupe, least of all since Benedict XIV. gave it so high an ecclesiastical standing. But the light strong hand of Leo XIII. has magically touched the sacred subject, and has beautified what was already very beautiful.

It might not have been supposed that this American devotion would demand any special action on the part of the present Pontiff. All needful privileges seemed granted. The fondest clients of Holy Mary of Guadalupe had enough to satisfy mind and heart. The Apparitions, to whose undoubted certainty they so cling, had long been liturgically sung, by the order of Christ's Vicar, in thousands of churches and cathedrals, and could therefore by no means be false. And the sweet Picture so revered in God's house, so praised in the very language of God's service, must clearly be as marvellous as it professed, and consequently no human invention. In presence of such sanction, cavil and contradiction were too weak to give much trouble, and pious affection had its way.

Yet the Mexicans wanted more—as love always wants more—and they asked and obtained it. Indeed they obtained so much that, these two years past, they are rejoicing as exultantly as if it were the first time Rome had ever done anything for their Holy Mother and her sacred Picture. A felicitous event, one that overtops all those most fortunate and glorious in their ecclesiastical annals, has come, the Metropolitan lately writes, to fill with unaccustomed jubilation as well his own heart as the hearts of his priests and people. The event is a thoroughly Guadalupan letter from Leo XIII.

There was already strong proof of paternal beneficence in ordering the Picture crowned, in his own name, with a crown of gold; and much graciousness in undertaking to compose for the ceremony a most pregnant and prayerful Latin inscription. But though the Mexicans lovingly appreciate these favors, their glad gratitude is mainly for the papal document. They understand its full significance —which to outsiders may not at first be quite evident.

In the Office approved in 1754 there was a summary of the Guadalupan tradition introduced into the sixth lesson. The brief account must have been considered sufficient, for it is all that was proposed at the time. Now the whole three lessons of the second nocturn are consecrated to the miraculous occurrences; and the decree which authorises their introduction is rightly regarded as a most explicit approval and confirmation. The sanction is all the more forcible, as well as the more consoling, that it came on the heels of bitter opposition. In fact appearances go to prove that irreligious underhand proceedings actually forced the Congregation of Rites to something like a review of the whole Guadalupan history. And as the victory came after a struggle and a test, it is strikingly decisive and must prove final.

"For some time," continues the Metropolitan, "the pious prelates of the Mexican nation have desired that in the Divine Office, which is recited in honor of the Most Holy Virgin of Guadalupe, there should appear complete, with all its tender details, the consoling history of the Apparition of our heavenly Lady to the favored Indian, Juan Diego, on the blessed hill of Tepeyac. They wanted to read there her categorical message to the first bishop of this church, Don Fray Juan de Zumárraga, of holy and imperishable memory; with the prudent and reserved conduct of that prelate as long as the celestial mandate was not confirmed by miracles. They wished to hear of the presentation of the marvellous flowers, which, gathered in the depth of Winter on the ridge of Tepeyac, Juan Diego brought rolled up in his poor mantle, and offered to the bishop with all candor and simplicity; and, finally, of the admirable transformation of these flowers into that most beautiful miraculous Picture of Mary, which, supernaturally painted on the same fortunate garment, we have now, for nearly four hundred years, venerated with the fondest devotion and most loving enthusiasm, in the renowned sanctuary of Guadalupe."

The illustrious writer adds that delay arose from the tribulations which crowned the last days of his predecessor, Archbishop Labastida, and still more from difficulties raised in Mexico and carried as far as the Eternal

City. Anonymous writings were clandestinely circulated, one of them falsely professing itself a Madrid publication. They finally took the form of a "Book of Sensation" and an "Exquisitio Historica," one being prentice-hand Latin of the choice passages of the other. Such as the translation was, however, it was audaciously forwarded to Rome; and it received a consideration which neither its form nor matter deserved, but which, as the event seems to indicate, was meant to render the pending decree more entirely unequivocal.

Difficulties formulated from this "Exquisitio Historica" were sent back from Rome to every Mexican bishop, and replies were demanded. All the prelates answered quickly and gladly; for, as the Archbishop of Mexico writes, it was 'a most sweet task,' *tarea dulcisima,* because it was work for the Holy Mother and because it was easy to do it well.

Every difficulty having been satisfactorily solved, the Congregation of Rites issued the new approbatory decree which is now causing such joy in the land of Holy Mary of Guadalupe. Then the Holy Father despatched to the Mexican Archbishops and bishops his very beautiful letter. And as this papal utterance most effectually inculcates devotion to the American Virgin, I think it well to give it here in quite literal translation. It runs as follows:—

"*Venerable Brothers, health and apostolic benediction:*

· "With complete satisfaction We have determined to "accede to your request, that We should enrich with some "special additions the Office already granted by Our illus- "trious predecessor, Benedict XIV., in honor of the Most

"Holy Virgin Mary of Guadalupe, the principal Patroness
"of your nation. For, indeed, We are aware how close are
"the links that have ever united the beginning and the
"progress of the Christian Faith among the Mexicans
"with the worship of this Divine Mother, whose Picture,
"as your histories relate, an admirable providence made
"famous in its very origin. We know, too, that in the
"Tepeyac Sanctuary, for whose repair, enlargement, and
"ornamentation you show yourselves so solicitous, the
"manifestations of piety go on increasing day by day,
"since to that spot as the common centre of their vows
"frequent devout and crowded pilgrimages flock from
"every part of the Republic. For this reason, not many
"years ago, We too ordered that in Our name and by Our
"authority the Picture of your august Queen should be
"crowned with a diadem of gold.

"Now also, Venerable Brothers, We have great
"pleasure in seeking to give special testimony to the
"satisfaction which your perfect concord causes Us, a
"concord that happily reigns in your hierarchy as well as
"among the whole clergy and people, and is the means of
"drawing closer and strengthening more and more the ties
"that bind you to this Apostolic See. Since, therefore, as
"you yourselves recognise, the most loving Mother of God
"venerated under the title of Guadalupe is the author and
"preserver of this great harmony of souls, We with all the
"affection of Our heart exhort through you the whole
"Mexican people to see that they always retain this
"reverence and love for the Divine Mother, as their most
"signal glory and a very fountain of every best blessing.

"With regard especially to the Catholic Faith, which
"is at once the treasure most precious and, in those days,

"the one most easily lost, let all be persuaded and intimately
"convinced that it will last among you in all its purity
"and strength as long as this devotion, entirely worthy of
"your ancestors, is fully maintained. In it, therefore, let
"them grow every day, loving with more and more warmth
"of affection so sovereign a Patroness; and they shall find
"that the blessings of her most efficacious patronage will
"flow down daily more abundantly, for the salvation and
"peace of all classes in society.

"Earnestly wishing you these blessings, We, in proof
"of Our intimate affection, send you, Venerable Brothers,
"to all and each one of you, and to the clergy and people
"entrusted to your care, the Apostolic Benediction.

"Given at Rome. The 17th year of Our Pontificate.

"LEO P. P. XIII."

Though farther on I shall have to give the Spanish-Indian narrative of the Apparitions, it may be a satisfaction to some readers to see, at once, what the new historical Lessons of the Breviary—referred to by His Holiness—are able to state on the same subject. This brief account is now part of the Liturgy, by the authority of the Congregation of Sacred Rites, and the special sanction of the Holy Father himself.

The Lessons run as follows:—

Lesson IV.

In the year of our Redemption fifteen hundred and thirty-one, the Virgin Mother of God presented herself, as it has been handed down by a long-standing and constant tradition, to the eyes of a pious and simple neophyte on the hill of Tepeyac in Mexico; and, addressing him most affectionately, bade him go to the bishop and say that on that spot a temple should be erected to her. The local prelate, Juan de Zumárraga, deferred his answer, being resolved to search diligently into the truth of the affair; but as the neophyte, through a second apparition and command of the Most Blessed Virgin, renewed his embassy with tears and supplications, he ordered him to go and earnestly ask a sign by which might be attested the wish of the great Mother of God.

Lesson V.

As the neophyte had to go in to Mexico to call a priest, so that his uncle who was dangerously sick might not be deprived of the last Sacraments, he took the path farthest from the hill of Tepeyac; but the most benign Virgin, now for the third time, came forth to meet him, and, in his sadness, assured him of his uncle's recovery. Then, arranging in his cloak most beautiful roses, which, in spite of the sterility of the place and the rigor of Winter, had just burst into bloom, she bade him take them to the bishop. Diego obeyed; and when the roses fell to the ground in the presence of the bishop, there was seen marvellously painted on the cloak the picture of Holy Mary, exactly as she had appeared on the hill near the city. Profoundly moved at the sight of so great a wonder, the inhabitants of Mexico took care that the sacred picture was reverently guarded in the episcopal chapel. Soon after it was transferred with solemn pomp to a temple built for it on the hill of Tepeyac, and its renown spread because of the singular veneration with which all the people honored it.

Lesson VI.

Later on it was placed in a magnificent shrine which the Roman Pontiffs ennobled by granting it, for the splendor of divine worship, a Chapter of Canons. There it became famous for the concourse of people and the frequency of miracles, exciting immeasurably the piety of the Mexican nation toward the Mother of God. Wherefore the Archbishop of Mexico, and the other bishops of those regions, in accord with all classes of society, regarding her as their most powerful Protectress in public and private calamities, elected her principal Patroness of the whole Mexican nation. With apostolic authority Benedict XIV. declared the election canonical, and granted a Mass and Office under the title of the Blessed Virgin of Guadalupe. Now Leo XIII., graciously acceding to the repeated petitions of the Mexican prelates, has, by a decree of the Sacred Congregation of Rites, allowed that this latest Office be recited. He also ordered that, in his name and by his authority, the Picture of the Virgin, famous for miracles and for the cult rendered it, should be solemnly crowned with a diadem of gold.

These special lessons are, of course, the most distinctively Guadalupan part of the Office; though the whole of it—and still more the Mass—points with marked significancy to the miraculous events in this New World. The light rising upon those who were in the shadow of death; the Virgin Mother, under the attribution of Wisdom, taking root in an honorable people and having her inheritance among the chosen; the great sign appearing in the heavens—of the Woman clothed with the sun, having the moon beneath her feet, and the stars, if not as a crown, at least strewn all over her vesture—these and other passages of the lessons and antiphons recall at once to a Mexican's mind the share Guadalupe had in bringing to the first neophytes the saving knowledge of the Incarnation.

The Mass is still more explicit, and is, plainly, altogether ordered with a view to the traditional celebration. I have seen the choice of the Prayer and the Gospel attributed to Benedict XIV.; but, though the learned Pontiff may have influenced the final form of the Mass, I find no proof that any part of it was first suggested by him.

In any case the parts mentioned are very suitable. The acknowledgment of continual divine favors to those who have taken refuge in Most Holy Mary's singular patronage, and the supplication to see her whom they are commemorating, are of easy reference for a Guadalupan. Then the Gospel, telling of Mary's visit to the hill country, and her embassy of sanctification to the unborn Baptist, most directly suggests her visit to Tepeyac and her exceptional blessings on the infant American Church. The similarity is no mere fancy: it was manifestly in the mind of Benedict XIV. when he donated his own Guadalupan picture to the *Visitation* Monastery at Rome.

The Gradual most poetically recalls the first and the last Apparitions, as well as the fruits of Mary's visit. Who is she, it asks, who comes up like the rising morn, fair as the moon, brilliant as the sun? As the rainbow when it glistens amidst clouds of glory, and as the rose-blossoms in the time of Spring. . . . The flowers have burst forth in our land, and the pruning season is come.

The words of the Offertory: I have chosen and sanctified this place, that here may be my name—have but one application; the hill of the Apparitions and the Shrine are clearly indicated. And finally the Communion *Non fecit taliter*, which is already familiar to us in connection with the Mexican cause in Rome, sums up the best authorised views of the whole Guadalupan question.

The examination of this Office of Holy Mary of Guadalupe, and the knowledge of the sanction and publicity lately given it by Leo XIII., sufficiently explain the enthusiasm with which the Holy Father's name is at present hailed by Mexican Catholics. The cause of their Mother, Patroness, and Queen, is so dear to them that whoever strengthens or furthers it gains their affection. And when it is Christ's Vicar who goes out of his way not only to praise but to preach the Guadalupan devotion, their childlike gratitude knows no bounds. They exult beyond measure at hearing the Sovereign Pontiff inculcate that the progress of Christianity in New Spain has always been closely linked with the worship of that divine Mother " whose Picture an admirable providence made famous in its very origin." Their joy is, if possible, fuller when they find the same high authority still attributing to Guadalupan influence the present 'harmony of souls' and 'concord of bishops' and 'purity of faith.'

What more can the fondest clients of Holy Mary wish to hear? The great Pontiff tells them that their Guadalupan devotion is altogether worthy of their ancestors, that it is a most signal glory, and a very fountain of blessings. He even predicts that if they cling to it and grow in it, it will prove for all a source of peace and salvation.

This most authoritative and most welcome teaching has made the Holy Father indescribably dear to the people of Mexico. They know, of course, that the Office is not all his gift, and that the Mass has long been theirs; but they also understand that those new detailed Lessons, with the letter that accompanied them, are a bulwark and a crowning glory to Guadalupe. The faithful feel like their chief pastors, who now cry out—'behold how the Holy See has deigned to confirm our constant faith in the most blessed fact of the Apparition of our Queen and Sovereign Lady;' or 'hitherto we have held the tradition piously and rationally, but now we believe it on the unerring authority of the Church;' or 'what need to speak any more when Rome has spoken?'[1]

If anything were wanting to enhance Pope Leo's popularity in the Mexico of to-day, it would be found in the action of his present representative in that country. The Pro-delegate, Archbishop Averardi, has already won much Guadalupan sympathy by his striking manifestations of reverence for the Shrine and the devotion. In a recent proceeding of his I find the most significant fact with which I can close this chapter. Last July he went to the limit of his power of granting indulgences, by attaching *eighty days* to the recital of one *Hail Mary* with the invocation: *Holy Mary of Guadalupe, pray for us.*

---

[1] Pensam. Obisp. sobre Guad., Mex., '94.

CHAPTER IV.

GUADALUPE AND THE MEXICAN HIERARCHY.

WE have seen that the Sovereign Pontiff, Leo XIII., highly commends the actual Hierarchy of Mexico. He praises the bishops for their union both among themselves and with the Holy See. He also intimates the root and source of so excellent a fruit, for he reminds the prelates that the author and preserver of this harmony and fidelity is none other than Holy Mary of Guadalupe.

Very beautiful, indeed, has been the relation between the pastors of the specially Guadalupan flock and Our Lady in her wonderful Apparition. Were all the circumstances brought to light and moulded into a narrative they would, I think, form as delightful a chapter of church history as any that is uninspired.

From the beginning the Mother of God seemed to trust to the bishops for all that she wanted done among the people of this continent. To them, in the person of the first bishop, she confided the miraculous representation of herself; and on them, in the ordinary exercise of their pastorate, she depended for the propagation and maintenance of her devotion. But of course she did more than show confidence and impose obligations; she afforded most special protection, and dispensed such manifest guidance and help that the bishops themselves never tire of proclaiming their indebtedness and gratitude.

They have also been admirably faithful. From the day that their predecessor and representative, the venerable Zumárraga, had his sufficient proofs that the Apparitions were heavenly, Guadalupe has found them reverent in belief, strong in defence, and loving in practice. The whole weight of their authority, and the resistless force of their example, have gone to exalt Holy Mary, the Patroness, the Queen, the Mother of the Mexicans.

That in such a matter there should have been complete episcopal unanimity seems almost miraculous. Many of these prelates lived far from the Shrine and might never be able to go there or see the Picture; their people, for the most part, had no hope of ever making the pilgrimage, and were, moreover, occupied with their own Sanctuaries and devotions; yet hardly a single bishop appears to have been satisfied until he and his whole flock were ardent Guadalupans. With no uncertain tone the grave unbroken episcopal voice kept on declaring that, as the neophytes expressed it, 'the most clean Mother of the True God' had appeared in the land; that from Mary's visit and words the definitive conversion of the people dated; and that the love of the Virgin of Tepeyac was at the birth and in the growth and through every vein of the nation's faith and morality. Whatever else was forgotten, this was to be remembered: the Mother of God had specially come to declare herself their Mother, and to leave her miraculous Picture in their custody.

The constant profession of these faithful prelates has been recalled and strikingly echoed in a comparatively recent declaration. In the year 1886 all the archbishops and bishops of Mexico signed the following formula: "That ancient tradition of our nation, of which a summary is found at the end of the sixth lesson of the Office granted by Benedict XIV. to the Mexican Church, concerning the Apparitions of the Blessed Virgin Mary to a pious neophyte on the hill of Tepeyac, and concerning the miraculous production of the holy Picture of the same Blessed Virgin Mary which is preserved and venerated in the Tepeyac sanctuary, both we and the faithful of our dioceses firmly believe and all with one voice profess." [1]

This they have been proclaiming all along. And yet the history of New Spain might make us apprehend that the best traditions risked being blurred or defaced or forgotten. Guadalupe had to keep its light burning in the darkest days of turmoil and tyranny, and had to rise above the storms of revolt and war and persecution. And it did so. For the bishops, in all circumstances and through all adversities, turned to the Patroness of Mexico, the Virgin of America, and directed thither the eyes and hearts of the faithful.

During the Spanish domination many of the viceroys were bishops, and they were always unwilling to enter on their onerous office without going first to consecrate themselves to Holy Mary of Guadalupe. Most instructive is it, also, to find frequently marked in the national annals, that when looked for in the Capital the Viceroy-Bishops were out keeping a vigil at the Shrine, or had gone there on retreat. Nor should their munificence be forgotten, for it spoke their faith and devotion. They rivalled their lay compeers in enriching the Sanctuary. But more glorious even than their generosity to Guadalupe was their heroism in going out to beg for it. This

[1] El Magisterio de la Iglesia, p. 115.

very year, two centuries ago, the saintly Archbishop and Viceroy, Ortega, was painfully making his way from door to door in the poorest as well as the richest quarters of his metropolitan city, soliciting alms for the rebuilding of the Tepeyac Shrine.[1]

During the struggle for independence, and the successive civil and foreign wars that have rent and distracted the land, the thought of the chief pastors, whether at home or in exile, has always been fixed on Guadalupe. There was their hope. They were confident that as long as the Temple raised to the Mother of God at her request was worthily served, as long as the Picture left as a pledge of her maternal affection was lovingly treasured, things would finally go right with their flocks and their country.

It is touching to find recorded that the late suffering Metropolitan, Archbishop Labastida, always found it possible, during his eight years of exile, to say the Mass of the 12th of each month at an altar or, at least, before a picture of Holy Mary of Guadalupe. The fact is given as a proof that the devotion was wide-spread, for the venerable exile had tarried in three continents: I find it also proves and exemplifies the traditional fidelity of the Mexican hierarchy to the great national Patroness. They cling to this 12th day celebration and to many others. Besides their frequent diocesan functions, and their part in all the great annual and exceptional celebrations, they at certain times claim the Collegiate Church for themselves. All want a share in the service and enjoyment of Our Lady's Shrine. We find constantly announced in Mexican newspapers and calendars that

---

[1] Hist. Comp., p. 105.

such and such days at Guadalupe belong to Puebla, or Colima, or Querétero, or Guadalajara, or San Louis Potosí, or other dioceses a thousand miles from the Shrine.

On those days the pastors and the people bring offerings —if none other are required, myriads of bouquets natural and spiritual—to the Hill of the Apparitions, and make it a time of glad festivity with the Holy Mother. Her praises are sounded by the Bishop, who also leads his children in every simplest act of piety. Or if he should be absolutely hindered from coming, some other prelate, with beautiful fraternity, takes up the pilgrims, and officiates for them in the Ordinary's name.

Though always much in evidence the Bishops' Guadalupan devotion is naturally most prominent on great occasions. Every opportunity of honoring Our Lady is, certainly, seized on by them; but in religious circumstances of peculiar import they show their feelings more unreservedly. The late Coronation of the Picture is a case in point. As they all had labored for it, they all took part in it, every one of the six archbishops and twenty-two bishops having either a share or being represented in the great act of fealty and homage. And though this Coronation is not my present subject, I must here dwell on some details of it that brought out the episcopal bearing and sentiment on the whole Guadalupan question.

There was strong unanimity of belief, with corresponding zeal and generosity. But better still, there was much evidence of childlike love for the Mother of God. I know few treatises of devotion to the Blessed Virgin that are as moving as the collected sayings of these venerable prelates concerning her Coronation under the loved title of Guadalupe. They exulted as faithful and affectionate children. Enthusiasm and delight carried them away. They published and pronounced panegyrics and sermons and addresses; they wrote and circulated and sang odes and hymns and choruses. Though some of them paused to prove critically and expound theologically the Guadalupan traditions and decisions, yet their general tendency was to put glad fervor into emotional language. Indeed several of the younger members of the episcopal body seemed competing for the palm of excellence in combining Guadalupan devotion and Castilian sweetness in joyous though stately metre.

These devoutly poetic effusions had high exemplars to follow. Leo XIII. had sent his polished Latin distichs, which the dean of the Mexican hierarchy, the renowned Archbishop of Guadalajara, though in the forty-fourth year of his episcopate, undertook to interpret in Spanish verse.[1] The lines of these two most venerable men have such ecclesiastical, and will have such historic, interest, that it may be well to give them here with a free English rendering.

These are the Pontiff's lines:

> Mexicus heic populus mira sub imagine gaudet
>   Te colere, alma parens, praesidioque frui.
> Per te sic vigeat felix, teque auspice Christi
>   Immotam servet firmior usque fidem.
>
> Leo P. P. XIII.

(Imagini augustae Mariae D. N. Guadalupensis in Mexico subscribendum.)

Romae ex aedib. Vatic. die XXVI febr. an. MDcccvc.

[1] Vid. Tiempo Supl., Oct. 12, '95.

Rendered by the Archbishop:—

> En admirable imágen,
> Santa Madre nuestra
> El pueblo Mexicano
> Gozoso te venera,
> Y tu gran patrocinio
> Con gozo y gratitud experimenta.
> Feliz y floreciente
> Por ti así permanesca
> Y mediante el auxilio
> Que benigna le prestas
> La fé de Jesucristo
> Fija conserve con tenaz firmeza.
>
> ✠ Pedro, Arzob. de Guadalajara.

> In thy portentous Picture treasured here,
> The Mexic race, O Gracious Mother, joys
> To honor thee and reap the golden wealth
> Of thy unfailing aid. In happy strength
> Still make it grow, that blessed by thee it hold
> In ever tightening grasp the changeless Faith of Christ.

The thoughts and feelings of the other prelates are expressed in various forms and tones; but all are strong and jubilant, while many are full of the tenderest emotion. Some, like the fervent Archbishop of Mexico, pray that their people may experience the blessed fruits of the Guadalupan devotion as they themselves have, in their long pastorate and pilgrimage on earth. Some rejoice that their country is now safe, that neither its faith nor its independence can fail as long as its real crown is on the head of the Mother of God. Others, involving their joys, gladly congratulate themselves on the glory they receive in having her who is their Patroness and Mother so gloriously crowned.

So ardent and so affectionate is the language of all these Bishops, that it must seem exaggerated to one who does not know them, or who loves Our Lady less than they do. To them it is a poor and wholly inadequate expression of what they personally feel. But some passages from their published correspondence will better indicate their dispositions than any account or description.

I find specially characteristic the address of a bishop who was not able to come to the solemnity. He wrote to apologize, not to his Metropolitan, not to his flock, not to the assembled nation, but to Our Lady herself. "Impute it not to want of love," he says, "O Queen, Mother, and Sovereign Lady of the Mexicans, that the Bishop of Sonora is absent on this most solemn occasion, when nearly the whole episcopate of the country is assembled in your august sanctuary of Tepeyac, assembled to crown you in that precious Picture which was stamped by the finger of the Almighty on the coarse-webbed humble texture. My desires were great; and greater was my anguish when I saw that the immense distance which separates me from the capital of your Empire, the infirmities that afflict me, and the fewness of my priests, should debar me from this pilgrimage that would have been so dear to my heart. But though absent in body I am present in spirit; and from here, associating myself with my Venerable Brothers, I offer you the homage of my love and veneration.

"And as you spontaneously condescended to make yourself the special Mother of the Mexicans, O exalted Queen, obtain for us, by your powerful intercession before the Throne of Mercy, that we may worthily thank you for the singular blessing of having appeared on our soil, and of having been willing to leave us your miraculous Picture. Obtain for us all that we love you as our most cherished Mother. Pray in particular for the Bishop of Sonora and his beloved flock. Pray that the religious indifference which kills faith be banished from amongst us; that the light of the Divine Redemption may illumine the intelligences that are blinded by the errors of protestantism, masonry, and liberalism; that the reign of Satan who pretends to rule over us may be replaced by the empire of your Most Holy Son, the Divine Saviour and Master, Jesus Christ Our Lord.

"O Mother, O Queen, O Sovereign Lady, look with compassion on the whole people of Mexico!"[1]

Episcopal words, like those of the bishop of Sonora, sound sweet in Christian ears. Happy the countries and the ages that expect and understand them!

The simplicity of faith and piety in this Guadalupan letter is rivalled in others by dignity and formality splendidly ecclesiastical. Circumstances connected with the Coronation again offer examples. The Orator for the occasion was solemnly chosen and commissioned by the Archbishops of the country. The Metropolitan words their wish and urges compliance in these terms:—

"*Illustrious Lord and much Esteemed Brother,*

"As we have appointed the Coronation of the Most Holy Virgin of Guadalupe for the 12th of next October, we are beginning to make arrangements for the solemnity. The choice of an Orator for so propitious a day being one

---

[1] *El Tiempo*, Oct. 12, '95.

of the most important points, I sent out a note to the Most Rev. Archbishops; and we have unanimously fixed on your Right Rev. Lordship. I therefore ask you, Most Illustrious and Reverend Lord, in the name of God and of the episcopate, to kindly accept the sermon for the day of the Coronation of the Most Holy Virgin, our admirable Patroness.

"Kissing your hands, I remain your Lordship's affectionate friend and faithful servant and colleague,

✢ Prospero Maria, *Archb. of Mexico.*"

The Bishop answers:

"*Venerable Brother and much Loved Lord,*

"I have received the esteemed letter of your Most Illustrious and Most Reverend Lordship, of the 21st of the present month, and what you announce in it fills me with confusion.

"You write that, according to the note addressed to them by you, the Lord Archbishops have unanimously chosen me as the Orator at the solemn Coronation of Our Lady of Guadalupe on the 12th of next October. I beg you to accept, yourself, and to kindly communicate to the other Archbishops, the expression of my gratitude and the assurance of my confusion; making known, however, that after reflection I have resolved to accept the delicate commission, because I see in this choice and in the revered action of your Most Illustrious Lordships something like a Divine order and an express desire of the Most Holy Virgin.

"Wishing you, Most Reverend Lord, every blessing, I remain your very devoted friend and servant, who dutifully kisses your hands,

☩ CRESCENCIO, *Bishop of Yucatan.*"

The sermon so courteously requested and promised proved most learned and eloquent. It was in the style of the great panegyrics of past centuries, with its magnificent exordium, its invocation and divisions, and its moving peroration. To quote from it in this connection would be pleasant, did the order of my subject allow it. Here also it would be agreeable to dwell on the manifest virtues of these admirable Prelates, on their out-spoken faith and grandly commingled piety and dignity. But the question would lead to such laudation as could hardly fail of being presumptuous. It may however be in place to transcribe a few sentences from an authoritative statement of the actual high standing—through Guadalupan influence—of the Mexican hierarchy and clergy. When extolling the love of Holy Mary of Guadalupe to his country, Dr. Ibarra of Chilapa says:—

"In our Church there are still Bishops who are worthy successors of the Apostles by their ardent love for Jesus Christ, by their zeal in seeking the glory of God and the salvation of souls, by their profound humility and their detachment from everything earthly. There are Bishops in whose footsteps, as they make their pastoral visitation, purity of life and ecclesiastical discipline flourish anew; and who also add to such virtues the inestimable treasures of human knowledge. The Mexican Church still rejoices to have in its clergy, whether of the secular order or of the regulars yet left us, venerable Priests who have grown grey in study and prayer, who for the good of their people have traversed all the realms of truth and sounded all the shoals of error; Priests who never let themselves be seen except in the sacred obscurity of the Sanctuary where they offer the most pure oblation and pour on redeemed souls the waters that flow from the perennial fountains of the Saviour; Priests who never pass the shadow of the temple except to carry God's pardon to the dying, to anoint the athletes of Jesus Christ before they enter on their last formidable combat, and to bear the Bread of Angels to those virgins that, like Elias, are about to commence the laborious way which leads to the holy mountain of God."[1]

These statements are true and of very general application. Guadalupan devotion and high excellence of ecclesiastical life are found, in Mexico, to be inseparable. It looks as if Our Lady paid back the affection of the Bishops and their clergy in special graces of the priestly spirit, which is so near akin to her own distinctive sanctity.

Now, perhaps, it is sufficiently evident to the reader that the members of the hierarchy in Mexico are personally devout to Holy Mary of Guadalupe; and it may be asked how far their pastoral authority is exercised in furthering her devotion among the people. Of course their enforcing what is of general obligation with regard to the national Patronage, and their conducting pilgrimages and other Guadalupan exercises, is a very authoritative

[1] Guad. Sermon, Oct. 13, '95.

sanction. Something more, however, is found in their ministry. They exert all the powers entrusted to them, whether powers of approval and condemnation or of reward and punishment, in the direct aim to defend and spread the devotion. They safeguard the reverence due to the received and ecclesiastically approved tradition by discountenancing vain controversy, and by absolutely prohibiting contradiction or denial. "We order," writes the Archbishop of Mexico, "in virtue of the authority with which we find ourselves invested, that none of our diocesans venture to write or read anything that is in any way contrary to the revered truth of the Apparition."[1] He and other bishops have repeatedly issued similar prohibitions, while for protestations of faith in the Miracle of the Apparitions and the Picture they grant all the indulgences they can. Such protestations are much recommended, and their recital is occasionally made obligatory. One formula I transcribe here, that Guadalupe's standing with the Mexican episcopate may be the better understood. It runs thus:—

"Most amiable Queen and Sovereign Lady of Guadalupe, powerful and most tender Mother of the Mexicans, while my soul overflows with unutterable consolation and my heart is full of sweetest gratitude, I come to prostrate myself at your sacred feet and to protest once again, before Heaven and earth, that I believe with lively and unshakable faith the most happy event of your loving Apparition, on the blessed hill of Tepeyac, to the favored Indian, Juan Diego, on whose cloak (*tilma*), filled as it was with the marvellous roses that had

---

[1] Carta Pastoral, 12 de Abril de 1894.

touched your most pure hands, you left stamped in bright and indelible colors your beautiful miraculous Picture, which, these three centuries and more, we preserve as a precious memorial of your maternal love and a sure pledge of your sovereign protection. For this rarest of favors, this most treasured escutcheon of honor that our country possesses, I from my heart fervently thank you; and I wish I could always praise you with that elevated piety and fond enthusiasm with which your loving Apparition has been celebrated and your bounties extolled by so many Sovereign Pontiffs, renowned Prelates, illustrious members of the Clergy and the Religious Orders, great Kings, distinguished Viceroys, and other high personages, as well as by all the pious and grateful generations that in the long course of 365 years have continued to bless your most sweet name of Guadalupe, and have publicly rendered you splendid homages of filial love, both on the blessed hill that your most pure footsteps ennobled and in the many magnificent sanctuaries that their affectionate hearts everywhere dedicated to you.

"Obtain for me, most amiable Mother, the grace to be day by day more thankful for your favors. And since you are happily the Treasurer of the rich and inexhaustible gifts which for our welfare are contained in the Sacred Heart of your Divine Son, cause to flow down on me the graces I need in order to be faithful to Him in the observance of His holy commandments and the fulfilment of the obligations proper to my state in life.

"I trust, sweet Sovereign Lady, that you will never cease to exercise in my behalf the office of the tenderest and fondest of mothers; for you showed that this was your most beneficent purpose with regard to all the Mexicans, when you let yourself be seen in such amiable majesty by the fortunate Juan Diego, and asked to have there erected to you a temple in which you would benignantly hear our supplications, a throne from which you would abundantly dispense your blessings.

"To correspond in some way with your maternal patronage, I promise to love you with all my heart, and effectually to avoid sin which so much displeases you. I resolve also to contribute as much as I am able to the extension of your devotion, and to the propagation of your worship under this most tender invocation of Guadalupe. Oh! through your love, most sweet Mother, may I obtain the love of the Sacred Heart of Jesus, and hereafter, as the reward of my fidelity, praise Him in your company, and in that of my glorious Patron, your most chaste Spouse, St. Joseph, in the blissful everlasting mansions of glory. Amen."[1]

This *Protesta de Fe* is much used in Mexico, especially in the Metropolitan province, in which its recital is enriched with an indulgence of eighty days. On certain solemn occasions its use is prescribed. It was formulated at the Chilapa synod in 1893, and was there recited by the assembled clergy and people. It was then entered on the statutes of the diocese, and the decree was passed that it should be publicly recited:—by all *children* on the day of their First Communion; by all *students* at their entrance into the seminary; by all *levites* before each ordination; and by all *priests* during the ceremony of taking charge of a parish.

[1] Propag. Catol., Mex. '94.

The significance of such legislation is unmistakable. Were not the Guadalupan tradition true and certain and hugely important, the decree, as well as the indulgence, just mentioned would be ecclesiastically impossible. No trifling or doubtful practice merits a share in the Church's treasures; nor can such things be at all imposed on the faithful. Yet in this Chilapa law we find that practically every Catholic in the diocese is called on to make the Guadalupan protestation of faith, for the prescribed act begins with the First Communion and runs up to the charge of souls.

It may, therefore, be affirmed that the bearing of the Mexican Hierarchy towards Guadalupe is strongly corroborative of the wonderful story and the admirable devotion. Of course no corroboration is needed, considering the declarations of the Holy See. Yet, as the daily life of the Church is the surest guide to belief and practice, we cannot fail to see what strength accrues to a good cause from the unanimous advocacy of so many actual Chief Pastors. These Archbishops and Bishops, who so strenuously uphold Guadalupe, are the teaching and governing body in a Church of twelve millions of fervent Catholics, of Catholics on whose faith in Our Lord and fidelity to His Vicar no shadow has ever fallen. That large section of the teaching Church must be right, and the devotion it preaches must be pleasing to Heaven.

CHAPTER V.

GUADALUPE AND THE MEXICAN NATION.

IT is difficult to make known, even partially, to one who has never been among the Mexican people, what to them Guadalupe signifies and is. With it they connect all that they hold great, sacred, glorious. The people cherish nothing, and boast of nothing, that can be wholly dissociated from the Tepeyac events; and every Mexican hallows whatever is dearest or holiest with the name and the remembrance of the admirable Patroness. Affairs religious or political, social or personal, never take on the national raciness till they are brought into due relation with Holy Mary of Guadalupe.

Such an example of the absolute committal of themselves and all their interests to a special devotion, no other nation displays at present, nor did, I believe, ever display. And here I speak of the whole nation; for the exceptions are few and, for the most part, estranged from Mexico and its people.

The true Mexican seizes every occasion of professing and proving that his love and trust are preëminently placed in the National Patroness. He glories in her praise; he is ready, not only to labor and give, but also to suffer and die for her honor. In public and private her name must be reverently introduced. Some representation of her must appear wherever the people work or pray, or even play. To uninformed or unsympathetic strangers the Picture may occasionally seem out of place; but the children of the land, even the least devout, would feel a sad want if it were not there.

The press of a country being, in the long run, ruled by the sentiments of its readers, that of Mexico has to respect or to eulogise Guadalupe. The admirable religious press—on the whole, perhaps, as good as there is in the Catholic world—is, through faith and piety, reverentially loving and enthusiastic. The truly patriotic press is, also, markedly favorable, from the knowledge and conviction that the nation's greatness was born and fostered and crowned at the Hill of the Apparitions.

If one or other ephemeral sheet, viciously subsidized and vituperatively unclean, presume to blaspheme what it does not understand, the faithful can well afford to let it pass unnoticed.

I have before me a Mexican daily paper of the 12th of December, 1894. It is an illustrated serio-comic journal, bearing the significant title of *Gil Blas*, and well known as an irrepressible organ of the Opposition. Its policy—so far as I can judge from a few years' intermittent acquaintance—is that Mexico should be ruled by the Mexican people, and not by cliques or cabals or the pensioners of foreign governments. Its advocacy of popular measures is strong and able; sincere, too, it must be added, if fine, imprisonment, and periodical confiscation be good tests of sincerity. It is not at all a religious paper; but being addressed to the people it has to take notice of their feasts. This number of the 12th of December has an article on the day's celebration. The piece is characteristic, and may, perhaps—better than a professedly religious one—help us to understand what Guadalupe is for the nation at large.

"Three great dates," the writer says, "shall live forever in the pages of Mexican history: the 13th of August, 1521; the 12th of December, 1531; and the 16th of September, 1810. On the first of these days the renowned envoys of civilization, after famous exploits and a memorable siege with its ninety-three fearful combats, unfolded the banner of Castile over the great temple of Anahuac. On the second the dawn of redemption for the conquered race spread its mantle of purple over the heights of Tepeyac. On the third there arose from centuries of subjection a State the more for America, and another daughter for illustrious Spain. The first date marks the birth of a civilization, the second of a race, the third of a nation.

"On this day, this great day, historical above all others, the land of Mexico awakens in festival. The whole country from Yucatan to California entones its jubilant hymn, the old dithyrambic strain of the natives, the happy song in which, these four hundred years, that heroic race has celebrated its incorporation into the great family of humanity. This is the feast of Mexican redemption.

"A renowned genius had drawn a new world out of the measureless abysses. His voice, like the Divine one of Genesis, had stilled the waters of chaos with the mighty fiat of a fresh creation; and at dawn on the 12th of October, 1492, the world evoked by that fiat wafted the kiss of its breezes to the brow of the great navigator, and to his ears such a hosanna of glory as had never yet saluted any human being. Civilization, which like a planet revolves round Science, followed in his track as in that of a sun, and traversed the American hemisphere.

"But civilization had to open itself a way with the sword; and our country was made the scene of one of the most stupendous conquests that the ages have witnessed. Led by a wondrously daring genius the little band of Spaniards gained the victory. Then followed for the native race the usual fate of the vanquished—an inevitable fate in that age of iron. From Tabasco to the prison of the last Aztec emperor, the struggle had been fearful, heroic, incredible. The Castilian soldiers had not had to fight with effeminate hordes like many of those conquered by Alexander; they faced powerful nations with whom valor was a dogma, the fatherland an idol, the foreigner a beast of prey, and the art of war the greatest, most glorious, most cherished institution of the State.

"The awful struggle undergone in conquering such a people, the frequency of cruel reprisals on both sides, the groans of the Spaniards horribly sacrificed at the top of the great *Teocalli*, and the madness caused by the sight of blood that flowed without ceasing—all fanned hate to a pitch of phrensy. Hence, when the native race saw Cuauhtemotzin surrender at Sandoval's vessel, it believed itself utterly doomed to extermination.

"Inevitable vengeance, indeed, fell on the vanquished Indians; and of the persecutions suffered by them the most sweeping and far-reaching was the pretence that they did not belong to the human species. Against such a theory protests were raised by many Spaniards, some of whom, like Las Casas, are on humanity's roll of honor. The Spanish throne wisely and christianly resisted the tendencies of so cruel a doctrine; and, yet, many powerful interests of the moment held doggedly to the declaration that the Indians were irrational creatures. This made perpetual slavery imminent; hence race hatred spread like the flames of an inextinguishable fire.

"It is then that a Woman descends from Heaven and appears on the rocky heights of Tepeyac. Her countenance is like the humble, graceful one of the daughters of Anahuac; her hands are joined in supplication; and her feet are upheld by a figure symbolic of divine power. This is she before whose image the lord and king of the conquerors prostrates himself; she whose name was on the lips of Cortez as he rushed into the battle of Otumba; whose mantle he had kissed a thousand times, imploring strength of arm and courage of heart. She is the Queen who rules, enlightens, elevates the conquering nation, in *the land of the Most Holy Virgin.*

"She appears and speaks to an Indian, and says to him: 'My son!'

"'My son?' the hailed one repeats in wonder; and this 'my son' resounds with lightning vibration in every corner of New Spain. 'My son!' the missionaries exclaim, in their fervent preaching of redemption; and this sublime salutation by which Heaven adopts the conquered Indian, vindicating his possession of reason and placing him in the special family of Mary, reaches in sweet harmony the throne of Spain and reëchoes, like Angel music, round the Seat of the Pontiff who was then the arbiter of nations.

"Both races, the conquered and the conquering, fall on their knees before this Indian Virgin, and drink in the same love as from one vase of nectar. The conqueror casts away the fatal sword; the native shakes off the chain of slavery, and expels from his heart all deadly hate. The Virgin of Guadalupe has united the two grand ideals, the Faith of one people and the Fatherland of the other. To cast the victor down before the representative of the vanquished race was the colossal enterprise; it was to found a new human family, to bind most truly and most closely two hemispheres together.

"The Indian was no longer an orphan; he had as Mother the Woman of whom the most powerful emperor of the earth was a vassal. There was no enslaving a race that was receiving incense in the oratories of kings and at the hands of Popes.

"A glorious dawn followed in the wake of this Virgin; a new epoch commenced, a new fellowship, a new people. The Mexican nation was born at Tepeyac, as was the Spanish at Covadonga. On this hill, which pious generations have climbed on their knees, was laid, in 1531, the hearth-stone of our country. The Virgin saluted the Indian with a branch of roses. It was the gift of civilization, the gift of peace and of fruitful motherhood. It was the beautifully poetic symbol of the new garden that was about to be planted in this North America.

"Therefore is the Virgin of Guadalupe the deepest and most ineradicable love of every Mexican. Therefore did Hidalgo raise her picture as the labarum of independence; and therefore does there resound in every home that grandest name which we all give to our first-born daughter. Hence comes there to Tepeyac, from every hamlet in Mexico, the ceaseless pilgrimage of our countrymen; hence does every garden in the land bear its best flowers for the Guadalupan altars.

"Amidst the worst clouds and tempests of scepticism the star of Tepeyac has never been obscured; all, believers or not, find something to love, and love intensely, in the Virgin of Guadalupe. Against her, in this land, no man blasphemes. She is the ideal, the light that shines above our strife and our incredulity. For this reason could Altimirano himself write the memorable words: 'Come the day on which the Virgin of Guadalupe is no longer venerated, and you have the sign that the very name of Mexico has disappeared from the catalogue of nations.'"[1]

In this newspaper extract we catch a sound of true Mexican sentiment. We get a glimpse of the emotion felt by a son of the land when there is question of the National Patroness. Guadalupe must be loved by all who love Mexico; there is no real patriotism without chivalrous devotion to the Holy Mother. The two thoughts of Our Lady and the country have been so admirably interwoven, so long regarded as one glorious thought, that they cannot, must not, be torn asunder.

More than that, there is a unanimity of measureless exultance in recalling and commemorating the grand historic alliance which gave to the new Mexican people so nobly unique an origin.

The *Gil Blas* writer gives also some indication of the true grounds of the people's great devotion. All who have really practised or known Christianity see at once that its redeeming power is centered in the Mystery

---

[1] *Gil Blas*, 12th Dec., 1894.

of the Incarnation. If it civilizes and saves men in groups, or men individually, it is because God became and is Man. He alone could elevate them; and His means was to take them by the hand, to be one of them.

But this Mystery He has unchangeably revealed, accomplished, and applied through the Blessed Virgin. From the beginning in promise and prophecy, later on in doctrine and definition, now and always in devotion, His way to us is our way to Him, His Mother. She is the Woman to crush the serpent, the Virgin to bring forth the Saviour, the Mother to guard the children in the wilderness. In every conjuncture her honor is found to be her Son's best safeguard—the safeguard, that is, of His Gospel, His Church, and His Divine prerogatives on earth. To be near her is infallibly to be near Him; to love her is to be all His.

In their simplicity of character and speed of thought, the native Americans at once grasped the bearing of this Divine Dispensation. They heard that the heavenly Lady who had come to visit them was the Mother of the True God and yet called herself their Mother. So they wonderingly asked themselves, if they were her children and He was her Son, whether He was not indeed their Brother. Conversing and pondering on this truth, they entered thoroughly into its significance, and by its means raised themselves at a bound to the true plane of Christian dignity—a plane from which nothing has ever since been able to dislodge them. Outwardly they may appear low and backward; but their own intimate feeling is that they, equally with all Christians, are brethren of God. Their sense of equality in religious matters gives them a noble air of independence, so noble, indeed, that it might seem to border on the arrogance of conscious superiority, if it were not for their most gracefully humble deference. They take the first place, or they yield it, as would a kingly saint.

Happily, the conquerors of Mexico, avaricious and cruel as some of them were, held the Catholic Faith themselves and also revered it in others. The one check on thirst for blood or wealth was awe of Christianity. That was the restraint which the worse adventurers meant to remove by pretending that the Indians were not members of the human family. To the more atrocious oppressors the report of the Guadalupan Apparitions was a staggering blow. These thralls, therefore, were not only men, but the chosen friends of Heaven, the incomparably favored children of the Mother of God! No wonder if many of the proud victors were, at first, unwilling to hear of the miraculous interposition and very slow to admit its reality and its import. Indeed it is known that the Prelate to whom Our Lady's mandate was addressed, and to whom was entrusted the defence of the neophytes, was insulted and calumniated and persecuted.

However, the chivalrous faith of the Spaniards was sufficiently touched to make them soon unwilling to see victimised the special clients of the Holy Virgin. We may doubt whether the reconciliation of the races was quite as prompt as the *Gil Blas* article might seem to imply; but we know that it was effected with strange and unhoped-for rapidity. From chronicles of the time, as well as from the brave though exaggerated denunciations of Las Casas, we learn that the enslavement and extermination of the natives was, in many places, gathering volume and violence just before the Apparitions, but diminished and practicably ceased in the years immediately following.

Religion was making itself felt. The mystery which had blotted out the distinction between slave and free, and Greek and barbarian, was striking the victors with awe and clothing the vanquished with dignity. Those who were made partakers of the blessings of the Divine Incarnation might well share the privileges of Spanish citizenship. If they were recognised as children by the Mother of God, they were manifestly fit to mingle with their conquerors and become the progenitors of the new free people. They were, therefore, preserved and grew into a nation; and Mexican patriots are right to reverence Guadalupe as the cradle of their country.

The people trace their civil existence, their freedom, and, still more, their Faith and Religion, to the help of Our Lady and the influence of her Shrine. The Licentiate Verdugo knew he was but voicing the best public sentiment, when at a literary meeting in October, 1895, he eloquently said: "Thought has to fall on its knees when it comes to count all that, in this land, the Guadalupan devotion has caused to germinate of good and pure and holy, of delicate and exquisite. To it Mexico may be said to owe its earthly existence, its preservation amidst the shipwrecks of which history speaks, and its visibly imposing vocation to the destinies that the future has in store for us."[1]

"By Mary of Guadalupe," the lamented Bishop of Puebla recently exclaimed, "hast thou, O Mexico, received being in the social, moral, and religious order."[2]

---

[1] *El Tiempo*, Oct. 23, 1895. [2] Album de la Coron., p. 169.

Similarly the Archbishop of Linares lately wrote: "After God it is to Our Lady of Guadalupe that the Mexican people owes both the existence it enjoys and the Christian civilization by which it has merited to take an honorable place among cultured nations. Who can reasonably call this in doubt? We Catholics have always so believed; and not a few, also, of a different religious profession have so acknowledged and publicly declared."[1]

It is not alone in the publications arising out of the recent extraordinary fervor of Mexican devotion, that Our Lady's share in the nation's life has been patriotically and religiously proclaimed. The same thing has been said and repeated in every available page for hundreds of years. As an example I may quote, from among similar documents, Dr. Sarmiento y Heredia's Guadalupan panegyric of 1801. The learned orator keeps in view America rather than Mexico; and commenting on the Gospel of the day, which was that of the Visitation, he says:—

"Have not, O Catholics, God and His Holy Mother glorified our Indies with like blessings? In its birth to the light of the Gospel, America, on this hill and in the person of Juan Diego, heard from the very lips of Mary words of supreme beneficence, . . . words by which, without limit or reserve, she pledged to us all the support of her power, all the defence of her arm, all the riches of her mercy, all the benedictions of her maternal sweetness. And whence, indeed, if not from her glorious visit, came that wondrous enlightenment which, like Zachary in Judea, America has here received

---

[1] Alb. de la Cor., p. 178.

in the Faith of Christ? . . . Through respect for her and for her intimate alliance with the loved ones she had visited, the Lord has been moved to pour the grandeurs of His mercy on this our common fatherland."[1]

During the Spanish rule Guadalupe had practically a legal recognition in national affairs. Ever since the last quarter of the sixteenth century it was customary for the new viceroys to stop at the Shrine, and pass a night there, before they entered the seat of government. Moreover, during the last century they were bound to go there to receive the insignia of office.

Great privileges were decreed to the Order of Guadalupe. It was considered the highest honorary body, and its distinctions were vastly prized. The first Emperor, Iturbide, made it an Imperial Order in 1822; and President Santa-Anna renewed or increased its privileges, on the occasion of his bringing to the Sanctuary, in 1853, Hidalgo's banner of independence. Maximilian took care to visit Guadalupe before entering the Capital; to the reëstablished Imperial Order he also gave extraordinary splendor.

But it was the struggle for independence, in the beginning of this century, that particularly intensified the nation's attachment to Holy Mary of Guadalupe. The religious love and the patriotic were thereby most solidly welded. The true type of a son of the land is universally recognised in the able leader, Father Hidalgo of Dolores. This learned and energetic pastor won the title of First Apostle and Martyr of Mexican freedom. When the cry for good government or independence was

---

[1] La Gloriosa Aparicion, pp. 41 et seq.

raised in September, 1810, Hidalgo took a copy of the Guadalupan Picture from a sanctuary at Atotonilco, and made it the people's standard.

At first, indeed, the rising seemed somewhat in the nature of a crusade. Spain, the ruling country, was in the hands of Napoleon, and was, as the Mexicans understood, being revolutionised into infidelity. They, therefore, determined not to be dragged into the same gulf, and hence took up arms for the defence of their religion and the maintenance of the older Spanish authority. That this was the cause and object of the revolt is made manifest by the inscription on Hidalgo's banner. It runs thus :—

"¡ Viva la Religion, viva Nuestra Madre Santisima de Guadalupe, viva Fernando VII., viva la America y muera el mal gobierno!"

The religious character of the purely Mexican movement was further seen in the measures taken at the First Congress, in 1813. Under the presidency of Morelos—the priest and general who took the place of the executed Hidalgo, and soon after shared his fate—there was decreed a Guadalupan celebration in conjunction with an *Independence Day*; and the reëstablishment of the *Company of Jesus* was voted for the sake of the schools and missions.

The course of events made the struggle one for separation and native government. In view of the results we can hardly regard the religious character of the incipient movement as less than providential. It linked forever in the public mind the best civil traditions with the most sacred ones of piety and devotion. For it can never be forgotten that as Guadalupe saved the native race at the beginning, so later on it served to inspire and unite the soldiers of freedom. The impression is ineffaceable that it was under Our Lady's aegis the people struggled for their rights and gained them; and the influence of this impression is strikingly salutary.

The thought of Guadalupe is for every Mexican a bulwark of faith. It is one of the most unassailable defenses against the insidious attacks of the Secret Societies and the Protestant Associations. These proselytisers—who, whatever their personal motives, must objectively be regarded as tools of hell—taking occasion of political troubles and partisan legislation, strive, with most vulgar arrogance, to spread among the simple faithful the theory that their Catholic piety hinders their temporal welfare. It could not be expected that every peasant would know enough of true history and true economy to refute even shallow sophists; but the most childlike Indian is able to answer that all he has ever known of good for soul or body was connected with Holy Mary of Guadalupe, and that, moreover, to love her one must be a real Catholic.

She is still, as she has been all along, their beacon light and tower of strength. Her name is a war-cry, and her remembrance an impenetrable shield. Devotion to her is a sheltering mantle for these guileless children of the Church. And, in the religious affairs of the day, I know few things more admirable or more consoling than the fact that here, in the New World, these ten or twelve millions of native Catholics cling with ever increasing tenacity to the Immaculate Mother of God, and by her means are kept in saving union with Our Lord Jesus Christ.

CHAPTER VI.

HISTORICAL GROUNDS OF THE DEVOTION.

THE history of Guadalupe has been admirably preserved. That such contemporary testimony and unbroken tradition can be adduced, both for the substance and the details of the story, is rare in matters of this nature. Predetermined critics may, of course, harp on the absence of several original documents in their original form; but the judicious reader will rather wonder that unexceptionable historical grounds can be clearly assigned for a special devotion that sprang up among the Indians of this New World nearly four hundred years ago. Even in times and places of comparative enlightenment the best-founded devotional movements are not always easily traceable: they are lived rather than spoken or written. To get a clear view of their origin and progress is usually difficult, often impossible.

At Guadalupe, however, we can follow all from the beginning; though there also the persuasion seems to have prevailed, in some measure, that the keeping of many records was, if not meaningless, at least unnecessary. The traditional devotion was felt to be living; the miraculous Picture was seen to be undecaying—what more history or evidence was required? The modern need of finding everything on paper was, at that time, neither experienced nor foreseen in Mexico. Nevertheless enough was written, as we shall presently see.

My way will be clearer if I premise two points: one on the relation of history to these special revelations, and the other on the evidence that can be called historical.

In the first place, we commonly find accounts of apparitions, private revelations, and miracles, prefaced by the remark that the question is merely one of history, to be judged on its own merits, like every other historical matter. This is done to mark off clearly the difference between such facts and the revealed truths of Catholic Faith; perhaps, also, to propitiate a dreaded non-Catholic or coldly-Catholic antipathy. Such apologetic statements are to be met with in English publications that treat or touch on Lourdes, Paray-le-Monial, Loretto, etc. And though admittedly just and necessary the distinction between matters of individual free devotion and matters of universal obligatory belief, still the qualifying of special revelations as merely historical questions may manifestly be inexact. Before the Church touches such facts they have certainly to stand on their own proper evidence; but when she has judged and approved they surely have gained something extrinsic. Be it more or less, according to the form and extent of approval, they undoubtedly take on an additional element of credibility; so that it cannot be altogether true to say that they are still just as they were before the Church took them up, mere open historical questions. Her sanction, even from the historian's point of view, is a testimony that cannot be overlooked.

The second point is that history, though loosely spoken of as something written, includes much that neither is nor can be put on paper. Elementary logic makes clear that monuments unanimously and deliberately erected, that common beliefs explicitly held and transmitted, are stronger evidence of facts than ordinary printed matter. It would be simplicity more than primitive to affirm that things are true because men have written them. All that can in most cases be said is that such or such a writer took this or that view of what he saw, or, much oftener, of what he heard. But satisfactory testimony of the past must include all that successive generations seriously believed and thought worth transmitting. Nor does it matter in what form they recorded and bequeathed their knowledge and convictions. Indeed tradition, in its best Church sense of all truth handed down (the *traditum*) and all truth to be handed on (the *tradendum*), is the only complete history.

This interpretation of historical evidence and its relation to Church affairs I keep in view in relating the Guadalupan story, which, however, might very well stand on documentary evidence alone.

Characteristically enough the earliest known writings on Guadalupe are Indian. The representatives of the people to whom Our Lady came and to whom she spoke, took every means within reach to communicate and transmit the knowledge of *the Miracle*—as the sum of the events connected with the Apparitions and the Picture is commonly styled in Indian as well as Spanish and Roman documents. In native fashion they pictured it on maps, wrote it out in hieroglyphics, and committed it by verse to the trained memory of the public chanters. Then, as soon as they had been taught to write their own language phonetically, they composed detailed *nahuatl* narratives in Latin characters.

Of these Indian histories of Guadalupe the earliest is probably the one that had long been kept in the archives of the Sanctuary, and of which a printed copy appeared in 1649. It was edited by the chaplain of the Shrine, Father Lasso de la Vega; but the Indian diction was at once recognised by scholars, as well as proclaimed by those more immediately concerned, to be of a century earlier—that is, of a time very little subsequent to the Apparitions. This native story has been repeatedly turned into Spanish; and I notice that the narrative section in the recent *Album de la Coronacion*[1] is a literal rendering of the authentic copy held by the Guadalupan Chapter.

The author of this original history is not quite certainly known, though excellent critics attribute it to Antonio Valeriano—a learned and influential Indian of the first century of Spanish rule. Valeriano is proved to have written a Guadalupan narrative which differs in no important particular from the one edited by Father Vega, but which found its way into other independent publications. It seems too that he was fit to be a historian of Our Lady of America. He was contemporary with the Apparitions, having been born about the time of the Conquest. As he was of the Moctezuma family he got a good education. Through the Franciscan College of Santa Cruz, founded in 1535, he passed with great distinction. He even acted there, for some time, as Lector and Prefect of the Indian students. Afterwards

---

[1] Edición de "El Tiempo," 1895.

he was much honored by the imperial authorities; and, from official documents found in the Boturini collection, it appears that for the latter part of the sixteenth century he was empowered to act as Governor of the Natives.

At Valeriano's death his papers passed to a younger and not less distinguished Indian. This was a descendant of the Tescoco kings, who had taken in Baptism the name of Fernando de Alva. Renowned European ecclesiastics spoke of this native American as 'their equal in science and their superior in virtue.' Alva loved knowledge and holiness. Among other native manuscripts he carefully preserved Valeriano's Guadalupan story, to which he added an appendix concerning the first miracles. This precious document reached the hands of the learned Oratorian, Father Becerra Tanco, who, from it and other trustworthy Indian sources, wrote in 1667, for presentation to the Holy See, an admirably simple and complete Spanish narrative which I mean to translate in my next chapter.

As these Alva-Valeriano papers are of great importance in Guadalupan history, it is well to find competent and most solemn attestation of their authenticity. In 1668 an author famous in the Old World and the New, D. Carlos de Sigüenza y Góngora, gave this categorical testimony: "I affirm and swear that this relation (the Guadalupan narrative) I found among the papers of Don Fernando de Alva, all of which I hold; and that it is the same that the Licentiate, Louis Becerra, declares he saw in his possession. The original Mexican is in the writing of the Indian, Don Antonio Valeriano, who is its real author; and at the end there are added some miracles, in the writing of Don Fernando who was also a Mexican."[1]

Both these distinguished Indians lived to an advanced age, Valeriano dying in 1605, and Alva about 1640.

Other lengthy native writings are mentioned by Guadalupan authors; but as it does not seem proved either that they were distinct from the Alva-Valeriano document, or that they are still to be found, I see no great utility in complicating my subject with a detailed account of them. Some incidental and very strongly probatory references to the Miracle it is necessary to record.

A will made in 1559, by a relative of Juan Diego, has this passage: "By his means (Juan Diego's) was accomplished the Miracle there over at Tepeyac, where appeared the loved Lady, Holy Mary, whose amiable Picture we see in Guadalupe."[2]

Two other wills, made as early as 1575, contain declarations which allowed Cardinal Lorenzana of Seville, who had been Archbishop of Mexico, to make this statement: "These documents, by their antiquity and their proximity to the Apparition, prove it to evidence; so that there is no need to seek others of less weight among the papers of Signor Boturini."[3]

In the Tlaxcalan Annals, kept in the library of the Mexican University, Bartolache could still decipher in 1790 these entries:—

"Year 1531, to Juan Diego appeared the loved Lady of Guadalupe of Mexico, called Tepeyacac."

---

[1] Fernando Cortez, cap. 10.   [3] Letters of Cortez: note at end.
[2] Can. Vera's *Contestacion*, p. 439.

"Year 1548, died Juan Diego, to whom appeared the loved Lady of Guadalupe of Mexico."

In the same Royal University there was and probably is still—at least in the State institution that replaced it—a very early manuscript history of Guadalupe. Dr. Uribe said publicly in 1777, when it was easy to verify his words: "The history of this same (Miracle), in the Mexican tongue, is to-day in the archives of the Royal University; and its age, though not known to the year, is recognised as running up close to the time of the Apparitions. This is made manifest both by the form of the letters and by the paper which is of agave, such as the Indians used before the Conquest."[1]

Guadalupan writers make frequent reference to the map and chant records of the natives. In Father Tanco's sworn evidence there is this statement: "I certify that I saw and read a Map of remarkable antiquity, written in the ancient figures and characters of the natives, which recorded events for more than three hundred years before the Spaniards came to this kingdom, and for many years after. . . . And among the events that occurred after the pacification of this city and kingdom of Mexico, there was figured the miraculous Apparition of Our Lady and of her blessed Picture of Guadalupe."[2]

In like manner the Jesuit historian, Florencia writes: "Before the great inundation of the city, the Mexicans were accustomed to assemble in immense crowds, with their festive dress and rich plumes, on the day on which they celebrated, at the Guadalupan Shrine, the feast of the renowned Apparition. Thereupon forming a circle

---

[1] Sermon, 14 Dec., 1777. [2] Felicidad de Mexico, p. 36.

that occupied the whole wide area before the church, they danced around to the music which, according to custom, two aged men produced on an instrument called Teponaztli. The musicians at the same time sang, in a metre peculiar to their language: The Apparition of the Most Holy Virgin to Juan Diego; the messages which he bore from the Sovereign Lady to the bishop, D. Fr. Juan de Zumárraga; the delivery of the flowers when the Mother of God gave them to him; the Apparition, when he showed the flowers in the bishop's presence, of the holy Picture figured and painted on his mantle or *tilma*. They chanted in addition the miracles that the holy Picture had wrought on the day of its collocation in the first chapel, as well as the praise and jubilation with which the event was celebrated by the natives."[1]

The same writer mentions, as known to his contemporaries, a canticle composed by a chief of Azcapotzalco and sung by the Indians on that great day of the first translation. But this document is lost, like so many other Mexican ones. Indeed the fate of the native manuscripts, not only Guadalupan but also civil and political, has been sad and even tragic. The two best and fullest collections ever made have dwindled to almost nothing. One was D. Sigüenza y Góngora's, the one that contained the Alva-Valeriano documents with a number of others. He left it to the College of Sts. Peter and Paul; and at the suppression of the Jesuits in 1767, it was scattered, or nominally transferred to the Royal University. But since the University itself was suppressed in 1857, not a manuscript has been accounted

---

[1] Estrella del Norte, p. 97.

for—though probably some of them are rather missing than irretrievably lost.

The other was a still greater collection, and it fared almost as badly. It was made by a Milanese gentleman, Signor Boturini Benaduci, who was an enthusiastic archaeologist, and who visited New Spain in 1736. Like most Catholic strangers who pass close to Guadalupe, he fell under the charm of the Picture and the Shrine; and so he determined to honor Our Lady by an original history. With self-sacrifice and endurance he spent years in the Indian villages and huts, gaining the confidence of the natives and inducing them to sell, or at least show, the ancient maps and manuscripts which, by that time, they had learned to secrete most cautiously.

Boturini's efforts were very successful. With precious materials for a civil history which he now contemplated, as well as for the religious one, he returned to live hermit-like and write his works at Guadalupe itself. His devotion to Holy Mary of the Apparitions went on increasing; and, though manifestly most meritorious, it led to a proceeding that some thought indiscreet. He, a layman and a foreigner, undertook something like what Leo XIII. and the Mexican Hierarchy have lately accomplished: he wanted to see the Picture solemnly crowned. He even obtained a decree from the Chapter of St. Peter's, in 1740, authorising the coronation. He then began to collect alms for the great ceremony. But there he came in collision with the Spanish Government.

Viceroy Fuenclara had Boturini arrested for meddling with such important affairs, and for being a stranger in the dominion without a passport. The noble and generous Italian saw all his cherished papers seized, and he himself was shipped a prisoner to Spain. He did not even get there without mishap; for the English fleet captured the vessel that conveyed him, and, after wearisome investigation, cast the prisoner and his conductors ashore near Gibraltar.

At Madrid the Guadalupan archaeologist was acquitted of every charge, and even adjudged considerable indemnification; but he neither got back to this continent nor ever recovered his treasured manuscripts. They were held by the officials of New Spain, and suffered as great disasters as their rightful owner. While lawsuits for their possession, after Boturini's death in 1749, were being carried on in both hemispheres, they were decaying and disappearing. The case was never decided, nor was it finally of much consequence; for the announcement had at last to be made that 'neglect, damp, rats, and curiosity-hunters' had practically demolished the precious collection. Some fragments of the maps and stronger parchments were recently brought to the National Museum of the City of Mexico, and may be seen there in one of the inner apartments.[1]

Guadalupan writers much regret the loss of so many native documents, and always hope for the recovery of some of them. But they find, meantime, a certain consolation in the well-grounded belief that nearly all the details consigned to writing by the Indians passed also by tradition or translation into the multitudinous Spanish works that treat of the Picture and the Shrine.

Spanish Americans have indeed been industrious in making known and glorifying Guadalupe. It is true

---

[1] Dicc. Univ., Art. *Boturini*.

that Father Florencia, two hundred years ago, accused them of showing less gratitude in that way to the Holy Mother than did the Indians; but he also added that if, in the earlier times, they forgot to write much about her devotion they did not forget to practice it. Since that period they have been prolific in Guadalupan illustration and defence.

The earliest Spanish account of the Miracle was Bishop Zumárraga's letter to his brethren at the Calahorra convent of Vitoria in Spain. Though this document cannot now be located, yet the references to it are too respectable and too definite to allow us to doubt about its having once existed. A Commissary of the Franciscan Order, in the latter part of the eighteenth century, Father Pedro de Mezquia, averred that "he saw and read a letter of the Prelate to the religious of that convent, recounting the Apparition of Our Lady of Guadalupe, as and how it happened."[1] The contemporaries of Mezquia neither doubted the statement nor hesitated about reporting it.

That there is found no other writing from the pen of Bishop Zumárraga on an event of such consequence in his episcopate, certainly demanded explanation—and explanations have been given abundantly. In the Brief of Benedict XIV. we find the fact recalled that (though Zumárraga was twenty years bishop) not even a signature of his could be found in Mexico. By necessity the archives were at first kept badly or not at all; and in the bishop's multiplied afflictions and forced absence, records were put astray or destroyed. Many of his documents found their way to Spain and are being published by

[1] Escudo de Armas, p. 329.

degrees; but even of these the latest notices are that some are now lost, some moth-eaten, and some illegible.

It has been inconsiderately asked why Zumárraga did not print accounts of the Miracle for his flock, as it was he that set up the first press in this Western World. Now, we know that as a fact he did much less printing than he wished. In his letters he complains pathetically of having no paper on which to print what he had prepared. Thus in one to the Emperor Charles V. in 1538, the seventh year after the Apparitions, he writes: "Little progress can be made with our printing, through scarcity of paper. This is an obstacle in the way of many works that we have prepared, and also of those that should be reprinted; for we are in want of the most necessary books, and few are coming from your side."[1]

It has been conjectured—perhaps fairly—that some of these obstructed publications were Guadalupan; yet, in the circumstances, it would seem unlike Zumárraga's prudence to write or speak much about a new Indian devotion. His position was delicate, dangerous, and uncertain. He undoubtedly showed that for himself he was not solicitous; but his loved work could be overthrown and his grand mission rendered wholly abortive. When in 1528 he first came, and still at the time of the Apparitions in 1531, he was only bishop-elect. He was, however, ecclesiastical superior and official Protector of the Natives. In this double capacity he kept silence in presence of no infringement of either Church right or Indian right, and hence he made many enemies. He was recalled to Spain in 1532, but he returned consecrated in 1534.

[1] Life by García Icazbalceta: Appendix.

From that time, as from the beginning, until his death in 1548, he was in toil and suffering a veritable Apostle of New Spain. Parts of his life read like passages of the Acts that treat of St. Paul. He has been compared to St. Patrick; and certainly in his dealings with his countrymen and the natives, there appears both the kingly strength and the womanly tenderness that we are accustomed to associate with the ministry of Ireland's Apostle. He was the benefactor of this whole Western World, in ways that have not as yet been even fractionally acknowledged. He brought into it not only religion and education, and the printing-press which should be their handmaid, but also every useful book, machine, plant and animal that could then be bought or begged in Europe.

Those who intelligently appreciate Spanish-American Catholicity will also mention as Zumárraga's highest glory his providential share in establishing and spreading the Guadalupan devotion. Yet it is not likely that he prominently preached it. In recognizing the Miracle and founding the Sanctuary he did what was required; attempting more might have been a hindrance. In his Spanish surroundings there were powerful and violent adventurers who little respected the rights of the natives, who even affected to believe that the natives had no rights, as they were not yet proved to belong to the human family! In such a state of affairs to come out loudly as the champion of an Indian devotion was practically to make a laughing-stock both of it and of himself.

The avaricious tyrants who temporarily replaced Cortez hated and ridiculed the unbending monk-bishop. The year of the Apparitions and the two preceding ones were marked by fierce struggles. Zumárraga resisted the oppressive injustice of those momentarily in power, and they plotted and persecuted in return. In his letters of 1529 we find these statements: "The president (Gusman) said at his table, before several credible persons, that if he had been present he would have thrown me down out of the pulpit. And as I am wont to reprehend them (licentious officials) they have fled my sermons, and usually go to hold banquets on Sunday." Again: "He (the president) made fun and mockery of me; . . . he said that if I meddled with this (a public scandal) he would order me and my clergy to be seized and thrown away on the island of the Azores."

As the persecution darkened and thickened around him, and governmental snares were laid for his feet, the bishop was forced to say: "In the whole land there is not a lawyer who ventures to counsel me, or to come to my dwelling or receive me in his. . . . The natives were terrified (by the threat of hanging), the Spaniards were in bewilderment, so that no one dared to speak to me any more than if I were excommunicated. . . . The persecution that the president and his judges now carry on against the monks and clergy is worse than that of Herod and Diocletian. . . . They abuse the little Indian pupils whom the missionaries send to preach and make known the things of God where they themselves cannot go very often: they give them blows and similar treatment."[1]

As churches and monasteries had been violated, and zealous preachers brutally dragged out of the pulpit, the firm prelate put the whole city under interdict in 1530.

---

[1] Life by G. Icaz., App.

That strong act really broke the power of the persecutors, but it exposed Zumárraga to endless accusations. When writing to the Empress, in March 1531, he mentions that "thirty-four chapters, full of calumny," were presented against him in the Indian Council. He gives a summary of the charges, and specially marks that one of them was to the effect that he was preaching "things troublesome and scandalous." Were not the letter earlier in 1531 than the Miracle at Tepeyac, this indictment would be understood to concern the new American devotion; for six years later he and the other bishops had to rebut the charge of "interfering with doctrine and not telling the truth to the Indians"—almost word for word the accusation brought against Zumárraga's immediate successor for sending his people to Guadalupe.

It is then, I think, pretty evident that the first Bishop of Mexico could not write or publish much about Indian revelations. He was satisfied to put the devotion on a good footing, and to see it doing its work divinely. Before he died the whole land was ringing with the name of Holy Mary of Guadalupe. It is related that during the pest in 1545, three years before the bishop's death, the Franciscan Missionaries led all the children, of seven and under, before the Holy Mother, and through them obtained a cessation of the scourge. The "Children's Pilgrimage" is a graceful tradition among the Indians.

It is a question with well-informed writers whether the Juridical Acts concerning the Apparitions and the Shrine, which are frequently referred to, were drawn up by the first bishop or by the second. A present day learned opinion is that Zumárraga could not act as judge, since he was personally favored in the Miracle.

That Acts were formulated is affirmed with all authority. The Public Records Departments of the City of Mexico admitted to the author Sanchez, in 1640, that they had had Guadalupan Acts but had them no longer. In the juridicial deposition of the same Sanchez, in 1666, it is attested that Dr. de la Torre, dean of the cathedral, once found García de Mendoza, who was Archbishop of Mexico from 1602 to 1606, " reading with great affection the Acts and Process of the said Apparition." In Benedict XIV.'s Brief their absence is referred to, but with the note that " it is certain they existed." And Cardinal Lorenzana, in his Guadalupan sermon in 1770, says: " We regret that the Acts of Authentication of the Miracle have been lost; but they do not fail us, for they remain written in the hearts of Spaniards and natives. When the event occurred there was no cathedral, no secretary, no notary, no archives; and their testimony is advantageously replaced by the tradition perpetuated in the works, hieroglyphics, and maps of the Indians."

Some Acts of which Cardinal Lorenzana may never have heard—for the documents have only recently been published—were drawn up under Zumárraga's successor, Archbishop Montufar. In the trial occasioned by the wanton attack on that prelate for his Guadalupan devotion, to which allusion has already been made, the fact was brought out that the Archbishop did not off-hand call Tepeyac events miracles, but that 'he was taking an Information on them.' That information apparently concerned miraculous occurrences of the years 1555 and '56 in which it was taken, but it also implied an earlier information on the original Miracle.

The trial established other facts very glorious to Guadalupe in that twenty-fifth year of the devotion. In the records of it we find a Royal Procurator, Juan de Salazar, testifying that since this devotion spread, the people had mostly given up spending the Sunday in pleasure-gardens (huertas) and losing Mass; and that " now no other thing is heard in the land but—Where do you wish to go? let us go to Our Lady of Guadalupe."

Almost in the same terms Gomez de Leon testifies: " Now they go where there are no decked gardens, nor other refreshment but to be before Our Lady in contemplation and devotion."

Father Francisco Salazar bore similar testimony, and added from his own observation that "children, when they reached the use of reason, and heard their parents and other persons speak of this devotion, importuned much to be taken there."

Concerning the Archbishop, who was impotently but viciously threatened with expulsion from the country, on the trumped-up charge of disturbing doctrine and violating Lateran decrees, it was testified that " the miracles His Grace preached of Our Lady of Guadalupe was the great devotion which the whole city had taken to this blessed Picture, the Indians as well as others; how the very highest and most delicate ladies walk out barefoot, with their staffs in their hands, to visit and commend themselves to Our Lady; and how the Indians finding this a great example do likewise."[1]

Montufar's preaching seems to have angered some friars of Lutheran tendency who invoked Deuteronomy

---

[1] Inform. sobre un Sermon del 8 Sept., 1556, . . . Mex., 1891.

against image-worship, and perorated about the danger of exposing *their disciples* to take a wonder-working Picture for God! His words, however, have great probatory force from his known conservatism and even severity. At the First Mexican Council, in 1555, he, as presiding Metropolitan, had decrees promulgated strictly prohibiting the use of unauthorised images and unapproved religious histories. Yet in his panegyric of Our Lady, on Sunday, September 6th of the following year, he fervently advocated the Guadalupan devotion and urged all the faithful to go to the Shrine. In 1556, therefore, the Metropolitan of Mexico found Guadalupe sufficiently approved.

The text on which he preached has been preserved in the Information; and it was certainly a striking one in its application to the events at Tepeyac: it was nothing less than the words of Our Lord: *Blessed are the eyes that see the things which you see.*

The flourishing condition of the devotion and the Sanctuary in Archbishop Montufar's time is unequivocally proved by certain viceregal correspondence with Philip II., which somewhat hampered the action of the next archbishop, Moya y Contreras. Montufar had added a church to the original Guadalupan chapel or hermitage, and provided dwellings for the priests and pilgrims. The offerings were so abundant that what remained, after all needful expenses, sufficed for the excellent purpose of giving annually a marriage portion of three hundred dollars to each of six orphan girls. Though few his priests, Archbishop Moya found it necessary to name two permanent chaplains for Guadalupe; he would even have appointed more—for he contemplated establishing a parish and a monastery—had not Viceroy Enriquez interfered. This official set himself in opposition to the Archbishop. He wanted the Guadalupan alms turned over to a Royal Hospital, and he advised King Philip not to authorise the erection either of the parish or of the monastery.

Enriquez did not take the trouble to inform himself very accurately about the Sanctuary; but he vaguely refers to the Picture, the first hermitage, the new church, the miracles and the pilgrims.[1]

The parish and monastery were hindered for the moment. The inimical report of the viceroy is, at the same time, an unexceptionable testimony to the importance and influence of Guadalupe at the early date at which this letter was addressed to Philip II., that is in May, 1575.

In other secular history of that first Guadalupan century, some references are of great weight. Bernal Diaz, a blunt soldier-companion of Cortez, wrote the story of the Conquest most generally regarded as trustworthy. In matters touching on religion this author shows reverence, but not much credulity: there is even a gentle irony in his rejection of certain Spanish reports of St. James or some other heavenly visitant having helped the Christian army against the idolatrous Aztecs. But when he, who had no more personal interest in Mexico and was permanently settled in Central America, comes to mention Guadalupe, in 1568, he exclaims: "Look at the Holy House of Our Lady of Guadalupe which is at Tepeaquilla, where was the camp of Gonzalo de Sandoval when we won Mexico; and see the holy

---

[1] Cartas de Indias, p. 310.

miracles that it has worked and is working every day."[1] Having to name Tepeyac farther on, he cannot refrain from saying—"which now bears the name of Our Lady of Guadalupe, where are wrought and have been wrought many admirable miracles."[2]

This incidental and disinterested mention of miraculous Guadalupe, as of something well-known and undoubted, has much evidential force; especially when it is remembered that in 1568 the soldier-historian had long left Mexico, but had been there at the time of the Apparitions and for the seven years immediately following.

There is another brief historical passage of similar significance. Suarez de Peralta wrote, in 1589, sketches of New Spain. When mentioning the arrival of a viceroy he says: "He came to Our Lady of Guadalupe which is a Picture of very great devotion, at two short leagues from Mexico. It has wrought many miracles (it showed itself among the rocks) and to this devotion the whole land hurried."[3]

This passing remark is of manifest importance. Though written in 1589 it refers to facts of a date fifteen or twenty years earlier; and its very inaccuracy gives it a peculiarly independent value.

Of the authorities for Guadalupan history in the last 250 years there is no need to speak at length. The books written on the subject are extant, excellent, and numerous. On an average every ten years may be said to have given an important Guadalupan work, with countless smaller publications. The authors and occasions, as well

---

[1] Hist. Verd., cap. 209.
[2] Id., C. 250.
[3] Hist. del Descubr., cap. 41.

as the literary qualities, of these compositions differ considerably; but the same beautiful story is always repeated. With minor divergencies that but indicate individual research, there is most impressive accord in all matters of moment. The politicians, artists, and scientists who have written on Guadalupe seem as exact in narrative and as fervent in advocacy as the priests and religious who have best treated the same great subject.

It is, moreover, remarkable that, as time rolls on, Guadalupan authors give proof not only of a wider but also of an intenser grasp of the national tradition. They are showing day by day an increasingly deep appreciation of what happened at Tepeyac a full year of years ago. And yet the laborious industry and pious affection of the first writers in Spanish seemed to defy competition. When the complete printed narrative of the Oratorian, Father Sanchez, was declared by the ecclesiastical censor to be in accord with 'the tradition and the annals,' and came out in 1648 enriched with its devout novenas, the Guadalupan world was satisfied and even enraptured. Nevertheless much better treatises soon followed; and those of the middle of this present century, like the deputy Tornel's *Aparicion Comprobada y Defendida*, or of the present day and of living authors, far surpass all that preceded them.

Besides books other important documents for Guadalupan history are furnished by these later centuries. The various informations drawn up for presentation to Rome are of great importance. There are the Acts of the juridical processes in 1663, 1723, and 1750. More important still is the apostolic process ordered by Alexander VII. in 1666. This latter document is conscientiously detailed and solemnly authenticated. Among other testimonies it gives the exact words of ten lay persons and eleven ecclesiastics—twenty-one witnesses who represented all classes of society. Their ages ranged from 55 to 115 years; but naturally none of them could be eye-witnesses, since it was already 135 years from the time of the Apparitions. However, they were able to swear to what they had individually heard from their own fathers and mothers and other friends and neighbours who had known Bishop Zumárraga and Juan Diego, and were acquainted with all the circumstances of the Miracle.

Thus, when his deposition was read to Marcos Pacheco, a mestizo of eighty years of age, he further averred "that all he had said was recounted to him and his brothers by his before-mentioned aunt—and with all clearness, because she had learned it from the mouth of the said Juan Diego: moreover it was at the time public in their whole village and outside it."

In the final asseveration of Gabriel Xarez, an Indian of 110 years, there is a ring of something like impatience at being questioned: "So," he concluded, "his said father had told him, and the thing was certain and evident."[1]

The native witnesses were also able to testify to what they heard and saw when they were first taken to Guadalupe. As some of them were very old they made, as I see in their evidence, the impressive declaration of their belief that Our Lady had got them length of days till they could make that solemn deposition.

The ecclesiastical witnesses included secular priests, Franciscans, Dominicans, Carmelites, and Jesuits. More-

---

[1] Inform. de 1666. Test. 1º· y 2º·

over, the presidents, deans, and superiors of both civil and religious bodies signed for the categories they represented. Then there was added the written report of seven master-painters and three diplomaed physicists, on the miraculous nature and conservation of the Picture.

A more completely satisfactory substantiation of a religious history, than this Mexican Apostolic Process of 1666, need certainly not be desired. The only collection of Guadalupan writings, that a modern reader might find more interesting and edifying, would be an exact copy of the Mexican Hierarchy's correspondence with the Holy See during the present pontificate. By the nation's prelates the tradition—ancient, unvarying, constant—has again been authoritatively stated, and the faith-inspiring history has been worthily repeated with love, learning, and unanimity.

CHAPTER VII.

THE INDIAN NARRATIVE.

THERE is reason to rejoice that the Guadalupan story was retold by the Oratorian, Father Louis Becerra Tanco. He had at command the best traditions and the best manuscripts, and he was capable of profiting by them.

As he was born towards the end of the first century of the Spanish domination, when the two civilizations and peoples were fairly blended, he got the fullest education that New Spain could afford. He was, as in his book he has occasion to mention, reared among the Indians, whose language, customs, and traditions he learned thoroughly. His studies were made at the Royal University of Mexico, in which he afterwards held different chairs of literature and science. Among his ecclesiastical and religious brethren he held, for more than thirty years, the position of *Minister of Doctrine.* Many fruitful labors are recorded of him; but, as things now appear, his greatest work was his elucidation and authentication of the Guadalupan history.

In writing he repeatedly feels called on to give his credentials; "not" as he ingenuously states, "to magnify his own littleness, but to give sufficient reason for what he is affirming and certifying." Having mentioned his various opportunities and obligations of learning thoroughly the native language, oral and written, he naively remarks: "To which may be added the more than common acquaintance I have with other languages, such as Latin, Tuscan, and Portuguese, as well as enough to read, write, and pronounce the Greek and Hebrew tongues."

As a redactor, Tanco certainly inspires confidence. Contemporary authorities, and his own writings, go to prove that he was a priest of the humblest piety, and, for the time, of very profound erudition. In his devout zeal he labored systematically, turning to account all the sources of tradition found among the Indians. Having examined the maps and hieroglyphics, and listened to the various family chants, he was able to testify that this specially native evidence was in perfect accord with what the general public held concerning the Shrine and the Picture. He thus thoroughly verified and digested the beautiful Indian narrative.

When putting it into Spanish he held closely to the Mexican diction, both because he much revered the original, and because he had to swear to the authenticity of his version. It was the Apostolic Commission of 1667 that imposed the work on his willing zeal; and the ecclesiastical judges stood by, waiting to take his document as a sacred deposition.

With regard to the translation, Tanco complains of the difficulty of rendering the diffuse simplicity and affectionateness of the Indian speech into ordinary Castilian. But manifestly the difficulty is much greater in the case of our coldly masculine English. Yet I give the narrative word for word, in the belief that it will read none the less racy and authentic, for its divergence from our commoner modes of thought and expression.

The Indian Narrative.

"In the year of Our Lord, 1531, when the Spaniards had ruled in this city of Mexico and province of New Spain for ten years and four months, the war having ceased and the Holy Gospel having commenced to flourish in this Kingdom, on the morning of Saturday, the ninth day of the month of December, a poor Indian peasant, simple and humble, one of those recently converted to the holy Catholic Faith, was on his way to the Franciscan mission at the church of St. James the Greater, the Patron of Spain, to hear the Mass of the Virgin Mary. Juan Diego, as he was called since his Baptism, was a native of Cuautitlan, which lies four leagues north of the city; and he was married to an Indian woman of his own class, who bore the name of Maria Lucia. The church mentioned was in the suburb of Tlatelolco, and the Indian was coming from the village in which he then resided, and which is supposed to have been the neighbouring Tolpetlac. He, therefore, reached, at the first gleam of dawn, the foot of the Tepeyacac, or *sharp point of the hills*—so called because it stands out from the other elevations which surround the lake and the valley, where lies the Capital of Mexico, and because it is nearest to that city. At the present day, for reasons to be given immediately, it is named after Our Lady of Guadalupe.

"Towards the hilltop and the rocky pinnacle which overhangs the plain on the lake-side, the Indian heard a canticle resounding sweetly, which, as he said, seemed to him like the warbling of many different birds that sang together in dulcet harmony and quired to one another with wonderful accord. The higher hills behind repeated and multiplied the echoes.

First Apparition.

"Lifting his eyes to the place whence he thought the canticle proceeded, he saw a white shining cloud, having around it a magnificent rainbow whose colors were formed by rays of most dazzling light that blazed from a central point. Absorbed and almost ravished out of himself, but otherwise calm and untroubled, the Indian felt in his heart an inexpressible joy and jubilation. So he asked himself: What must this be that I hear and see? Or whither have I been carried? Can it be that I have been translated to the heaven of delights which our ancestors called the origin of our flesh, the garden of flowers, the earthly paradise hidden from the eyes of men?

"While he was in this rapturous wonder the canticle ceased, and he heard himself called by his name, in a woman's sweet, gentle tones. The voice came from the brightness of the cloud, and bade him draw near. Advancing and hastening up the ridge he saw in the midst of the refulgence a most beautiful Lady—very like her whom we now see in the blessed Picture, and well represented in the description which the Indian gave before the Picture was produced or copied. Her apparel, as he described it, so shone that, struck by its splendors, the rocks on that rough summit looked like well-cut, transparent precious stones; while the leaves of the cactus and the brambles—which the exposed situation makes poor and stunted—seemed to be clusters of fine emeralds, with thorns, branches, and trunks of bright, burnished gold, and the very soil of the little tableland was as jasper of many colors.

"With an affable, encouraging look, the Lady spoke to the Indian, in his own language.

"'My son,' she said, 'Juan Diego, whom I tenderly love as a little one and weak, whither goest thou?'[1]

"The Indian replied: 'I am going, most noble Mistress and Lady mine, to Mexico, to the Tlatelolco ward, to hear the Mass which the ministers and substitutes of God show us.'

"Having heard him Most Holy Mary continued: 'Know, my son, my much beloved, that I am the ever Virgin Mary, Mother of the true God who is the Author of life, the Creator of all things, the Lord of heaven and earth, present everywhere. And it is my wish that here there be raised to me a temple in which, as a loving Mother to thee and those like thee, I shall show my tender clemency and the compassion I feel for the natives and for those who love and seek me, for all who implore my protection, who call on me in their labors and afflictions; and in which I shall hear their weeping and their supplications that I may give them consolation and relief.

---

[1] Tanco here interjects: "How we recognise in these words the Mexican turn of expression!" ... A note of Carillo y Perez may also be in place here. "These expressive words," he says, "which in our (Spanish) idiom may seem unsuited to the majesty and grandeur of the Most Holy Virgin, are not so in the Mexican in which the Lady spoke. They form the most appropriate locution in that tongue which conveys most reverence when it is most naive, most affable and caressing." Pens. Amer., 1793.

That my will may have its effect thou hast to go to the city of Mexico and to the palace of the bishop who resides there, to tell him that I have sent thee and that I wish a temple to be raised to me in this place. Thou shalt report what thou hast seen and heard; and be assured that I will repay what thou dost for me in the charge I give thee: for it I will make thee great and renowned. Now thou hast heard, son, my wish. Go in peace, remembering that I shall reward thy labor and diligence; in this, therefore, employ all the strength thou art able.'

"Prostrating himself, the Indian replied: 'I go, I go, most noble Lady and Mistress mine, to do as an humble servant what you have ordered. Fare-you-well.'

"Departing with profound reverence the Indian descended the western shoulder of the hill and took the road to the Capital. In fulfilment of his promise he went straight to the city, the distance being a league, and entered the palace of the Prelate, who was the Illustrious Don Fray Juan de Zumárraga, first Bishop of Mexico. Having gone in he began to ask the servants to tell the Lord Bishop that he wanted to see and speak to him. They did not do so immediately, either because it was so early, or because they saw that the Indian was poor and humble. They kept him long waiting; but finally, moved by his patience, they ushered him in.

"When he reached the presence of his Lordship, he fell on his knees and delivered his message. He said that the Mother of God had sent him; that he had seen her and spoken to her that very morning. He then reported all that he saw and heard, just as we have related it.

"The bishop heard with astonishment what the Indian affirmed, and marvelled at the strange occurrence; but of the message, to which he gave little credit, he seemed to make slight account, thinking it was mere imagination on the Indian's part, or nothing better than a dream. Perhaps, too, he feared it might be a delusion of the demon, as the natives were but lately converted to our holy religion. Though, therefore, he questioned the man closely on his story and found all his answers consistent, he nevertheless sent him away, promising to hear him more at length and to consider the affair more thoroughly if he came again after some days. It is evident that he wanted time to deliberate and to get information about the character of the envoy.

"The Indian was very sad and disconsolate as he left the bishop's palace, both because he saw that he was not believed and because the will of Most Holy Mary who had sent him was not to be accomplished.

Second Apparition.

"The evening of that same day, about sunset, Juan Diego was returning to his village, which, as far as it can be traced, was Tolpetlac, situated below the slope of the higher hill, at a league's distance northeast. Tolpetlac means the place of the cat's-tail mats, for at the time the only occupation of the villagers was to make mats of that plant. Passing, therefore, by the height on which he had that morning seen and spoken to the Virgin Mary, he found her waiting to get the answer to her message. As soon as he saw her he prostrated himself before her and cried out:—

"'O little one, most dear! (a Mexican address of affection to a superior) my Queen and most high Lady, I did what you told me. Though for a long time I was not let in to the bishop, I finally saw him and gave him your message just as you ordered me. He listened to me with kindness and attention; but from what I noticed in him and from his questions, I gathered that he did not believe me: for he told me to come again that he might at leisure inquire into my affair, and examine it more closely. He supposed that the temple you demand was an imagination or whim of mine and not your will. I therefore beg of you to send some noble and influential person, some one worthy of respect, to whom credit ought to be given; for you see, O my Sovereign, that I am a poor serf, a mere lowly peasant, and that I am not fit for this embassy of yours.

"'Pardon, O Queen, my boldness, if I have at all failed in the respect due to your greatness. Far be it from me to incur your indignation, or to displease you by my reply.'[1]

"Most Holy Mary heard the words of the Indian benignly, and then said:—

"'Hear, much loved son, and understand that I am not without clients and servants to send, for I have many that I might employ if I wished, many that would do whatever they were ordered; but it much befits that thou undertake this affair and conduct it. My wish and desire has to be accomplished by thy means. So I ask

[1] "This colloquy," Father Tanco parenthetically remarks, "is found as here reported in the historical writings of the natives, and contains nothing of mine but the translation, phrase by phrase, from the Mexican idiom to the Castilian." Felic. de Mex., p. 9.

thee, my son, and I order thee, to go back in the morning, and see and speak to the bishop. Tell him to erect me the temple I demand, and say that she who sent thee is the Virgin Mary, Mother of the true God.'

"Juan Diego answered: 'Be not offended, Queen and Lady mine, at what I said. For I shall go with great good will, and obey your order with all my heart. I'll bear your message, for I am not offering excuses, nor do I think the journey any trouble. Perhaps, indeed, I shall not be received nor willingly heard; or if the bishop listens to me he may not believe me; but all the same I will do as you tell me. And here, Lady, in this spot, I shall be waiting to-morrow evening at sunset to give you the answer that I shall have received. So peace be with you, my little one most high, and may God keep you.'

"The Indian took his leave with profound humility and went to his home in the village. It is not known whether he mentioned the occurrence to his wife or any one else, for history says nothing on that point. Perhaps being confused and ashamed that he had not been believed, he did not dare to speak till he saw how things would turn.

"The following day, Sunday, December 10th, Juan went to the Church of St. James to hear Mass and assist at the Christian doctrine. And when the Ministers of the Gospel had as usual gone through the whole list of the native Christians of the parish, ward by ward, he went again to the bishop's palace to fulfil the mandate of the Virgin Mary. The members of the household were very slow to announce his arrival; but when he was let in, humbling himself in the bishop's presence, he told, with tears and sighs, 'how he had again seen, in the same place, the Mother of God who awaited him for the answer to her message; how she had ordered him to come back to the bishop and tell him to have a temple erected to her where she had appeared and spoken; and how she certified that she who sent him was the Mother of Jesus Christ, the ever Virgin Mary.'

"The bishop heard with greater attention this time and was less disinclined to believe. But to make surer of the facts, he questioned and requestioned the Indian, warning him to take good care what he asserted. He made him describe the Lady who sent him; and from the description he had to recognise that the man had neither been dreaming nor inventing. Nevertheless, to acquire greater certainty, and to avoid the apparent levity of believing an Indian peasant's simple tale, he told Juan that 'his story was not enough to start such an enterprise as he proposed; and that, therefore, he should tell the Lady who sent him to give him some signs by which it might be known that the message was really from the Mother of God, and that it was indeed she who wished the temple erected.'

"The Indian replied 'that the bishop might see what sign he preferred, and that he would ask it.'

"The prelate noticed that the man neither doubted nor hesitated about asking the sign, but that utterly unruffled he had said to name any sign desired. He then called the two most trusted persons of his household, and, in the Castilian tongue which was unintelligible to the Indian, bade them look closely at the man and be ready to follow him as soon as he left the house. He directed them not to lose sight of him, but without his notice to keep after him till he reached the place where he said he had seen the Virgin Mary. They were to observe with whom he spoke, and bring back an account of all they saw and heard.

"They did as they were ordered. When the Indian was dismissed from the bishop's presence, they followed him and, without his knowledge, kept their eyes on him.

"But as soon as Juan Diego reached the bridge on the eastern side of the city, where a stream passes and, almost at the foot of the hillock, runs into the lake, he vanished from their sight. They eagerly sought for him, and searched both sides of the hill, but all in vain. Indignant with him, therefore, they called him an impostor and liar or else a wizard. So when they came back and gave their account to the bishop, they besought him not to believe this fellow, but, if he returned, to punish him for his imposture.

Third Apparition.

"When Juan, who had gone on in advance but yet within sight of the bishop's servants, reached the summit of the hillock, he found Most Holy Mary again waiting to get the answer to her message. Humbling himself in her presence he related 'how, in fulfilment of her order he had returned to the bishop's palace and delivered her message; how he had been questioned and requestioned, and finally told that his simple story was not enough to decide so important an affair, but that he must ask the Lady for a sure sign; in order,' he added, 'that it may be known that it is you who sent me, and that it is you who wish a temple to be here erected to you.'

"With tender words Most Holy Mary thanked him for his care and diligence, and bade him come there next day that she might give him a sure sign by which the bishop would believe him. Promising obedience the Indian reverently took his leave.

"However, the next day, Monday, the 11th of December, passed without Juan's being able to return as he had been told. For when he reached his village he found his uncle Juan Bernardino, who was as a father to him and whom he loved most deeply, sick unto death of a malignant fever which the natives call *Cocoliztli*. Having much compassion for him he spent most of the day seeking the help of a relative of his, a medical man; who, indeed, came and administered some medicines, but with no better result than an increase of the malady. Hence the sufferer, feeling himself failing that night, besought his nephew to set out before daybreak for the Convent of St. James at Tlatelolco and call a priest to give him the Sacraments of Penance and Extreme Unction, as he judged his sickness mortal.

"Juan Diego was away before dawn, hurrying with all speed to call one of the priests and return with him as guide. Therefore, towards daybreak, on Tuesday the 12th of December, he came to the place where he should cross, from the east, the summit of the hill. It then occurred to him that he had not come back the preceding day in obedience to the order of the Virgin Mary, as he had promised. Thinking, therefore, that if he passed the place in which he had seen her, she would reproach him for not coming as she told him, he imagined in his simplicity that by taking another path round the lower slope of the hill he should escape being seen or detained by her. This he did, saying to himself that his present business required haste, and that once free of it he could come to ask the sign and take it to the bishop. But when he had passed the spot where the spring of aluminous water rises, and was about to turn the shoulder of the hill, Most Holy Mary came forth to meet him.

Fourth Apparition.

"The Indian saw her descend to cross his way, from the summit of the hill, surrounded by a white cloud, with the same brightness as on the first occasion.

"She said to him: 'Whither goest thou, my son, and what road is this thou hast taken?'

"The Indian was confused, afraid, and ashamed. So he threw himself on his knees and answered perturbedly:

"'My little one most beloved, and Lady mine, may God keep you! . . . How early you are around! . . . I trust you are well. . . . Be not displeased with what I shall say. Know, my sovereign, that a servant of yours, my uncle, is dangerously sick of a grievous and mortal malady. And as he appears very low I am hurrying to the city, to the church of Tlatelolco, to call a priest who will come to confess and anoint him—for in fine we are all born subject to death. But having despatched this affair I shall return here to obey your orders. Pardon me, I beseech you, my Lady, and have patience a little; for I am not seeking an excuse not to do what you commanded this servant of yours, nor is it a false pretext I give you: to-morrow I'll come without fail.'

"With gentle look Most Holy Mary heard the apology of the Indian, and thus replied:—

"'Hear, my son, what I now say to thee: let nothing trouble or afflict thee. Fear neither pain nor sickness nor other grievous accident. Am not I here, I who am thy Mother? Thou art beneath my shadow and protection. And am not I life and health? In my lap art thou, and counted as mine. What more dost thou need? Have neither sorrow nor anxiety on account of thy uncle's sickness, for he will not die of this attack. Be even assured that he is already well.'[1]

"When Juan Diego heard these words he was so much consoled and so fully satisfied that he cried out: 'Send me, then, O my Lady, to see the bishop; and give me the sign, as you said you would, that I may be belived.'

"Most Holy Mary replied: 'Go up, my son, much loved and cherished, to the summit of the hill where you saw me and spoke to me, and pluck the roses which you will find there. Gather them in the lap of your cloak, and bring them to my presence, and I shall tell you what to do and say.'

"The Indian obeyed without a word, though he knew for certain that there were no flowers in the place; for it was barren rock and produced nothing. Having reached the top he saw there a beautiful rose-tree with fresh, odorous, dewy flowers. Arranging his cloak or *tilma* in the native fashion, he plucked as many roses as he could put into the lap of it and bore them to the presence of the Virgin Mary. She was waiting for him at the foot of a tree which the Indians call Cuauzahuatl, that is *the tree of the spider's web* or *the fasting tree*. It is a wild

---

[1] "And so it was," Father Tanco incidentally adds, "as was afterwards known, and as we shall relate farther on."—Felic. de Mex., p. 18.

tree that produces no fruit, but in its season gives some white blossoms. From the position I think it is the ancient trunk which still stands on the slope of the hill, and at whose foot is the path leading up the eastern bank. In front of it is the aluminous spring.

"Here, doubtless, was effected the miraculous painting of the blessed Picture. For when the Indian humbled himself in the presence of the Virgin Mary and showed her the roses he had gathered, holding them up in his cloak, Our Lady herself took them out all together and put them back in the lap of the garment, saying:—

"'Here thou hast the sign to take to the bishop. Tell him that by token of these roses he is to do what I ordered. Attend, son, to what I say, and remark that I place confidence in thee. Neither show what thou carriest to any one by the way, nor open thy cloak till thou art in the presence of the bishop. Then tell him what I have just said, and thou wilt dispose him to raise my temple.'

"Having so spoken the Virgin Mary sent him away. The Indian was delighted with the sign, for he understood that he should now succeed and that his embassy should have its effect. So he brought the roses with great care, never losing one, but snatching a glimpse of them from time to time and enjoying their fragrance and beauty.

Apparition of the Picture.

"Juan Diego reached the episcopal palace with his latest message and asked several of the servants to tell the bishop. They did not do so till they were tired of his importunities; but noticing that he carried something in his cloak they wanted to see what it was. Though he resisted all he could, they discovered by a slight opening what he carried. Seeing the roses so beautiful they then tried to take some of them; but when they put in their hands, as they did three times, it seemed to them that the flowers were not real but skilfully painted or woven into the cloak. They reported this to the bishop, and the Indian was led in.

"He delivered his message, saying that he brought the sign which he had been ordered to ask from the Lady who sent him. As he then unfolded his cloak the roses fell out of it to the ground, and on it there was seen painted the Picture of Most Holy Mary as it is seen to-day.

"The bishop was struck with wonder at the prodigy of the fresh, odorous, dewy roses, just recently gathered, as it was the most rigorous winter time of this climate; but much more was he in admiration at the sight of the holy Picture which he and those present of his household venerated as something heavenly.

"He undid the knot from behind the Indian's head and carried the cloak to his oratory. There, fittingly placing the Picture, he gave thanks to Our Lord and His glorious Mother.

"That day the bishop was kind to Juan Diego and kept him in his palace. On the following morning he bade him come and show him where the Most Holy Virgin Mary had ordered her temple to be built. When they reached the place Juan pointed out the location and the spots in which he had the four times seen the Mother of God and spoken with her. He then asked leave to go see his uncle, Juan Bernardino, whom he had left so sick. The bishop allowed him and sent with him some of his household, telling them that if they found the uncle cured they should conduct the man to his presence.

Fifth Apparition.

"When Juan Bernardino saw his nephew arrive at his house, accompanied by Spaniards and honored by them, he asked the cause of the unusual proceeding. The nephew then gave an account of his having been sent to the bishop, and of the Most Holy Virgin's assuring him that his uncle was cured. Whereupon, Juan Bernardino, having asked at what hour and minute he was said to be cured, affirmed that at that very point of time he saw the same Lady, exactly as described, and was by her restored to perfect health. She likewise told him 'that she wished a temple raised to her at the place in which she had appeared to his nephew; and moreover that her Picture was to be called Holy Mary of Guadalupe.' For this no reason was given.

"The servants heard all and then led the two Indians back to the presence of the bishop who examined the elder man on his sickness, on the manner of his cure, and on the appearance of the Lady who restored his health. The truth being made manifest, he took the uncle and nephew to his palace in the city of Mexico.

"Already the fame of the Miracle had spread abroad, so that the inhabitants of the city were crowding to the episcopal residence to venerate the Picture. It was therefore taken to the principal church and placed on the altar by the bishop, that the people who were coming in great numbers might all enjoy it. There it remained till, on the spot indicated by the Indian, there was built a hermitage to which it was transferred in procession with most solemn festivity."

"This," says the historian, "is the whole simple tradition, without ornament of words."[1] That the narrative little needed ornament of words most readers will feel. There is about it a delicious fitness and verisimilitude. As it has convinced and charmed multitudes in the past, so may it for all time.

---

[1] Felic. de Mex., p. 23.

CHAPTER VIII.

THE PICTURE.

ONE who has seen the Tepeyac Picture must hesitate about describing it. The best thing he can say is—go and see it. Description, while felt to be utterly inadequate, is liable to appear exaggerated and not to be believed. Most of us have some experience of the enthusiastic admiration which certain persons express for certain pictures; but thereby we are hardly moved to join in such praise, or even to think it necessarily deserved.

However, some account of the Picture of Holy Mary of Guadalupe has here to be inserted. Laudatory, too, that account must be, perhaps even to apparent excess. The Picture is usually referred to by Mexican writers, as true, amiable, admirable, prodigious, portentous, miraculous, sovereign, sacred, holy, heavenly, divine. Of course, its historical origin may give it a claim to these titles; such qualifications are, at the same time, intended for itself in its actual state and influence. Those who are acquainted with it think no other picture even remotely comparable. The idea of comparison can scarcely present itself. Such sacred beauty is not seen elsewhere, nor such sweetness of power: it is like a living beneficence.

To have looked on *Holy Mary of Guadalupe* is counted a high privilege. Clavigero (1785) speaks of the favored ones who "have had the immeasurable happiness, *imponderable felicidad*, of seeing the most beautiful, sovereign Picture of Guadalupe." Florencia (1675) says that for those "who enjoy the bliss of feasting and beatifying, *recrear y beatificar*, their eyes with the sight of so sovereign an object, every other picture will be a blot." Sanchez (1648) writes: "Here the Most Holy Virgin Mary appears so noble, so graceful, so beautiful, that the miraculous Picture is easily seen to be a wondrous copy of that Original whom St. Augustine thought worthy to be called 'the beauty of God.'"

The author of the *Pensil Americano* (1793), who exults in having spent his youth near Guadalupe and in having seen the Picture without glass and kissed it innumerable times, says of its appearance: "Its celestial beauty draws the least devout attention with such attractive force that the eyes can turn to no other object in the temple but to that divine Figure. Its mere sight is enough to melt the most stubborn and obstinate hearts into affections of love, of gratitude, of respect, of veneration for so portentous a Picture."

In the Brief of Benedict XIV. we find quoted these remarkable words: "In it there is nothing that is not wonderful: a Picture from flowers gathered in midwinter on a soil entirely sterile and fit to bear only thorns: on a cloth so thin that through it as through a lattice, *transennam*, the temple lay easily open to the eyes: and that after two centuries the nitre of the neighboring lake, which erodes silver, gold, and brass, has not in the least injured its supreme beauty, *summam pulchritudinem*, nor its most vivid colors."

That the beauty of the Picture immediately excites admiration is a fact of long experience. It is not, however, the passing admiration of technical excellence, not the admiration merely of the artist or of the lover of the Beautiful. The sentiment is more moral than aesthetic. There is pleased wonder that the representation should be so worthy of the subject, should in fact be so sacredly fitting; and a sense of genial mystery mingles with the devout emotion. The *Madonnas* of some of the great painters are capable of evoking the deepest and noblest human feelings. While Murillo and Fra Angelico have canonised Virginity, Raphael and Correggio have divinised Maternity. Other Masters in other ways have thrown all dignity and all tenderness round the figure of Our Lady. Yet in their best productions the work attracts attention to itself; the style, the school, the man, proclaim themselves.

In *Holy Mary of Guadalupe* it is different. The Picture has nothing to say of itself—though when critically looked at it puzzles all skill. It but presents her who came in the light and the music, who spoke the sweet words declaring who she was and saying what she wished. With unearthly simplicity and most winning heavenliness this silent figure conveys its permanent message to the minds and hearts of believers.

From the beginning it is recorded that the first sight of the Picture on the Indian's cloak left all, learned or unlearned, under the impression that its origin was supernatural. Then this opinion was confirmed by close inspection, by scientific research, and by religious inquiry.

In the first place it was and is quite evident that, humanly speaking, the work was done on very unsuitable ground. The poor stuff which the peasants wove for clothing and other purposes is there visible. Some eye-witnesses compare it to a net or open web. Without saying so much I can affirm that it is of thinner texture than ordinary sacking, and that I saw the rough vegetable fibres standing out on its surface. A description of it given by Father Sanchez, 250 years ago, is still considered exact. He writes:—

"The cloth, on which from flowers there appeared painted the holy Picture, is of a very coarse texture, in which the warp and woof are of many badly twisted threads of *iztle*. This the Indians get and manufacture from the *maguey*—a plant very useful in these countries and famous in foreign lands. Others say that it is from a kind of palm from which, to-day as formerly, there are made blankets, called in Mexican *zzotilmatli*. The name of this cloth is *ayatl*, vulgarly *ayate;* with it the poorer Indians are dressed; and it is much coarser than the canvas of Europe. There are two oblong pieces sewed together with cotton thread; and as the seam runs up the middle of the cloak, the face of the Picture would have been cut in two did it not turn to the right where it is not disfigured. The whole cloth is more than two yards in length by more than one in width."[1]

A hundred years later, Cabrera, the Master painter, inserted a description substantially the same in his artistic study of the Picture. He sensibly observes that it is unnecessary to decide whether the material be palm or aloe, for "both are the most unsuitable material that a human artificer could choose." Concerning the actual

[1] Quoted in Estr. del Nor., p. 36.

cloth he calls attention and testifies to a striking peculiarity. "What for the moment should more excite wonder," he says, "is the smoothness felt in this *ayate;* for, all that roughness which appears to the eye—and which should be there, since the material is so ordinary—is, to the touch, converted into a soft smoothness like that of fine silk. This I have experienced on the repeated occasions on which I had the happiness of touching it; and certainly other *ayates* of the same kind do not enjoy this privilege."[1]

How the colors were laid on so strange a 'canvas' no one can explain. The cloth neither got a priming coat, nor was at all prepared; and, in any case, all known specific preparations would have been insufficient. That, as a matter of fact, there was no preparation is proved by a statement quoted in the papal Brief, and by much expert testimony. Several witnesses swore that, standing behind the Picture, they could distinguish the figure with *all its lines and colors,* and, at the same time, see the church clearly. With the poorest canvas most poorly prepared, nothing similar could happen; for, *preparation* has exactly the effect of compacting the cloth and preventing the colors from going through.

That, therefore, evidence of miracle is found in the Picture itself can be no surprise. Taking the figure on the Indian cloth, and making abstraction of every accessory circumstance—as of its humanly unaccountable origin and preservation—scientific examiners have again and again admitted and attested a supernatural intervention. Thus the Painters' Commission, of 1666, "certifies

---

[1] Marav. Amer., p. 4.

that it is impossible, humanly, for any artificer to paint or produce a thing so excellent on a cloth as coarse as is the *tilma* or *ayate* on which appears this divine Picture; . . . that having employed all the diligence to which they were bound, in conformity with their art, they have not been able to find or discover in the holy Picture any one thing that is not mysterious and miraculous; that no other but God our Lord could effect so beautiful a production; . . . and that they hold without doubt and affirm without scruple that the imprinting of the said Picture of Our Lady of Guadalupe on the *ayate* or *tilma* of the said Juan Diego, was, and must be understood and declared to have been, a supernatural work and a secret reserved to the Divine Majesty. They conclude that what they have deposed is, to their knowledge, in conformity with the art of painting; and for greater completeness they swear to it in due form of Law."[1]

The seven painters that signed this professional finding were distinguished laymen, who held jealously to the canons of criticism in what might now be called legitimate art. But they had the wisdom to bow before an inexplicable, more than earthly masterpiece.

Similar testimony, solemn, categorical, and expert, was again furnished in 1750, in preparation for the embassy to Benedict XIV. The Masters of painting then in Mexico were invited to form a commission for the close, detailed inspection of the Picture, and for an authoritative report on its apparent nature and actual condition. Miguel Cabrera was named president with six competent

---

[1] Hist. Comp., p. 259.

assessors. The new Commissioners, having taken down and uncovered the wonderful 'canvas,' saw, touched, and minutely examined it. Their affirmation of the miraculous nature of the Picture was, if possible, stronger and more explicit than that of their predecessors a century earlier. The substance of their declaration is found in these words of their president: "The plan of this holy Picture is so singular, so perfectly accomplished, and so manifestly marvellous, that I hold for certain that whoever has any knowledge of our art must on seeing it at once declare it a miraculous portent. .... Its most beautiful grace of symmetry, the perfect correspondence of the whole with the parts and of the parts with the whole, is a marvel that amazes all who see it and are at all acquainted with sketching. Every line and turn of it is so clearly a miracle that there actually palpitates in the admirable work the supreme power of its author."[1]

Another happy fruit of this Commission was a book by the chairman. Though more accustomed to wield the brush than the pen Cabrera was induced to detail in writing the result of his observations. His *Maravilla Americana*, or 'Conjunct of rare marvels, observed under the guidance of the rules of the art of painting, in the portentous Picture of Our Lady of Guadalupe,' did good service in Rome as well as in Mexico. The treatise, which cost the author much labor, and which he simply styles his '*mal escrita pero muy veridica declaracion*,' touches every material and artistic aspect of the Indian *tilma* and the sacred figure it bears. The unpretentious exposition and keen technical analysis make the evidence

---

[1] Marav. Amer., p. 6.

for the supernatural readily admissible. Indeed every chapter puts the Picture clearly outside human possibilities.

At the end of the work I find letters of accord and confirmation, signed by the Professors of Painting: Ibarra, Osorio, Ruiz, Vallejo, Alcivar, and Arnaez.

A characteristic of the Picture, which has much excited the wonder of painters, is the appearance of several kinds of coloring in the same figure. It is noticed that the face and hands look like *oil-painting*, while the mantle seems in *water-colors*. Then the tunic, with the supporting Angel and the clouds, resembles what the artists call *distemper* or *gum-coloring*; and lastly a part of the background appears to be *labored distemper*, or thick laying on of color, as in wood or wall painting. If the 'canvas' was naturally unfit for any one of these methods, much more was it for their unexampled combination.

The colors themselves have also been a cause of astonishment and admiration. The curious and the artistic have puzzled, as well over the nature of the coloring matter, as over the manner of applying it. The poetic imagined some relation between the Picture tints and the tints of the flowers carried in the mantle; or they saw a resemblance in the beautiful plumages of the native birds. Experts sensibly admitted their inability to determine the substance of the pigments, while strongly affirming that the work was superhuman. The abundant gold of the stars and rays seemed to many to be a layer of the ordinary precious metal. Close observers thought they could perceive that it was dust thrown on, as they expressed it, like the bright coloring on butterflies' wings; but, unlike the insect gold, it was found when touched not to be removable but to be wrought into the texture.

The preservation of the Picture is as wonderful as its formation—more wonderful, indeed, for the wonder is growing every year. Naturally neither the cloth nor the colors should have remained as they are. Already in the time of Becerra Tanco—whose Indian Narrative I gave in the preceding chapter—the enduring freshness of the Picture was a cause of wonder. In his reflections on Guadalupe the distinguished author says:—

"An additional thing to be admired is its not having grown dim or changed in the one hundred and thirty-five years which have passed since the Apparition, that is from 1531 to this year in which I am writing, 1666, even though it was always treated with decent reverence."

As if forestalling objections he adds: "And even though the texture that bears the figure should decay with time which consumes everything naturally corruptible, this would not make less true the Apparitions of the Most Holy Virgin, nor less certain the fact that the sacred Picture was imprinted on the cloth which served as a mantle to the Indian Juan Diego. For what the faithful reverence is not the material of pictures but the truth represented by them."[1]

When Becerra thus wrote he had no apparent reason to fear the ravages of time. For, in the very same year, 1666, we find a scientific Board testifying to the miraculous duration of the Picture. The three professors of the Royal University, who held the chairs of Physics and Medicine, were appointed an examining Committee.

---

[1] Felic. de Mex., p. 43.

Their professional report, sworn to and signed before a Notary Public, contains this statement:—

"The continuance through so many years of the holy Picture's freshness of form and color, in the presence of such opposing elements, cannot have a natural cause. Its sole principle is He who alone is able to produce miraculous effects above all the forces of nature."[1]

In Cabrera's book there is a similar scientific note. "It is certain," he writes, "that the fabric on which is delineated the holy Picture did not need such powerfully opposing elements in order to make it quickly decay: the sole material was enough to cause it to fall to pieces in very little time. Therefore, I judge that we must attribute this rare preservation to the special privilege it enjoys because it bears painted on it the holy Picture."[2] With the eye of a painter for a safe canvas, he also calls attention to the thin cotton thread which holds the two pieces of cloth together, "This fragile thread," he wonderingly remarks, "resists and, for more than two centuries, has resisted the natural force, weight, and drag, of the two pieces which it unites, and which are themselves of much heavier and grosser stuff."[3]

Experience certainly shows that Diego's cloak has exceptional enduring qualities, qualities naturally unaccountable. Similar garments fell to pieces in ten or twenty years at most, not to speak of two or three centuries. It matters not whether the fibre is of palm or of aloe; neither lasted long in these coarse common textures. Indeed much better Indian fabrics held together but little time. When expressing their wonder

[1] Hist. Comp., p. 133.   [2] Marav. Amer., p. 2.   [3] Ibid.

at the sight of the favored *tilma*, Mexican writers have reasonably asked: Where are all the well-wrought stuffs of Moctezuma's palace, and the gorgeous cloaks of contemporary Indian chiefs? Even the strong textures and the skins used for maps and charts, though carefully kept from contact with the very air, have hardly left a few fragments hanging together.

Attention must also be called to the fact that Guadalupe is not a good place to preserve any fragile material. It is exposed to winds, at times moist, at times dusty. Moreover, a corrosive exhalation from the lakes and the undrained marshy surroundings eats into everything. Ornamental works, especially if colored, even cut stone and solid cement, have quickly decayed and crumbled in the biting atmosphere. That this universally penetrating, deleterious influence should be withstood by the frail *tilma* alone, is cause of legitimate admiration. And the climax of wonder is capped by the continuance of the delicate colors in their rich freshness.

Guadalupan writers do not forget, when extolling the marvellous preservation of their Picture, that contemporary and older paintings are also preserved elsewhere. They are acquainted with the European masterpieces of the fifteenth and sixteenth centuries. But they see a difference. They know that those great works of art demanded the experience of ages and the labored skill of colossal geniuses, to secure a relative permanency of canvas and color. Many canvases remain; the colors also are distinguishable, though mostly dimmed or deadened when not periodically renewed or retouched. There is no abiding representation on a texture as open as a lattice, and in coloring matter as thin as that of the rose-leaf or the violet. Even the best of comparatively recent paintings have suffered decay. Before there is an exhibition of Sir Joshua Reynolds's portraits, we hear of their being retouched and almost repainted. Yet the English artist, of a hundred years ago, is known to have industriously scraped off the thick coating from many old and faded Italian masterpieces, in order to discover the secret of fairly permanent coloring.

Neither have miraculous pictures been commonly exempt from the ravages of time. Of this fact we were lately reminded. Eighteen-ninety-six was the centenary of the miraculous manifestations witnessed in many sacred images, at Rome and elsewhere, towards the end of the troubled pontificate of Pius VI., and commemorated annually in the Office of the *Prodigies of Mary*. The preparation for the festivities of the centenary included the *restoration* of many of the miraculous pictures *which had grown dim with age*. Yet they are young in comparison with *Holy Mary of Guadalupe* —of which, indeed, one of them is a copy.[1]

Circumstances have, therefore, been taken into account by the authors who dwell on the unexampled endurance of the Guadalupan Picture. And, without doubt, circumstances often are the most irrefragable, though not the most striking, evidence of providential or miraculous intervention. If no similar case has occurred, or demonstratively could occur, in the course of nature, we are justified in looking higher.

Some may imagine that the canvas and the colors lasted because of the extreme care bestowed on them.

---

[1] Vide infra, p. 168.

But the truth is that they have been rather badly treated. The 'decent reverence,' of which Becerra speaks, was not always sufficient. We learn that the Picture was left open and uncovered for more than a century; since it is mentioned that 1647 was the year in which it was first put under glass. In all that long period multitudes treated it as if they really thought it indestructible. They rubbed against it all sorts of pious objects, and some that were profane. Men touched it with their swords, and women with their bracelets. Impetuously devout people rushed in and cast themselves on it to embrace it. The hands and even the face were ceaselessly kissed. Many aching limbs touched more than the hem of the garment, and of shreds and fibres of it daring thefts were committed.

Even after the glass was placed it had to be removed annually or oftener. Then the number of objects offered for contact with the Picture was literally countless. Cabrera says, somewhat pathetically, that once in 1753 he saw, while he stood by for two hours, the sacred canvas touched more than five hundred times with objects handed up from the crowd. The touching was then done, it is true, by the careful hands of ecclesiastics; but even so it could hardly fail in course of time to make injurious impressions.

The Picture was also exposed to dangerous accidents. It is related that on one occasion the goldsmith, who was employed to clean the frame, spilt a bottle of nitric acid down the length of the cloth. Yet no more trace remained than what sufficed to show that the accident had occurred.

There were also some very stupid attempts to improve on the miraculous work. In the first century of the

Picture's existence, certain misguided guardians thought it might be well to fill up the raw margin of the *tilma* with a border of Seraphim. They had this decoration added, touching also the moon beneath Our Lady's feet and other parts outside the figure. The effect of their absurd fancy was soon manifest. Every one found the new border so horrid that it had to be washed off, to the great danger of the frail texture and the beautiful tints. Then the silver put on the crescent and the other added colors faded and blackened, leaving some abiding blotches to warn off all future irreverent hands.

Age can scarcely be said to have affected the Picture. Whatever gloss it has lost, or whatever slight abrasions it may show, came from negligence or from inconsiderate familiarity. Even imprudent devotional proceedings caused no apparent injury. It was long and openly exposed to the heat and smoke of candles, of incense, and of other burnt perfumes; yet it remained untarnished. To-day, in spite of time and—what we may gently call—abuse, it is still a wonder of undecaying beauty. And it is pleasant to know that now, as for a good while past, the care taken of it is as wise as it is loving.

Those who have not seen it may form some idea of its actual appearance from the accompanying copy of a recent photograph. The outline is here very exact; but, of course, the tints are wanting, as well as the warm, life-like glow. Indeed neither photograph nor direct copy is satisfying to one who has seen the original. This is, perhaps, true of most great works of art; but much more is it true of *Holy Mary of Guadalupe*.

For a long time it was thought and found to be quite hopeless to attempt copying the Tepeyac Picture. Many had tried and as many had failed. "The greatest masters of the art of painting," wrote Becerra in 1666, "confess now and have, as many as closely examined, already confessed that a beauty of countenance so modestly joyful is humanly inimitable." Long after the same thing was acknowledged and insisted on by the painter Ibarra. Writing in the middle of the eighteenth century he mentions many of his contemporaries and predecessors in the art, both Mexicans and Europeans, and then adds: "Not one of them, nor anybody else, has been found capable of sketching or copying *Our Lady of Guadalupe;* . . . nor was this effected till a profile was taken from the original itself; . . . singular uniqueness which proves the Picture to be the invention not of a human artist but of the Almighty."[1]

By aid of what the painter calls a profile, recognisable copies were obtained before photography came to the assistance of art. It was allowed to lay oiled paper over the glass of the Picture, and draw the exact outlines, marking every turn and peculiarity. Then many artists got copies of this tracing and transferred it to their canvas, producing what they humbly styled "something resembling the original as far as that was possible."

As it was hard to copy the Picture so it is also to describe it. The Virgin stands alone; she is the Woman of the Apocalypse with the vesture and ornaments of sun, moon, and stars. The stature is perfect life-size for a maiden of fourteen or fifteen years. The head bends slightly, the hands are joined, and the expression is one of ecstatic adoration. The hair and complexion

---

[1] Marav. Amer., p. 10.

are dark; the face is oval; and the features are of ineffable delicacy. The rose-colored tunic is flowered, and lighter or deeper according to prominence; and the blue-green mantle, which falls gracefully from the head, is slightly gathered under the left arm. In a background of softly reverberating light, above sixty golden rays diverge most regularly from each side of the figure, while forty-six stars of similar tint glisten on the azure field of the mantle. A niche is formed by the surrounding clouds.

When the Indians gaze on their beautiful Picture they sometimes see, in the finely proportioned form and the sweetly dignified countenance, a heavenly prototype of the noblest native maidens; but they, like other Catholics, always find there the incomparable, unlocalised semblance of the Virgin Mother. Occasional pilgrims may be startled by the reminder which the grand though delicate features bring them of Veronica's *Holy Face*.

We saw in the *Indian Narrative* that Our Lady told Juan Bernardino her Picture was to be called *Holy Mary of Guadalupe*. This name requires some observations. It is not likely that the Indian said exactly *Guadalupe*; for the sounds of *g* and *d* were unknown to the natives and not easily acquired by them. What, then, appears to have happened in this case, as in the case of many other Mexican names, is that the Spaniards represented Juan Bernardino's pronunciation of the title by a form congenial to their own speech. If the Indian said something like *Guadalupe* that name at once suggested itself as being already dear and familiar. Not that they could find any outward resemblance between the *Picture* on the *tilma* and their *statue* of Guadalupe at home in

Extremadura—a statue in which the Divine Mother holds the Child on her left arm and a sceptre in her right hand; but because what they heard sounded like that cherished name.

Scholars have sought out the Indian expressions that a Spanish ear might catch as *Guadalupe,* paying attention to the way in which the more rustic natives still pronounce that word. Father Becerra found that either *Tequatlanopeuh* (she who originated at the summit of the rocks) or *Tequantlaxopeuh* (she who put our devourers to flight) would be the probable equivalent. The present Bishop of Cuernavaca, who is an authority on this as on all other Guadalupan points, suggests coa-tlalo-peuch (she who cast down the serpent)—an expression very close in sound and very appropriate in meaning. For, the title *Mother of God* was long taken as synonymous with *Guadalupe;* and the Indians, by a rare instinct of faith, always saw that to be Mother of God, and to overcome the serpent—or be entirely clean—were things practically identical.

That the Picture represents the Immaculate Conception is accepted as certain and evident. For centuries this has been unhesitatingly affirmed. "If instead of the dragon," wrote Sanchez in 1648, "she has at her feet an Angel, the fact strengthens the opinion of those who maintain that she was conceived not only without sin but even in the splendors of glory (*in resplandores de gloria*)." Bachelor J. J. Montufar, writing about the Picture, in 1744, entitles his book the "Marvel of Prodigies and Flower of Miracles, which appeared at Guadalupe, giving clear testimony of the Conception in Grace and Glory (*en Gracia y Gloria*)[1] of Mary Our Lady." The artist Cabrera, also, affirms that the Picture is "the most faithful and appropriate representation" of the Immaculate Conception. Nor did Benedict XIV., in his Brief of 1754, a hundred years before the Definition, hesitate to call Our Lady the "*Blessed Mary Virgin Immaculate of Guadalupe.*"

The interpretation is, therefore, an authorised one. Indeed any beholder, who is accustomed to distinguish between the different representations of the Mother of God, will immediately call the *American Virgin* an *Immaculate Conception*. The lone queenly figure, the prayerful attitude, the glad absorption in God—all suggest the mystery of favored sinlessness.

The beautiful Angel, from whose presence and action arguments were drawn for the glorious privilege of his Queen, should not escape our attention. In himself he forms a delicious picture: but he is not there for himself. Learnedly and lovingly he has been maintained by some devout clients to be Michael, and by others to be Gabriel; the strong truth, however, which Montufar and all the disputants deduce from his willing ministry is, that, at the moment of her Conception, Our Lady was already immeasurably above the highest of the Seraphim.

Good comes of looking at this Angel. His face is a mirror of a child's joy and a mighty spirit's power. His action is eager, as he bears aloft his precious burden, stretching out his arms to catch the fringe of the mantle on one side and that of the tunic on the other. His

---

[1] Whether by *glory* these writers meant more than fulness of grace and confirmation in grace, with, perhaps, transient sights of God, they do not make clear.

expression of heavenly exultance almost says aloud—See what I can show you!

In noting and studying every detail of this most wonderful Picture, art critics have remarked that the position of the wings of the Angel indicates a ceasing from flight: they bear a relation to Our Lady's attitude which is one of walking, the right foot being firmly placed on the crescent and the left knee bent in the act of advancing. She came and seems always coming.

Truly the gift of the Mother of God to the young Church of America is endlessly amiable; and this Western World possesses no material treasure that can be mentioned in comparison. Her Picture has been for many generations, and is to-day for many millions, a centre and an occasion of much most happy holiness. Its very copies are capable of making every church a home and every home a sanctuary. The Jesuit poet, Father Abad, expressed but the truth when he wrote: "More beautiful or more lovable than it, there is nothing in this world: *Qua neque amabilius quidquam est nec pulchrius orbe.*"

The Shrine at Guadalupe.

CHAPTER IX.

THE SHRINE.

ERECTING temples of Religion has always been recognised as a work most distinctively sacred. To the eyes of faith there is something grand, almost pathetically grand, in giving to God for His own use a small piece of the Earth that is His, and in putting up a roof under which He may freely hold intercourse with His exiled children. Such a place is so determinately holy, so surely the scene of the creature's best aspirations and the Creator's kindest response—in fact, of the Scriptural Kissing of Justice and Peace—that to have had a part in marking it off and sheltering it over is one of life's most ennobling experiences. This holds universally. Be it the Patriarch consecrating the pillow stone of the Vision, or the King the shining Temple, or the pontiff the mighty basilica, or the missionary his hut of clay—the divine assignation is ever of most sweetly solemn import.

It may be said that church-building establishes a sort of solidarity with God. In some strange heavenly way what we give Him is more ours afterwards than it was before. The site and the stones that have become His house call still with blessings on the name of their original owners, who can hardly fail to be influenced for good by the consciousness of this joint possession.

A thing sacred to God is partly theirs—so they must be sacred themselves.

Like individuals and families, countries receive a measure of sanctification by raising religious edifices. Temples, indeed, however rich and numerous, are no proof that a religion is true; but they offer some evidence that the professors of that religion are sincere. On the whole it is a good sign of a land to bear many marks of church expenditure. There may, of course, be pretence and hypocrisy and vain display; yet money is not given for nothing, and, in the long run and the generality of cases, its free religious donation argues the devotedness of personal belief. This, I think, is true whether said of the pennies of the generous poor or of the lavished gold of the unworldly rich. Where contributions were large and constant, faith was probably both strong and abiding.

The sacredness of generosity to God's house has marked no country more deeply or nobly than the land of Holy Mary of Guadalupe. From end to end Mexico is sown with churches. Many now are sadly ruined, many still more sadly secularised; but many, too, thank God, are yet richly beautiful in structure, adornment, and frequentation. Cathedrals, monastic and parish churches, wayside chapels and shrines, hold every coign of vantage and give every landscape a religious aspect. The concomitant educational, medical, and charitable establishments are usually entensive enough to form a strong, sacredly humane centre for each town or village. In this grandly Catholic country you find squares and markets almost always flanked by church walls; and wherever you turn your gaze you see towers and spires that unmistakably declare the national character of the people's piety. As these are the strongholds it is evident Who holds the sovereign sway.

The Spanish conquest of Mexico was, doubtless, marked by ambition and greed, though much less so than English readers are accustomed to think. The fact, however, that Faith overruled both victors and vanquished is in this church-building, as in other matters, abundantly demonstrated. It required the earnest coöperation of all classes to put up and keep up so many pious edifices; and with unsurpassed devotedness every category lent its willing assistance.

A narrow, shallow view of New Spain's ecclesiastical wealth may represent the many works undertaken as a mere pastime of the ruling classes, or a crafty expedient for greater impunity of extortion. But it must not be forgotten that the money was actually expended, most religiously expended, with self-sacrificing magnanimity. A single basilica or convent often had devoted to it the whole fortune of a rich family, while also sharing the free labor of an entire generation of the surrounding peasantry. And the number of such erections was so great that, in less than three hundred years, Mexico was made to look as anciently and thoroughly Christian as were the European countries in ten or fifteen centuries.

The number, indeed, joined to the cost of the churches of the Catholic Republic, is sometimes made a matter of reproach. Even well-meaning—though spiritually blind or dull—people are heard to ask what use there was in raising them so numerous, so rich, so close together. But the Spanish American and the Catholic Indian, to whom every great Church devotion was a living reality and many Saints were as cherished friends, knew why shrines were fittingly and profitably multiplied. Moreover, the disproportion between their number and the number of the people's habitations was never really what it now seems; for, the ecclesiastical buildings, being better constructed, have often remained standing while the dwellings between and around them have wholly disappeared. What looks like a village of churches and convents was once the centre of a large town.

Some butterfly tourists and commercial travellers sententiously express their regrets that railways, factories, and other monuments of modern progress, did not engross the attention given to these religious edifices. As such people comfortably lecture the ages, without chronological or other restraints, and get their own superior enlightenment mainly from hotel *Guides* and train *Itineraries*, it can hardly be advantageous to argue with them. Yet, even to them it may be suggested that, as a matter of experience, church-building is not found to prevent secular industries. It may, also, be recalled that the money religiously spent by the Mexicans and their rulers had, at the time, hardly another outlet except luxury and self-indulgence. Nor is the fact to be overlooked that to the converted Indian the grandeur of the sacred edifices was a prime source of civilization, and that their beauty—especially when he had contributed to it—was for him, indeed, "a joy forever."

As New Spain so readily raised shrines on every side, we might expect that many of them would bear the name of the Virgin of Tepeyac. She certainly was not forgotten. Wherever you pass among the people, be it in city or hamlet, both young and old can direct you to *Our Lady of Guadalupe*. They may look their innocent astonishment that you have to ask for so well known a place; but gladness breaks over their features as they point or guide the way. And if you should have occasion to enter their homes, you may feel sure of meeting the Guadalupan chapel, or altar, or, at the very least, the picture.

But all these shrines, up and down the land, be they private or public, are but representations and reminders of the one at Guadalupe itself. This is the Temple which Our Lady asked and which the people gave, making it the place of custody of the Picture she had left them. Where her virgin feet seemed to touch the ground, the Shrine arose and grew—indeed, is still growing in magnificence and power for good. Its beginnings were small, but the hearts of the people cherished it; and its history is one of the most edifying episodes in the annals of church-building.

As the direct and reiterated demand of the Virgin of the Apparitions was a temple at Tepeyac, the bishop to whom her message was addressed felt anxious to erect one as speedily as possible. He had, also, the portentous Picture to place; and, though its location had not been explicitly indicated, it seemed fitting to preserve it where it originated. Moreover the pilgrimages had begun and were divided between the episcopal residence, with its new treasure, and the hill favored by such wonders. The cry was, therefore, to show the Picture of Holy Mary of Guadalupe on the spot sanctified by her presence. So, just where she stood to arrange the roses in the *tilma* of the Indian, he and his friends, under Zumárraga's direction and with crowds of enthusiastic helpers, raised quickly a small adobe chapel.

All accounts state that this first shrine was ready for the Picture at Christmas; but good historians inclined to the opinion that it could not have been the same year—that is, barely two weeks after the Apparitions. They would even make it the third year following; for, the Picture seemed to have been some time venerated at the bishop's church; and he himself in 1532 and 1533 was absent in Spain, while he was certainly present at the inauguration of the Guadalupan chapel.

Nevertheless, the weight of authority, with the special testimony of the oldest Indians, is for the very year of the Apparitions. The shortness of time allowed for the erection of the chapel offers no difficulty; since, in the secular history of the early Mexicans it is shown that, when urged to it, they came in such numbers and so zealously labored at their simple architecture that they put up monasteries and even whole villages in ten or fifteen days.

On the Feast of St. Stephen, therefore,—as all are agreed—the inauguration took place. The Indians had the Shrine, provisional as it might be, tastefully prepared. Then Bishop Zumárraga, with his clergy and the Franciscan and Dominican religious, brought the Picture from the city in solemn procession. The fragmentary records of the day sufficiently attest that the exultation was great and general. The impressionable natives were beside themselves with joy. They had lined the way with green boughs and strewn all the approaches to the chapel with sweet smelling herbs. Their boats on the canal that then skirted the road were fantastically adorned; and the men that walked brandished their bows, playing at mimic war. They danced and sang, the burden of all their canticles being the pathetically boastful but magnificently Catholic words: "The Virgin is one of us, the Indians! Our clean Mother! Our Sovereign Lady! The Virgin is one of us!"[1]

The enthusiasm, which was great, received a hundredfold increase from the sight of a manifest miracle. Consternation came on the sham fight when an Indian was seen to fall, pierced through the neck. His comrades, having picked him up, hurried in and threw him down before the Picture, seeming innocently to say to Our Lady—See what you have done! They then drew out the arrow, and the man stood up healed. He continued to take part in the sport and rejoicing.

This first chapel, inaugurated by Bishop Zumárraga, was, as already stated, so much improved in 1554 by Archbishop Montufar, that he is sometimes spoken of as its founder. In 1600 it was improved and enlarged, almost to the extent of being rebuilt. The viceroy, metropolitan chapter, and other dignitaries, civil as well as religious, took part in the ceremony of reopening. For already the Shrine of Holy Mary of Guadalupe was an object of universal veneration. Pilgrims came, wonders were wrought, and all eyes and hearts were turned thither. The patriotic called it the Citadel of New Spain; the pious styled it the Cenacle of the New World.

This earliest Guadalupan edifice, successively improved, served to shelter the Picture, and those who

---

[1] Hist. Comp., p. 45.

came to venerate it, for about ninety years. It is still a place of pious interest: it is recognised in the actual sacristy of the parish church.

The more the history of the Apparitions was known and examined, the less the faithful were satisfied with what they had done in response to Our Lady's demand. Singular favors, also, were constantly urging them to new efforts of gratitude. The pastors only corresponded with the people's desire when, in the beginning of the seventeenth century, they authorised the amassing of money and materials for a better temple to their heavenly Visitant. At once free offerings poured in in great abundance. Silver, precious stones, and costly ornaments, were lavishly contributed. When the donations reached fifty thousand dollars it was allowed to commence the building, on whose continuation and completion several hundred thousands were expended. The viceroy, Salvatierra, gave three thousand ounces of silver to make a throne for *Holy Mary of Guadalupe*. Sixty sanctuary lamps of the same metal are also mentioned among the gifts of the faithful.

With great and solemn rejoicing the new Shrine was dedicated in 1622; and there the miraculous Picture held its place in splendor and profound veneration for seventy-six years.

But it always seemed, as it seems still to-day, that the Mexicans cannot be fully contented with anything they do for the Mother of God who once called herself their Mother. The same century which saw them put up this costly temple saw them eager to replace it by a grander and richer one. In 1694 some leading citizens of the Capital presented themselves before Archbishop

Aguiar, asking permission to take up subscriptions for a great church to the Virgin of Tepeyac. As they offered eighty thousand dollars of their own to head the list, they were authorised to undertake the good work.

One point of their preparation for building was characteristically whole-hearted and reverent; it also indicated significantly the public estimation of the Picture. The best site for the new edifice was the ground occupied by the actual shrine. That, therefore, should be taken down. But what in the meantime were they to do with *Holy Mary of Guadalupe?* They would not move the sacred Picture till they had erected a suitable, though a temporary, shrine for it. So, with a devotedness which displayed faith and must excite admiration, they spent a year constructing a regular church in which to place the Picture till the great temple should be completed. Though meant to be temporary, this building was so well put together that it still serves as the parish church of the town.

In 1695, the very day that the Picture was fittingly placed for the time being, the archbishop, attended by the viceroy, the canons, councillors, judges, and other dignitaries, blessed and laid the foundation stone of the third and greatest temple to Holy Mary of Guadalupe.

The building operations and the adorning of the new shrine took fourteen years, and called forth heroic generosity and devotion. Reference has already been made to the admirable example of Artega who, though viceroy and archbishop, constituted himself door-to-door collector in the city. Not being recognised he received some rebuffs; but less, perhaps, than most other church-collectors; for his people gave readily when asked in the name of Guadalupe. Indeed the amount contributed, considering the certain poverty of the Indians and the alleged rapacity of the Spaniards, seems nearly incredible. Historians put the expenditure above eight hundred thousand dollars, not counting at all the free materials, or the free labor of man and beast.

The miraculous Picture being the central object of veneration, the perpetual memorial of the Apparitions, and the pledge of the affectionate promises, no expense was spared in its setting and location. The new inner frame was of pure gold, and the throne, as well as the supporting back, of beaten silver. The lamps, chandeliers, railings, and other ornaments, were proportionately expensive.

On May Eve, 1709, the translation of the Picture from its temporary resting-place to its finished and definite throne was gorgeously conducted. Equally devout celebrations may have been before at Guadalupe, but certainly none so magnificent. All the bells for miles around rang out in wild exultance, and all classes thronged to the noble Sanctuary. The whole hill was surrounded by the rejoicing Indians, who also covered thickly the league of highway back to the Capital. They are always in striking evidence when there is question of the Virgin of Tepeyac whom they lovingly claim as their own.

After the dedicatory services there opened a grand novena; and, for the first nine days of that beautiful month, Mexico presented a spectacle which might gladden the Angels in Heaven. There was a devout rivalry between all the responsible bodies in Church and State, to get each a day on which to bear the expense and labor of the festive celebrations. The Metropolitan Chapter and the Religious Orders wanted their turn; the Viceroy claimed his, as did also the Royal Audience, the Courts, and the Nobility. But the closing days had to be given to the Mexican Clergy, the representatives of those dearest to Our Lady, and to the Municipality of Guadalupe that held within its territory both the Hill and the Shrine, and almost claimed the Mother of God as a former citizen.

Forty years after this solemn dedication an opportunity again offered to elevate and aggrandise the Sanctuary. There was no need of erecting a new temple, but something similar was done in a liturgical way. The church of Our Lady was made collegiate, a chapter of canons being established and the choir services inaugurated. The necessary funds came from a devout legacy; the occasion was also seized to make many offerings to Holy Mary of Guadalupe. To enhance the splendor of the Collegiate, a capitular choir was constructed in admirable richness and beauty. The stalls were hewn out of mahogany, with ebony and other rare woods in the inlaid symbolical ornamentations. The hand-rails were of silver. Fine sculptures ran around the cornices, all tending to a central piece modelled on the Picture. An addition of vast consequence to the church services, now very solemn and practically ceaseless, was a magnificent organ whose sweet tones long rejoiced and inspired Our Lady's simple pilgrims.

The next honor for the Guadalupan Sanctuary was its being created a *Lateran Basilica* by Benedict XIV., in 1754, with all the privileges attached to that high title.

Thirty years later there was raised, adjoining the Basilica, a convent and church of the Capuchin Nuns. The Sisters had long desired an abode in the immediate vicinity of the Shrine; and one of them, Sister Mariana Veytia, finally got permission to start the work. She began with fifty cents, but collected enough to put up buildings that must have cost a quarter of a million dollars.

These are not the only edifices around and on the holy Tepeyac. As you stand facing the Basilica, which looks magnificent with its domes and many octagonal towers, you have immediately on the right the convent buildings and the Church of the Capuchin Sisters. Still to the right, but considerably farther back, is the Parish Church, or Church of the Indians, whose sacristy was the first Shrine. Beyond the pretty park, on the street parallel to the Basilica, you meet the Church of the Well, near where Our Lady stood when she bade Juan Diego go up for the roses. This building, not large but very tasteful, is of Moorish style, and was completed about a hundred years ago. It contains fine paintings, which are attributed to Cabrera; and its vestibule covers the mineral spring of which mention is made in the Indian Narrative.

A little farther on you turn to the left and mount by a broad winding staircase, with Stations and commemorative stone sails,[1] to the Hill Chapel on the spot where

---

[1] The meaning of this peculiar monument is indicated by the following inscription: "A ship being caught in a violent tempest, and its helm as well as its compass lost, the crew, at the point of despair, invoked with all their strength the Most Holy Virgin of Guadalupe; they vowed that if saved they would carry and offer in

the Apparitions first occurred. From the beginning, the place was naturally one of devout resort. The present substantial building was erected some two hundred years ago. A few rooms were afterwards added, for the use of the chaplain and of the citizens who came out there to go through the exercises of a retreat.

There lies behind the chapel a very beautiful cemetery. As pious souls were anxious to live near *Holy Mary of Guadalupe,* so many of the faithful wished to sleep their long sleep on her sacred hill. From the plain, therefore, they laboriously brought up in baskets enough clay to form the required depth of soil on the bare rock. They then planted and adorned this special Field of God. The elevation, the view, the hallowed surroundings, render the place very impressive. The valley, lakes, and mountains, are in sight, but the cloudless sky is best seen; and in all the earth I doubt if there be a calmer spot in which to still the vain emotions of the hour, or a sweeter in which to rest "after life's fitful fever."

From the height we can see, clustered round the foot of Tepeyac, the town of Guadalupe. It is not large, but since 1743 it has had the rights of a *villa* (municipality)—hence its popular appellation of *la villa;* and since 1822 those of a *ciudad* (city), with the official name

---

her Sanctuary the mast of their vessel just as it stood. The Most Holy Virgin compassionately heard the supplications of her children, and the shattered bark was able to enter safely the port of Vera Cruz. The crew fulfilled their promise. On their shoulders they carried to the Sanctuary the whole masting of their ship and enclosed this their votive offering in a stone construction, to save it from the ravages of time."

10

of Guadalupe-Hidalgo. It may have been as well that its situation was not favorable to growth, for it has remained just sufficient to be the quiet environment of a sanctuary. Its population of four or five thousand was as high three hundred years ago as it is now; though tens of thousands of persons often pass there in a day. Stretching back to the Capital we see the broad highway with its pleasant mule-trams and many pedestrians. To its right is the old pilgrims' road to the Shrine, now partly occupied by a railway. This has still remaining some of the fifteen massive structures that contained paintings of the Mysteries of the Rosary, and served as halting-places on the prayerful journey. They were being erected when the historian Florencia was writing, more than two hundred years ago, for the devout man expressed a great desire to see them zealously completed. He says this causeway was to be a " Via-Sacra, but more peaceful; one that we should call a 'Flowery Way to Heaven,' on which the blossoms are to be Ave-Marias. The object was that on days of greater frequentation and devotion, such as Saturdays and Feasts of Our Lord or His Mother, those who went to visit the holy Picture might pass along reciting the Fifteen Mysteries of the Rosary, one in each Oratory, beginning with the first (near Mexico) and ending with the last (at Guadalupe); or, according to their devotion, a decade from one to another, so as to finish the Rosary and make an offering of it in the Church of Guadalupe. Thus they might reach the Holy House with the silence and devotion that so venerable a sanctuary demanded."[1]

---

[1] Estrella del Norte, p. 33.

However inspiriting may be the hill-top and however interesting its environs, the centre of attraction at Guadalupe is always the actual shrine of the Picture. During the seven years preceding 1895 the favored place was the Capuchin Church; but now *Holy Mary of Guadalupe* is back again in her Basilica, more nobly enthroned than ever before. The fine building needed internal repairs, and has been completely renewed. Commonly the restoration of beautiful old structures is a doubtful advantage. Tasteless vandalism too often removes and remodels unsparingly. The Collegiate has not been so treated. It has been both preserved and further beautified. Indeed the late reopening astonished even those who expected much, so manifest was the triumph of lavish generosity, of delicate taste, of perfect harmony between the older and the newer decorations.

The main improvement in view was the erection of a great altar with a fitting baldachin, throne, and setting for the miraculous Picture. For this it was found necessary to open and disencumber the choir and sanctuary. But the Mexicans are never satisfied—at least at Guadalupe—with what is just necessary. They do things on a grand scale. So they have now practically rebuilt the whole interior of the Basilica in rich Byzantine, with splendid columns, arches, and domes. They have gone to great depths to lay firm foundations for the new crypt which supports the sanctuary, and contains several altars and cineraries.

The canons' choir is now in the apse, behind Our Lady's altar, which is itself the centre and focus of all the artistic beauty and magnificence. It is of Carrara marble and workmanship, pearly white and most graceful of design. The baldachin is commanding and proportionate. It rests on shafts of shining granite that have bronze and colored marble in the pedestals and capitals. Above are statuettes of Archangels and figures of the Cardinal Virtues; and the inner side is heavily gilt. Here are beautifully traced Leo XIII.'s Latin distichs to Holy Mary of Guadalupe.

The aisle and end altars are also of white marble, while the floors are in black and white mosaics. The former famous choir-screen and silver railings are utilised and well placed, though they may make less impression now from the equal splendor of their surroundings. The prevailing colors in ornamentation are white and gold, to which the starred blue of the central and other domes seems to add lustre and richness.

The Litany scrolls and Mystery emblems are treated with the devotion that always enhances artistic church adorning. "Gorgeous" and "heavenly" are the spontaneous qualifications of the untechnical visitor; and closer criticism has but tended to strengthen the encomiums.

Yet better still than the work materially accomplished was the spirit that actuated it. This grand restoration of the Guadalupan Sanctuary speaks well for Mexican enterprise and taste; but more unmistakably it proclaims the energising force of Catholic piety. The expensive undertaking has been carried through in difficult times. It represents seven years' untiring zeal and self-sacrifice. That impoverished ecclesiastics, with their struggling or penniless flocks, should in those sad days voluntarily undergo such labor and cost is something really heroic. Not less than a quarter of a million dollars was required; and, though the noble and wealthy can always be counted on in the religious Republic, yet much of the money had naturally to come from the cents and dimes of the numerous poor.

All classes, however, are represented. The imported marbles and stained glass, the altars and statues, and other precious gifts, will perpetuate the names of many special benefactors. Fathers and mothers of families, young men and women, convent girls and school-boys,— all strove to prove their generous love of Holy Mary of Guadalupe. Their pastors preached liberal giving and nobly led the way.

One piece of princely magnanimity demands individual mention. Oil-paintings were desired for the Basilica, in keeping with the new decorations, and in harmony with the Guadalupan devotion. It was proposed to have executed a masterly picture of the often commemorated *First Miracle;* another of the *Vocation of the Indians;* one of the *Information of 1666;* one of the *Embassy to Benedict XIV.;* and finally one of the *Oath of Patronage.* To have these works made worthy of their destination required twenty thousand dollars, four thousand for each painting. And as so large a sum would prove a heavy draw on the common fund, five prelates took the burden on themselves. They are — Archbishop Zubiría of Durango, Bishop Camacho of Querétero, Bishop Carillo of Yucatan, Bishop Montes de Oca of San Louis Potosí, and Bishop Portillo of Zacatecas. The incomes—at least official—of these prelates must certainly be rather limited; yet they nobly gave four thousand apiece, to secure these artistic and most fitting ornaments to the renovated Shrine. Their memory will live with the admirable paintings; for the Catholic Mexicans are grateful.

A striking and characteristic commemoration of services rendered to Guadalupe is seen above the collegiate choir, in the high cupola of the apse. There aloft appear the faces of Benedict XIV. who first approved the national Patronage; of Leo XIII. who has granted the new Office; of Labastida, the late Archbishop of Mexico, who suffered and labored for the renovation of the Shrine; and of his pious successor, Alarcon, under whom the great work was continued and completed. There, too, is fittingly painted the escutcheon of the present abbot, Bishop Antonio Plancarte, to whose devoted perseverance and consuming zeal is largely attributable the success both of the material improvements of the Basilica and of the grand festivities of the subsequent Coronation.

Archbishop Labastida also appears in a white marble statue before the entrance to the crypt. The figure is kneeling, with joined hands, and eyes raised to the Picture. It is a good reminder of the pious fidelity of all the Guadalupan Archbishops of Mexico.

But of course no secondary figures attract, or ever will attract, so much devout attention as do those of Our Lady's messenger and of the prelate to whom he was commissioned. Kneeling left and right, just outside the altar but nearest to the Picture, and looking up with awe, affection, and confidence, the Indian Juan Diego and the Spanish Zumárraga are historically and artistically the most interesting concomitants of Our Lady of America, and the best preachers as well as exemplars of the sweet-spirited Catholicity of the Guadalupan devotion.

THE WELL CHAPEL.

CHAPTER X.

THE MIRACLES.

THERE is evidence for assenting to the statement that many miracles have occurred at Guadalupe, and in connection with the venerable Picture. Some of them a Catholic will call "miracles" only in a qualified manner: miracles, that is, as ordinary intelligent Christians may understand and report. Others seem to enjoy an ecclesiastical sanction, though, for the most part, rather in general than in particular. Of both kinds I shall treat, keeping in mind the restrictions demanded by the subject and prescribed by the Church.

That the Mexicans have, for centuries, attributed wonders to Holy Mary of Guadalupe and constantly counted on her miraculous intervention in their favor, is a plain fact of their history. In their minds the miracles at the origin of the devotion were a sign and a promise of others to follow. As it has been well argued in the case of Christianity itself, supernatural events at the beginning rendered not less but rather more probable similar occurrences in the sequel. So the Apparitions and the Picture being miraculous, it was very natural, the Mexicans thought, to look for and obtain miraculous help at the Shrine. Moreover, the heavenly Lady had said she wished a temple there that she might aid the Indians and all who came to her; hence, applying to her was all that was needed. They therefore asked; and their experience was that they obtained.

However, it is to be noted and insisted on that the devout clients of Holy Mary of Guadalupe have never been of the miracle-seeking class. They often, indeed, visited the Shrine or honored copies of the Picture with the desire and hope of getting speedy assistance; but the possible or probable miracle was not usually the determining object of their devotion. They turned to the Holy Mother because of their trusting love. Such, at least, is the impression conveyed by their words and conduct.

That supernatural favors were not the more prominent aim of Guadalupan pilgrims may, also, be easily explained. Mexican Catholics take miracles almost as a matter of course. They have heard of so many, they believe themselves to have witnessed so many, that they hardly think them special to any shrine. One finds scarcely a single old or much frequented church in that Catholic land, which has not a considerable space of its inner walls covered with votive offerings and memorials of supernaturally accorded benefits. There are hundreds of small wax figures representing the limb or part healed; there are signed, authenticated reports of the supposed miracle; there are especially, and most characteristically, crude sketches of the scene and circumstances of the recorded wonder. Sometimes it is the picture of a carriage-wreck, of a burning house, of an explosion; oftener it is the humble home with the sick bed and its failing occupant, and the medal or picture in the hands of the praying child or parent or other devout relative.

Indeed to the simple-minded faithful, asking a miracle is not a very different thing from praying for help in special needs. They cannot easily distinguish—nor can, perhaps, people of much more intellectual training—between God's action in granting our petition for rain, or sun, or calm voyage, or rich harvest, and his intervening at the request of those nearest to Him to stop disease or hold back death. At all events Mexican Catholics, of whatever race, confide with great freedom their wants and wishes to their heavenly patrons, and first and most to Holy Mary of Guadalupe, trusting that succor will come according to its necessity.

At the Shrine it has been noticed that the afflicted present themselves—whole families together—and, having put their case before the Holy Mother, go away contented, without asking or considering whether or not they have gained their object. It may be that fervent confidence gives them the assurance of having done all that is required in coming to Guadalupe, or that their devotion takes the higher course of leaving everything in the hands of Heaven and wishing only what God wishes. But certain it is that the general conviction of the apparitional Mother's efficacious intercession is deep, constant, and unshakable. In fact the unquestioning belief and the frequent experience that wondrous blessings could be obtained at the Shrine, have caused the records of undoubted miracles to be cursory and undetailed.

For long years every one acquainted with Guadalupe affirmed that it was the centre and source of much that was manifestly supernatural. No one contradicted; hence no methodical proofs were formulated. Even

Bustamente only blustered that so openly attributing miracles to the Picture would cause the Indians to call it God. Every report of a new favor made thousands anxious to deserve a like one, but hardly suggested to anybody the utility of an exact statement of what had occurred. What need to substantiate in writing what all the city witnessed? And if proofs were wished, there were the Apparitions themselves and the abiding Picture.

It is thus that we find, through the sixteenth and seventeenth centuries, unfailing reference to the numerous wonders wrought at Guadalupe, but with few details of particular miracles. We have seen, in the sixth chapter, how the earliest civil chroniclers, like Diaz and Peralta, mention Tepeyac as a place of many and most sacred marvels. Becerra Tanco regarded the Guadalupan miracles as too well known to need lengthy mention, and also too numerous to be given in detail. Writing for the Mexicans and Spaniards, in 1666, he says: "It is a fact that the Picture, since it was first placed in its chapel or hermitage, has worked and is daily working many wonders among the devout; and that copies which have touched it are the occasion of miracles where they are located." But he does not detail these wonders, for by themselves "they would require a large volume, and the Picture is its own greatest miracle."[1]

In the Juridical Process of the same period, the third Interrogatory calls the actual and past Guadalupan miracles—"innumerable."

The supplication for the Patronage addressed to Benedict XIV., and by him inserted in his approving Brief,

---

[1] Fel. de Mex., p. 56.

states that "miracles are declared to have occurred in all New Spain" in connection with the holy Picture. Also in the Office first granted by that learned Pontiff, and lately enlarged and reapproved by Leo XIII., it is stated that the Shrine at Guadalupe has been famous for '*frequentia miraculorum,*' the frequency of its miracles, or, as the words more strictly mean, for its constantly recurring miracles.

We see, therefore, that there is abundance of most trustworthy authority for the general assertion and belief that many real miracles have been wrought through the instrumentality of this New World Picture and Shrine, and through the intercession of Our Lady of America.

Among the first Guadalupan writers who took pains to collect and classify the apparently supernatural facts, the ablest is the Jesuit historian, Florencia. Forty years before him, in 1648, Sanchez, the Oratorian, had extolled and summarily mentioned the Tepeyac wonders. But the method of the Jesuit Father was better adapted to history. He sought out attested details, inquiring into the origin and significance of many ex-votos and inscriptions. He also suggested, in 1687, that it would be well to take an official information on each case though he explained and apparently justified its omission on certain occasions. Notoriety and openness to the public gaze seemed to dispense with formal documents. For this reason there was no information taken in a case which the historian was then personally investigating, and which, as illustrative, I give here, though somewhat out of its chronological order.

On the 19th of February of that same year, 1687, the stout, heavy Mrs. Sinoesio (the description is Florencia's) was the subject of a strange occurrence. She lived on the *Plateros* corner of the great *Plaza*, and was known as a pious mother of a family. Accidentally the good woman was precipitated into a deep well, dragging the ladder down with her. A child discovered the accident and shouted for Mr. Sinoesio. He came in haste but was unable to pull out the corpulent lady, so deeply had she gone headforemost into the water, and so tightly was one of her feet caught in the stakes. When he had procured ropes and help, there was, of course, no apparent hope of saving the woman's life; but a negro, who went under the water to help to lift the body, came up saying that she was still alive. It was an hour from the fall when she was extricated; yet there was little more wrong with her than a cut on her head where it came in contact with the bottom of the well, and a bruise on her foot where one of the ropes was tied.

The historian questioned her and her husband and many eye-witnesses. Their testimony he found perfectly consistent, and the escape plainly more than natural. The woman's own simple explanation was that, at the moment of her fall, she earnestly exclaimed: "Mother-of-God of Guadalupe, my children!"[1]

Florencia details most of the extraordinary occurrences which, at his time, were sufficiently authenticated to allow of a memorial being placed in the Sanctuary. They mainly concern deliverance from imminent perils on land and sea, or from personal physical evils. He mentions about forty cases, many of them at great length. From his narrative and those of other historians, I find the following examples most easily detachable:—

---

[1] Estrella del Norte, cap. XXVIII.

What is popularly called the *First Miracle* happened, as we have seen, when the Picture was being transferred from Zumárraga's church to the earliest Shrine. An Indian, not of the city but of a neighboring Chichimeca tribe, having been accidentally shot through the neck with an arrow, was taken up apparently dead—*dead*, the oldest account says. When the arrow was withdrawn, in the presence of *Holy Mary of Guadalupe*, the man stood up as if awaking. He retained only the marks of the arrow's entrance and protrusion; and, according to native traditions, he never after left the Sanctuary. Of this event innumerable representations have been produced. One of the oldest paintings is still in the presbytery at Guadalupe; the best one is in the right aisle of the restored Basilica.

In 1545 the fearful *cocolixtli* plague suddenly ceased among the Indians, when their children were led in procession to pray before the Picture. This is spoken of as a very public miracle, and as one of the powerful minor forces that attracted the native race to the Holy Mother. It is well commemorated by a large canvas in the Indian or Parish Church.

Another instance of the miraculous intervention of Our Lady is attested by both civil and ecclesiastical annals, in connection with the great flood of 1629 to 1634. It had at the time, rained much and the canals were full. Then an unprecedented rise in the adjacent lakes swamped the greater part of the Capital and caused immense loss of life and property. It is related that, at one period of the inundation, the plain on which the city stands was six feet under water, so that hardly a ground-floor, except that of the Cathedral, remained unflooded.

Most of the clay buildings, then so numerous, foundered immediately, and crushed or left homeless the majority of the poor. Thousands of Indians perished of drowning, hunger, and exposure; whilst many of the wealthier citizens hurried away to other parts of the country. What made the situation especially gloomy was the fact that the waters did not seem to diminish even when the great rains had ceased, but kept on rising or lodged heavily over the desolate streets.

Matters went so far in the second year and the beginning of the third that, after many official inquiries and reports, the provisional order came, from Philip IV. of Spain, to abandon the doomed Capital and build a new one on the high ground between the neighbouring towns of Tacuba and Tacubaya. But some members of the municipality opposed the execution of this royal order. They advised the people to have confidence in the stability of their city. It belonged, they said, to God and was consecrated to His Immaculate Mother whose sacred Picture they had among them: proper recourse to her was all that was required.

They had, indeed, brought in the Picture from Guadalupe; for, the extent of their dangers and disasters induced both civil and religious authorities to sanction that unusual proceeding. Now they renewed their supplications to their great Patroness, and eventually gained their object. For, though the waters did not immediately recede, sufficient confidence was inspired to endure and wait until God saw fitting to relieve His people. The city was saved and its ruined parts rebuilt; and, though the intervention of Our Lady may not, to the eyes of outsiders, seem very manifest or striking, all classes of the citizens, from the Royal Audience down, unanimously proclaimed her the preserver of Mexico. They publicly and officially acknowledged their preservation as a miracle; as such they entered it on their various Records, and wrote about it to Rome as well as to Madrid.

Laymen seem to have been most prominent in this avowal and thanksgiving; but the most intimate conviction of the reality of the miracle was held by ecclesiastics like Archbishop Manso and his successor, Dávalos, who heard and believed certain private revelations concerning the averted doom of the ungrateful or frivolous Capital, and concerning the destined duration of this punitive but remedial deluge.

The waters withdrew in the fifth year, as had certainly been predicted; and the Picture, which had been brought away from the Shrine with all the solemnity that a decorated fleet of canoes could afford, was borne back in triumphal procession, with gladness and song, in the month of May, 1634.

About the same time the remarkable case of a Franciscan priest, whose brethren and colleagues knew and examined all the circumstances, was well authenticated in the city of Mexico. Father Pedro Valderrama, of the monastery of St. James, suffered from an ulcerated foot. He grew so bad, and so hopeless of relief, that he had finally to resign himself to the decision of the infirmarians and surgeons who declared that there was nothing for it but to amputate the diseased member. However, before submitting to the operation, the good Father besought his superior to have him once carried to the Shrine at Guadalupe.

He had his wish; and, arrived before the holy Picture, he cast himself down in fervent supplication. Those who had accompanied and carried him were moved to pity at the sight of the Priest and Missionary so helpless that he could not stand by himself. But their joyous wonder was great when the crippled man bounded up and shouted that he was cured—vividly recalling a well-known apostolic miracle.

The cure was so real that Valderrama walked barefoot the three miles back to Mexico, and made soon after, as a practised pedestrian, an excursion of forty miles to the monastery of Pachuca.

In 1665 Bishop Tomás of Oaxaca authenticated a double miracle. At the Guadalupan shrine of his episcopal city the curtains before the copy of the Picture were unaccountably set on fire. A piece within one of the curtains and two within the other were seen to burn through, yet the stuff adjoining bore no trace of fire, nor did the string on which the burnt pieces were hanging. Much less was the picture or its veil touched; and, stranger still, the burnt parts did not fall out, though the curtains were drawn and drawn back.

There was commotion in the shrine from Saturday to Tuesday. Then the bishop came to inquire into the occurrence. He saw and wondered. The third time he made the curtains run on the string the burnt parts fell down in ashes on the Tabernacle. One of his priests, Father Quintero, had the happy thought to give some of these ashes in water to his sister, Crescencia de Quintero, who was sick of a dangerous malady—which, from the description given, seems to have been diphtheria. She arose cured next morning, and went immediately, with two other witnesses, to give testimony of her marvellous recovery.

The bishop was so impressed with what he saw and heard that he appointed a court of inquiry, composed of canons, doctors, provincials, guardians, rectors, and other dignitaries, whose names and titles are given at great length in the Information. Their decree has these passages :—

"Both occurrences (the burning and the cure) were brought about miraculously and in a way beyond all the forces of nature. . . . The portentous Picture of Our Lady of Guadalupe works and has worked miracles in this kingdom for the propagation of the Faith among the natives. . . . The copy of the said holy Picture having been so lately brought into this diocese, and the shrine so lately founded, it is clear that the most serene Queen of the Angels wishes to spread her devotion among the faithful by means of her wonders. . . . There shall be proposed to the people the miraculous effects which Our Sovereign Lady has wrought these days in this diocese. For the greater solemnity of the celebration, his Lordship shall assist, with the Venerable Dean and Chapter of his church. So is it provided, ordered, and signed. Tomás, Bishop of Oaxaca. Before me, Miguel Martinez de Escobar, Notario Público."[1]

Another miraculous deliverance of Mexico attributed to Holy Mary of Guadalupe concerns the Great Plague of 1737. This time the whole of New Spain was in question, for the strange malady spread over the entire country. It was a fearful fever, accompanied by violent

---

[1] Estrella del Norte, p. 149.

spasms, and ending generally in abundant bleeding from the nose and speedy death. The contagion began in woolen mills near the Capital, and ran like wildfire in all directions. Its ravages are described as appalling.

When natural remedies had failed, the people, led again by the metropolitan municipality, turned to Our Lady, "the Polar Star of the Nation," as many were accustomed to call her. Past experience made them look hopefully to the Shrine; and a striking fact of the moment vividly excited their confidence. For the plague, practically universal, had not touched the environs of Guadalupe. So they petitioned the archbishop to appoint them the proper means of recourse to the Holy Mother, in their extreme distress. After much prayer and most frequent reception of the Sacraments, it was decided, by a spontaneous impulse that spread on every side, to vow the Capital and the kingdom to Holy Mary of Guadalupe as Principal Patroness.

With great manifestations of public faith, with multitudinous civil and religious formalities—of which I may speak in another chapter—with an enthusiasm hardly ever before equalled, the vow was solemnly ratified.

Very quickly were its fruits experienced. All historians of the period agree that the plague seemed lifted off the land at the exact time at which the Patronage was decreed. As one of them puts it, "health then became epidemic." The Capital could record that, on the vigil of the solemn consecration, only three corpses entered its chief *campo santo* where forty, fifty, and even a hundred, had been received on other days. Similar reports came from all sides; and immediately the Great Plague was a thing of the past.

The miracle here seems sufficiently evident. A critical observer may, of course, be disposed to say that the contagion might naturally disappear as suddenly as it came—though that would be strange enough; but the conviction of a whole people, who were intimately concerned in the malady and its cessation, should count for something, and, in this case, will not be easily shaken. That generation of Mexicans, and all the generations since, declare that the decimating Plague of 1737 was stopped by Holy Mary of Guadalupe.

Those familiar with the history of devotion to the Sacred Heart may recall an incident of the Plague of Marseilles in 1720. The heroic Bishop Belzunce, who stood calmly at his post when fear made the very magistrates flee the stricken city, and who ministered day and night to his dying people, determined to seek help in consecrating Marseilles to the Sacred Heart. He did so amid circumstances and ceremonies of deepest pathos; and from that time the number of daily deaths began to diminish. The vow of consecration having been ratified on the 4th of November, the people had recovered sufficient courage at Easter of the following year to insist on opening the long-closed churches. The interval was considerable; yet all felt that the public vow had arrested the course of death. This persuasion had also lastingly beneficial results. "There is no doubt," Dalgairns writes, in his book on the Sacred Heart, "that the favor thus granted to Marseilles was a powerful cause of the spread of the devotion in France."[1]

[1] Introd., p. 57.

Now it may be admitted that the benign intervention was more remarkable in Mexico than in Marseilles. No wonder that Holy Mary of Guadalupe is declared in the new Office, as in the older one, to have been an ever-ready help in public and private calamities: *praestissimum adversus publicas privatasque calamitates praesidium*.[1]

As an example of a particular favor and a fully authenticated miracle, it may be well to mention the case of a nun of St. Catharine's convent in the city of Puebla. The facts occurred in 1755, when juridical depositions and verbal processes were more attended to than they had been earlier. Hence, in this case we find every detail given, and the medical as well as the ecclesiastical decision in perfect form.

Sister Jacinta had suffered, since the time of her novitiate, from an ulceration or perforation of the stomach that caused daily hemorrhages. She dragged on for years; but at the age of twenty-eight, worn out with vomiting and nausea, she was completely prostrated by acute peritonitis. Many swear, in the processes, that they saw her on the sick bed utterly unable to move; that she was speechless; that her eyes were insensible to the light; that breathing was most difficult; and that the medical opinion declared her dying. In that condition she was anointed towards midnight on the 11th of December; and the hope was devoutly expressed that she would be called to her reward on the morrow—the day of Holy Mary of Guadalupe.

The fervent Pueblans had made preparation to celebrate the Feast with unequalled splendor that year, on

---

[1] Hist. Comp., p. 75 and fol.

account of the special Office and Mass just granted by Benedict XIV.

In the forenoon of the 12th the confessor was waiting to give the dying girl the final absolution, when she made known to him that she was not going to die. It does not appear whether the nuns paid much or little heed to this communication, for they merely put in the sister's hands a copy of the Picture. This she held close to her breast. She was in prayer, insisting—as they afterwards learned—that her recovery would be for the honor of the Virgin of the Apparitions and the fame of her holy Picture at Guadalupe.

At noon she suddenly sat up in perfect health. She was radiant and full of life. She immediately asked for food which she ate with the appetite of a person who had long fasted and had never been sick. She wanted to dress and go down to the choir; but the superiors refused permission, being still impressed with the fact that the sister was in her agony only a moment before. She had to content herself with proclaiming the miraculous cure and giving thanks for it in her cell that afternoon and evening. But at the community hour next morning she was in choir, followed all the exercises, and took up again her function as sacristan.

In good health she lived and labored in the convent for thirty-seven years, dying as late as 1792, at the age of sixty-five.

The Bishop of Puebla caused the depositions of doctors and other witnesses to be methodically taken and the juridical process instituted. Then he issued the decision of the episcopal court which stated that "there was a real miracle wrought by God, through the intercession of the Virgin of Guadalupe, in the instantaneous and complete cure, on the 12th of December, 1755, of the Religious, Sister Jacinta Maria de San José."

I find that the medical notes of this case, taken more than a century ago, were lately submitted to a number of doctors in Mexico. Their detailed opinion, formulated by the most distinguished scientist among them and fully corroborated by the others, ends with this passage: "I have considered the way in which this sick person was cured, and, after close study, I cannot help saying: This is extraordinary; this is physically impossible. Why should I not continue and say: This is a miracle, this is directly the work of Him who can suspend natural laws; . . . who, being able to work mediately through man's science, works immediately by Himself when so He fulfils His inscrutable designs? *Mexico, June 1st, 1883.* Manuel Carmona y Valle."[1]

Close on the year in which Sister Jacinta ended the length of days granted to her through Our Lady's intercession, another miracle widely increased the fame of the Guadalupan Picture. This time the event occurred amidst circumstances particularly favorable to its attestation and publicity. It was at Rome, in a great church, under the eyes of thousands of the faithful and of many ecclesiastics.

In a certain true sense the miracle in question may be said to have needed special evidence and sanction; for, it was of the kind that is least readily accepted, and most likely to be ill-judged—even by Catholics. The self-sufficient world has so often laughed at all reports

---

[1] Hist. Comp., p. 83.

of supernatural life-appearances in sacred pictures and images that ignorant members of the Church may sometimes think it due to their own strength of mind to be also, in such matters, peremptorily incredulous. They forget—though only heresy should here be supposed to forget—that God has chosen and chooses the things that are weak and foolish, to confound the wise and the powerful. What circumstance of a miracle can appear unworthily little or simple to one who believes that the Scriptural *dry bones*, and *handkerchiefs*, and *shadows*, healed and raised to life?

Non-Catholics, indeed, may be expected to reject scornfully the story of the *Crucifix* moving its arm, or the *Madonna* its eyes: though, accepting no ecclesiastical miracles whatever, they can hardly think one more unlikely than another. But in these questions they are not accustomed to reason. "Would any amount of evidence," Newman asks, "convince the Protestant of the miraculous motion of a Madonna's eyes? is it not in itself, prior to proof, simply incredible? would he even listen to the proof? His First Principle settles the matter; no wonder then that the whole history of Catholicism finds so little response in his intellect or sympathy in his heart. It is as impossible that the notion of the miracle should gain admittance into his imagination, as for a lighted candle to remain burning, when dipped into a vessel of water. The water puts it out." (Pres. Pos. of Cath., Lect. VII.)

Earlier in the same Lecture the great controversialist, emphasising the fact that miracles abound in the Church, says in his enumeration: "Crucifixes have bowed the head to the suppliant, and Madonnas have bent their eyes upon assembled crowds." Farther on, to make it clear that he was not shrinking from a statement of his own belief, he adds, among other professions: "I think it impossible to withstand the evidence which is brought for the liquefaction of the blood of St. Januarius at Naples, and for the motion of the eyes of the pictures of the Madonna in the Roman States."[1]

The miraculous Roman *Madonnas* to which Newman makes reference included a copy of the Guadalupan Picture. It was much spoken of at the time he wrote; and it has been, in Rome, the centre and object of much devotion this whole century. During the Vatican Council it was brought into particular notice. Pius IX. had restored and decorated the Church of St. Nicholas, in one of whose chapels the painting was kept. To accord with this representation of Our Lady, the title of the chapel was changed from *St. John the Baptist* to the *Immaculate Conception*. There was, also, celebrated in that Church of St. Nicholas a great Guadalupan solemnity, on the 12th of December, 1869. More than sixty of the Vatican Fathers who represented America and Spain took part in the proceedings; and the fame of the Tepeyac Virgin was most auspiciously proclaimed.

Last year the Catholic world was again particularly reminded of this American wonder in Rome; for, 1896 was the centenary of the "Prodigies of Mary," and the annual feast—found in many calendars on the 9th of July—was given unusual prominence and splendor.[2]

---

[1] Lect. VII., p. 312.

[2] An interesting and exhaustive article on the general subject is found in the *American Ecclesiastical Review*, July, 1896.

One of the "prodigies" consisted in the miraculous movement of the eyes in the Roman copy of *Holy Mary of Guadalupe*. The picture is mentioned by name in Cardinal Somaglia's Decree of Approbation, published in 1797. Its history is interesting.

It was brought to Rome by a Jesuit missionary after the Expulsion from Mexico in 1767. The good Father was zealous in making known its origin and meaning; and by its instrumentality he drew many to the love of Our Lady's American title. His picture finally came into the possession of the Church of St. Nicholas.

It is an oil painting on canvas, very closely copied after the impression on the *tilma* of Juan Diego, and in consequence very beautiful.

On the 15th of July, 1796, the people praying in the church suddenly raised a cry, for they saw the *Madonna* look down like a living person, and raise and lower the eyelids and move the eyeballs. Their inspiration of the moment was to rush and ring the bells of St. Nicholas's and of the neighboring churches. Crowds hurried in, among them the Archpriest, Father Reboa, who says of himself in his sworn testimony: "At the sight of so stupendous a prodigy I at once felt the influx of a sacred awe and was, as it were, rapt out of myself; but immediately there possessed my soul a sweetness and consolation that no words can explain, and that can be understood by those alone who had the same experience."[1]

As the miracle occurred day after day, the crowds became enormous, and the church had to be left open at night. All Rome was now anxious to see the Ameri-

---

[1] Hist. Comp., p. 237.

can *Madonna*. Even in the formal, unornamented details of the Juridical Process, we can perceive that the old Collegiate of St. Nicholas witnessed during that second half of July, 1796, scenes of wonderful and most moving devotion. The enthusiastic multitudes could restrain neither their voices nor their tears. They shouted in admiration and gratitude; they wept in joy, or contrition, or tenderness of affection. They even called on the Holy Mother, when the eyes resumed their painted fixedness, to look at them again; and she did so, to their new and greater enthusiasm.

But it was not merely the crowds of simple faithful that witnessed the miracle. Artists, scientists, and theologians, drew near the wondrous *Madonna*, taking the closest possible observations, as we can see by their testimony. They studied the optical conditions of the strange occurrence, took in turn the best positions, and spent long hours in verifying the facts. They could see that in this painting, as in the original at Guadalupe, the eyes are half-covered by the upper lid, only part of the iris with a little of the white being visible; and that the glance is turned gently downward. But when the miracle occurred the lid sometimes rose, the whole iris with much of the white was clearly seen, and the glance was up or forward as well as down; at other times the eyes moved in their sockets with free natural action, looking gravely and majestically from side to side. The specialists witnessed, also, the unusual continuance or the repetition of the wonder when the people eagerly and devoutly besought it of Our Lady.

In the attestation of Father Tallepietra, a theologian and physicist, there is this categorical passage: "For me the miracle was not only certain but demonstrated to physical evidence. Because, depending on the sure principles of Optics—which I had both studied and taught in the schools—I was perfectly sure of making no mistake, and sure also that my sight was subject to no illusion internal or external."[1]

So great was the edification derived from witnessing the miraculous phenomena in the Guadalupan and other *Madonnas*, that many Romans clamored for the juridical process in which they might record their grateful testimony. The court was constituted under the presidency of Cardinal Somaglia, Vicar General of His Holiness, Pius VI. It sat from October, 1796, to February, 1797, examining eighty-six witnesses, who were above all suspicion and who swore to what they had seen. Depositions were taken on many pictures in which extraordinary manifestations had, at that troubled time, appeared for the consolation and strength of menaced Rome.

The Decree, issued on the 28th of February, 1797, mentions the pictures which its approval covers—the Guadalupan copy being among them [2]—and concludes with the statement that "the truth of the aforesaid wonderful and prodigious occurrence has been sufficiently and superabundantly proved:—*satis superabundeque comprobatam fuisse veritatem antedicti mirabilis prodigiosique eventus.*"

In this sketch of the Guadalupan miracles I have not thought it necessary to treat of the ameliorations or cures

---

[1] El Magist. de la Igl., p. 169.

[2] "Bmæ. Virginis Mariæ denominat. *Guadalupe,* existentis in Sacello S. Joanni Baptistæ dicato in Collegiata et Parochiali Ecclesia S. Nicolai *in carcere Tulliano.*"

effected by the use of the water from the *Pocito*. This well, in the porch, of the *Iglesia del Pocito* at the foot of Tepeyac, is turbidly mineral and bubblingly abundant. It is not accredited, by any tradition that I have seen, with a supernatural origin; but it bears an ancient and wide-spread reputation for remedial qualities. The physical good effected by drinking of this water or applying some of it with the hand—for bathing is neither practised nor provided for—is said to be incalculable. All classes have recourse to it, and thousands proclaim its value to them individually. Few seem to ask whether the *Pocito* water works naturally or by miracle; but very many, after a happy experience, advise confident reliance on its healing properties.

The Mexicans drink of it devoutly because it has some historical connection with the Apparitions of Our Lady, because it is found in the vestibule of one of her churches, and because multiplied instances of its good effects are on record among them; but they are neither curious nor presumptuous about determining its exact character. Perhaps the author of the *Pensil Americano* indicated the popular impression as exactly as is possible, when, in 1793, he said of the *Pocito:* "Experience has caused these waters to be regarded (more from supernatural than natural virtue) as an almost universal remedy for all pains and infirmities." The common view at the time of the *Informations* in 1666 is expressed by the third witness, Andres Juan, an Indian of 112 years, who testifies: "Through washing with the water of a Well which adjoins the said hermitage, and through drinking it—though it is not very sweet—there occur and have occurred prodigious miracles; but for this, look to those who have written papers and acts of the said Apparition, before as well as since the said hermitage was constructed."[1]

Foreign visitors to the Aztec Capital go to drink at the *Pocito*, with a certain respect and a vague hope of benefit. Frequently, too, they report most happy results. I have heard Englishmen and Scotchmen, as well as people of the States, who habitually dwell in the City of Mexico, declare that the cures and improvements effected by that water are numerous and undoubted; and that they appear too varied and too opposite—not to say too sudden—to be all referred to the natural efficacy of any merely mineral remedy.

This is the opinion which common sense suggests, even though we may see no need of pressing the question of manifestly supernatural cures.

From the facts adduced in this chapter, and from other similar ones, it must, I think, be rigorously concluded that Guadalupe has been glorified by continued miraculous favors. Such a conclusion is far-reaching and important. God alone can work miracles, and when He does so He gives a truly unmistakable distinction and sanction to persons, or places, or practices. If this direct intervention of the Creator can be obtained by believing that the Mother of Our Lord has appeared among us and left us tokens of her visit, or by giving her new titles, new love, new honor, because of that belief, then surely no doubt remains about the truth of what we believe. But more than that: it must be very specially God's will that we piously occupy ourselves

---

[5] Inf. de 1666; Test. 3°.

with such Apparitions and with the devotions founded on them. Here is plainly indicated a walk of Christian life over which Heaven is open, and on which falls abundantly the dew of saving grace.

CHAPTER XI.

OTHER REPORTED MIRACLES.

EXTRAORDINARY facts which have sometimes been styled miraculous, and which may or may not be so, abound in Guadalupan traditions and annals. The record of them is interesting, while it puts no more strain on our credence than the details of each individual case may themselves reasonably impose. These facts are handed down by respectable writers, without, however, being clothed with undue authority; and most of them have been commemorated by votive offerings and festive celebrations at the Shrine or elsewhere in New Spain. They help to manifest and explain the ever-ready trust and recourse of Mexicans to the intervention of Holy Mary of Guadalupe. The relation of them may entertain and edify. From the *Estrella del Norte* I transcribe and abbreviate the following accounts:—

Don Antonio de Carvajal set out from Mexico for the town of Tullantzinco, accompanied by Antonio, his son and namesake. As they rode along, the young man's horse became restive; it took the bit between its teeth and soon pitched the rider out of the saddle. Antonio remained hanging from the stirrup and was dragged half a league over rugged, thorny, and stony places. His companions, who followed and were sure that they should find him dead and battered to pieces, came up

with him as he still hung by the foot from the saddle.
The horse was standing inclined forward, with its fore
legs bent as if attempting to kneel, and its mouth to
the ground as if kissing it. The beast now seemed
altogether gentle and tranquil. The youth was alive,
well, and uninjured. Having freed his foot from the
stirrup, they asked him for the explanation of this
apparently prodigious miracle. He said that, as they
had seen, when passing by the Sanctuary of Our Lady
of Guadalupe he went in to make a visit and pray before
the miraculous Picture; that then on their way they were
speaking of the wonders she works in favor of those
who invoke her. So when the accident happened and
he found himself carried away by the horse, the con-
versation being fresh in his mind, he began to call
with all his heart on the Virgin of Guadalupe. She at
once appeared and, restraining the horse with the bridle,
brought him to a stand-still. The animal, as it seemed
from his posture, wanted to kneel in her presence, and
kissed the ground that her feet had trodden. His own
persuasion was that he could never have escaped were
it not for the miracle wrought through the Mother of
God. . . . This admirable occurrence, depicted on
canvas by a skilful hand, is seen in the Sanctuary of
Holy Mary of Guadalupe; and Don Andrés Carvajal y
Tapia, son of the gentleman on whom the Immaculate
Virgin conferred the favor, erected at Tullantzinco, in
memory of it, an artistic and costly reredos on which
the facts are painted to the life. There the feast of the
Apparition is every year celebrated with the utmost
solemnity.

Captain Lucas García Montaño, coming from Maracaibo to Vera Cruz, was driven for eleven days before a fierce north wind. He continued to implore God's mercy. On the Feast of St. Andrew, 1685, towards midnight, all human hope of escape was finally abandoned. Then the captain and the crew began to invoke with their whole hearts the Virgin of Guadalupe of Mexico. From that moment the hurricane abated, and in a few days they arrived safe at Vera Cruz. Every soul in the ship believed that it happened through the intercession of the sovereign Lady; and Captain García had the occurrence represented in a painting, which, as a memorial of thanksgiving, he sent to the Sanctuary.

About the end of August, 1668, there left Vera Cruz for Habana a frigate, with Miguel de Lete as captain, and Christobal de Ledesma as pilot. For some days they sailed with a favorable wind; but toward the twenty-fourth parallel there came on them a tempest so violent that, their ship's sides not being fit to bear the fury of the waves, they had to turn the stern to the wind and to send where fortune carried them. The helm soon became unmanageable and was lost; both the mainmast and the foremast were broken; the cookroom and forecastle were torn away by a furious wave; and the smashed side let in so much water that the forty-seven persons who labored at the two pumps, were unable to exhaust it. As they saw that, humanly speaking, they were lost, they all made their confession to four Priests who were on board, one secular, one Augustinian, and two Franciscan. When they had made this Christian provision, a passenger, named Rodrigo de la

Cruz, who was a native of Mexico, commenced to implore the protection of the glorious Virgin of Guadalupe, his country-woman (*su paisana*), and to urge his companions to do the same. All together, with the contrition and devotion that such perils usually excite, they cried out to her, promising to amend their lives, and also to be her true servants for the time to come. So, during five days, the ship ran on without helm or sail, guided rather by the favorable breeze which the Holy Virgin sent it than by the opposing blast of the north wind. And on the 2nd of October they found themselves at the shore of Barlovento in New Spain, at a point so good and favorable that they could all land without the least danger—though on most of that coast the land is more dangerous than the high sea. Every one attributed the escape from so great and manifest perils to the protection of Our Lady, through her miraculous Picture of Guadalupe of Mexico; and, in memory of the favor, the said Rodrigo de la Cruz put a painting of the occurrence in the Sanctuary.

While a man was once in the Chapel Major of the Shrine, praying before the sacred Picture, the cord of a lamp over his head happened to break. The lamp was heavy enough to kill him, or at least to wound him seriously. It came down on his head—yet he was not hurt at all. And that the favor of the miraculous Virgin might the better be recognised, the glass was not broken, the oil was not spilt, the light was not put out, though the lamp fell over on the ground. Those who were present were struck with admiration, at the sight of the many wonders that accompanied the fall of the lamp.

As the Licentiate Juan Vazquez de Acuña, who had been many years Vicar of the Sanctuary, was once going up to the altar of the holy Picture to say Mass, a strong wind, of the kind that often sweeps over that locality, extinguished the candles. While the server went back to look for a light, the priest, who was waiting, raised his eyes to the holy Picture through devotion; and—oh wonder! he saw two rays, from the sun which surrounds it, extend themselves to the candles on the altar and miraculously light them. The other persons present saw the same thing.

When the server returned and found the candles lighted, he thought immediately of a miracle, even before he heard what had happened; for he knew the trouble which it cost him to bring in the light, and he judged that no one could have anticipated him in doing so.

Admiring and revering her prodigies, let us ask the Holy Mother, adds the narrator, as often as we go to worship in the sacred Temple, that she would send us rays of her light to enkindle our affections, so that with fitting dispositions we may enter her House and go up to the Altar of the miraculous Picture.

Juan Pavon, sacristan of the holy Picture had a child, a son of his, very sick with quinsy. Taking a little of the oil from the lamp that always burns before the Holy Virgin, he anointed the boy's throat with it, and he was immediately cured. This, among other favors of Our Lady, is commemorated in her Sanctuary.

Catalina de Monta suffered from dropsy eleven years and could find no remedy. She went to the Sanctuary to make a novena and to invoke Our Lady of Guadalupe. She drank of the well, where the Most Holy Virgin appeared to Juan Diego when she gave him the flowers; and though water, considering the person's sickness, should be her enemy, it became to her, through the intercession of the Holy Mother, both medicine and life. There is a tablet, commemorating the fact, raised in the church.

Eight ecclesiastics were driving to the Shrine at full gallop, when an Indian, with his mule, came up the middle of the highway. The mule, being from the mountains, took fright at the sound of the wheels and bolted, throwing the Indian to the ground. He fell so near the carriage that, before the drivers could pull up, the wheels were upon the wretched man and passed over his body. Those in the carriage were calling loudly on the Virgin of Guadalupe to deliver the Indian; and just as they feared they had killed him they saw him stand up, well and unhurt, and run away after his mule. The eight ecclesiastics, some of whom were priests, were eye-witnesses of this extraordinary event; and it was inscribed in the church, among other favors of the Most Holy Virgin.

For a long time Bartolome Granado suffered such fearful pains in the head that they used to deprive him of consciousness, and seemed to be hurrying him to his death. Having got himself carried before the Picture, he presented a silver head, which still hangs in the Sanctuary, and he was immediately cured.

Don Juan de Castilla was suffering from an inflamed leg that became ulcerated. As he had been treated by many surgeons and saw himself without human remedy, he took the advice of Father Pedro de Valderrama (who was cured at the Shrine) and sent to Our Lady of Guadalupe a leg in silver of the dimensions of his own. No sooner was the silver leg brought in sight of the holy Picture than the leg of flesh was cured. So sudden was the miracle that the person who carried the offering found the sick man, whom he thought he left dying, sound and nimble enough to set out immediately, on foot, to the Hermitage, in order to give thanks to God and His Blessed Mother for the favor he had received.

Having narrated what precedes—and much more—the author of the *Estrella del Norte* then says: "I leave here, in order not to increase the bulk of this History, fourteen other cases for which painted tablets are found in the Church, and in which the Virgin of Guadalupe seems to have miraculously succored her devout clients; .... and I give two which the Vicar, D. Juan Altamirano de Villaneuva, assures me he thoroughly verified, and which not only yield honor to the holy Picture, but also instruction to us:—

"On the 13th of August of last year (1685), a native boy, who serves in the Vicar's house, went to the Well Chapel to light a wax candle before the principal copy of the Picture of Our Lady of Guadalupe. The Indians practise this devotion in memory of *El Transito* of the Virgin Mother of God, which is thought to have been on the 13th, as on the 15th was her Resurrection and her Coronation at the right hand of her Son. I know not what connection the lighted candle has with the mystery on that day more than on any other. Perhaps it is because, as St. John Damascene and other saints relate, the Apostles and Christians assisted at her passing-away, and held lights in their hands. Be the reason what it may, the devotion is praiseworthy, and as such the Lord seems to have qualified it in the case of this boy.

"For, as he was coming back from the *Pocito*, after having placed the candle before the picture, there joined him, near the Vicar's house, three other boys. They all seemed of his own age and size; they were dressed with neat elegance; but they went barefoot as the Indians go. Their faces were very handsome; and, together with their beauty, what most strikingly manifested itself was an exceedingly joyful affability. This was so great that, though the boy did not at the moment imagine they could be other than human, he was lost in astonishment at the strange gladness and jubilation which they appeared to enjoy one with another.

"One of them asked him whence he was coming. He replied that he had been offering a candle, through devotion to the Guadalupan picture of the Well Chapel. *Happy* (then said the boy, or whoever he was) *those who serve Our Lady of Guadalupe! Oh! if we, there where we are, could wait on and serve her!*

"As he spoke thus they arrived in front of the church; and then, with an affection so intensely moving that, as the little Indian affirmed, it melted his heart, he added: *If all knew what it is, and what it avails, to serve Our Lady of Guadalupe!*

"As he said this, the native boy, who was accompanied and surrounded by them, turned to look, and they were gone! he knew not how. He hastened his steps, not troubled nor afraid, as he declared, and as he declares to-day, but so full of gladness that his heart could hardly be contained in his bosom. The moment he entered the house he told the Vicar, bidding him at the same time put his hand to his breast and feel the jumps of joy and delight his heart was giving. The Vicar testifies that he did so, and that he found it as the boy said.

"As for the truth of this story, I do not affirm that it is infallible, but merely that he who relates it is *Homo Sacerdos de semine Aaron, et non decipiet nos.* The boy to whom the case occurred is not unworthy of credit for being an Indian, since Juan Diego was one, as well as Juan Bernardino, and they were found worthy to be believed by the Archbishop, and to be visited by the Sovereign Queen of the Angels, who looks not to the condition of the person but to the innocence and simplicity of the soul.

"I do not say that these were angels, though the circumstances point to something more than common mortality; but it cannot be denied that the three sentences, which they pronounced for our instruction, are worthy of the reverence and respect which the angelic hosts must show to Our Lady. Putting aside the question whether they were angels or, perhaps, the souls of some little Indians who, through devotion to the Holy Mother and through her intercession, are now living in God and enjoying Him present to them, let us follow and keep their words: *Happy those who serve Our Lady of Guadalupe! Oh! if we, there where we are, could wait on and serve her! If all knew what it is, and what it avails, to serve Our Lady of Guadalupe!*—and be they men or angels we shall not go astray.

"I remark only, in the supposition of their being blessed spirits, that their manner and way of speaking—desiring to serve Our Lady where they are and where we are—is not because they have not the felicity of serving her both there and here, so that holily envious of our lot they should desire to do so, but because there is for them such glory in waiting on their great Lady and Queen and showing her reverence, that while they are actually serving and obeying her they wish to do so more and more. Thus the Apostle St. Peter affirms that while the angels are gazing on the essential glory, which is God, they still increasingly long to look on it and enjoy it: *In quem desiderant angeli prospicere.* And if the angels, who incessantly wait on Mary in Heaven, want more and more to wait on her, and are as it were anxious to serve her in her miraculous Picture of Guadalupe: *Oh! if we could wait on and serve her!*—what should we men do, we who have not the happy lot of seeing her most blessed countenance? What we should do is to entertain a most heartfelt devotion toward all her images, especially toward the miraculous one of Guadalupe, *for they are happy who revere and honor her in them all.*"

"The second case concerns the extraordinary music which at times is heard, either at the place of the Well or at the site of the Chapel, where the Holy Virgin appeared on the last two occasions to Juan Diego, when she ordered him to climb the hill and cut the roses, and when she sent him with them to the Ilmo. Sr. D. Fr. Juan de Zumárraga. Once, among other times, the harmony was so heavenly that the natives, who live in the neighboring village of San Lorenzo de Guadalupe, came out to know what music was this so sonorous, and went to the Chapel where it seemed to be. Arriving there they thought it was at the Well, and thither they went; but then they heard it resounding toward the Chapel! So it passed from the Chapel to the Well and from the Well to the Chapel, as they went or returned from one to the other.

"To this music I attach no more importance than what it derives from the veracity and authority of the well qualified person who asserts that the principal men of the quarter told him of it, and testified that they had heard it. To me there seems in it a certain congruence; for it is known that, the first time Our Lady of Guadalupe showed herself to an Indian, there was that music of the heavens which I mentioned in the *First Apparition*. And if the angels then sang because their Sovereign Queen appeared on the hill, why could they not now sing at the place where she showed herself twice to the same Indian? We are thus taught the harmony which the excessive condescension of this admirable Lady should always produce in our souls, and the attentive veneration with which a grateful memory should make us frequent the spots that were sanctified by her virginal footsteps."[1]

In some Guadalupan writings much stress is laid on the fact that after the Apparitions of the Mother of God nothing more is heard in Mexico, or in any part of New Spain, of demoniacal possession or interference.

---

[1] Estr. del Nor., p. 143.

The Indians are said to have particularly noticed the change, being painfully familiar with blood-exacting, speaking idols and other diabolical impositions. Many afflictions, corporal and spiritual, were attributed to the immediate influence of evil spirits; and, allowing for much probable exaggeration, it may still be concluded that where snake worship and human sacrifice were rampant the enemies of God and man made some striking manifestations of their power. On the subject of Guadalupe's miraculous action in casting down or expelling them, historians like Father Florencia remind us that the matter is not one easily attested, that the authority is mainly public rumor and general opinion. They report what was commonly said in their time, but to such testimony they assign no definite historical value.

Of course they recognise the sacred fitness and complete likelihood of Our Lady's having always a great part in crushing Satan's head, most especially in a region of the world in which she had made so admirable a revelation, and left so unique a memorial, of her Immaculate Conception. They also bear witness to the fact that the voice of the people universally declared the outward display of satanic agency, where the Picture or a copy of it was actually present, to be both unheard of and impossible.

As an illustration of this popular belief and a proof of its far-reaching influence, I give, in substance, one last case from the *Estrella del Norte:*—

An Andalusian of some wealth and standing was maltreated by a demon that had got possession of him. For his deliverance from so cruel and perverse a guest, he had recourse to the exorcisms of our Mother the Church, to the prayers of many good souls, and to the intercession and relics of various Saints. These are always salutary remedies, but, in the deep designs of God, they are not always efficacious.

Accidentally—and yet not without the counsel of Heaven—this Andalusian heard, from an acquaintance of his who had been in New Spain, that those regions, and very particularly the City of Mexico, enjoyed immunity from infernal spirits, through the blessing of the miraculous Picture of Our Lady of Guadalupe, the people's most special Patroness and Advocate. The traveller told him of the admirable Apparition, of the faith and devotion of the Mexicans, of the favors and miracles of the Holy Mother, and how she was an asylum and city of refuge in all dangers and necessities. He spoke to the possessed man's heart, for he touched the point of his affliction.

When the sick are given up by the good physicians whom they have at hand, they easily believe that one who is absent could heal them. So this spiritually sick man persuaded himself that in the Picture of Guadalupe he was to find the cure of his malady, since the Lord, in His supreme dispositions, did not wish it to be found in the remedies of the Church, nor in the Saints that were the accredited healers of similar infirmities. Therefore, without saying anything to anybody, lest his departure should be interfered with, he set out for Cadiz. Then taking some merchandise, in order to conceal the object of his voyage, he embarked and sailed to Vera Cruz.

While still on sea he had felt some relief, which he attributed to the fact of merely approaching New Spain; when he disembarked and touched the land, he found himself entirely unafflicted by the evil companion whose presence had hitherto been so heavy on him. He went up to the City of Mexico, visited the Sanctuary, and venerated the Picture. He was then in great consolation and in the full confidence that, through Holy Mary of Guadalupe, he had obtained the complete cure which he came so far to seek.

He remained some time in this kingdom, for the most part in Mexico, being at peace and made glad by the propinquity of the Picture, to which his visits were very frequent. However, the love of country which is always a powerful magnet, attracting some with sweet violence and wrenching others from the sphere of their highest advantages, was calling on him to return to Spain. It whispered to him that his ancient guest had now lost sight of him, and that if he went back to his own land there was no reason to fear that the demon should get back into him. It is said even that in his special pleading he began to doubt (no uncommon blindness) whether his deliverance had really been a miraculous effect of the holy Picture's influence, or if it did not merely coincide with the allotted term of possession. He finally determined to make the experiment; and he was undeceived at his very great cost.

He had hardly arrived in Spain when he found himself again possessed by the evil spirit, and in so violent a manner that it was immediately necessary to have recourse to exorcism. Being compelled, during the ceremony, to say why he had not molested this man in New Spain and yet when he returned home had taken up his ancient possession of him, the demon replied that in New Spain he was baffled by the Picture of the Virgin of Guadalupe, whose virtue makes hell tremble and puts to flight all its emissaries. Hearing this the man took warning, and, having repented of his want of faith and piety toward his Liberatrix, he came back to Mexico once for all. The Most Holy Virgin of Guadalupe, forgetting his inconstancy and compassionating his repeated labors, restored peace to him, delivering him again from the evil spirit that had continued to molest him. And the well-warned Andalusian took good care, as long as he lived, not to go away and absent himself from so benign a presence.

Though the author of the *Estrella del Norte* is learnedly reserved—like the good Jesuit historian he is—in proposing this case of the possessed Spaniard, he makes in connection with it some forcibly beautiful reflections. Applying St. Bernard's homily, *Vineae florentes*, to Our Lady of America, he says: " Mary blossomed like a vine in the mantle of Juan Diego: *Ego quasi vitis fructificavi;* from the hill of Guadalupe she spread abroad her miraculous flowers and the odorous breath of her heavenly fragrance. *Et hic odor fugavit serpentes, et omne reptile venenatum excedere loco coactum est:* and she put the demons to flight, obliging all the infernal spirits to quit this land and kingdom. Already we see the flight of those malign spirits from the thousands of thousands of gentile souls that, delivered out of their claws, have been restored to the noble liberty of the sons of God by Faith and Baptism."[1]

The moral miracles, of which we are here reminded, are not as prominently treated by Guadalupan writers

---

[1] Ib., p. 132.

as are the physical ones. They are, perhaps, too well-known, or too ordinary, or too little susceptible of rigorous demonstration. That they are not, however, overlooked, I may evidence by a passage from Dr. Heredia y Sarmiento, with which I can fittingly close this somewhat disjointed chapter. In his Guadalupan panegyric of 1801 he asks an audience that could understand him, what affliction America had suffered, since the day she saw in her bosom the Mother of her God, which had not found its remedy at the Hill of Tepeyac; or what greater proof of love for Americans Our Lady could give than the protection accompanying her Picture; then he exclaims: "Her blessings to us, how many are they not in number! how opportune in conjuncture! how ready in effusion! how efficacious for our true felicity! What is it that has melted into tears of contrition, so many scandalous highwaymen, so many cruel assassins, so many sacrilegious thieves, so many lascivious gallants, so many furious seekers of revenge, so many habitual sinners, so many dying impenitents? It is, I will not say an attentive contemplation of this Picture, but a momentary devout look into this Sanctuary, a single Christian glance at the exterior of this Temple, even a distant religious curiosity concerning this blessed Tepeyacac. For here abides the attractively sanctifying power of that glorious Benefactress, who, in spite of distance, of indisposition, of resistance, effectually breathes into the soul her practical exhortations to sanctity."[1]

---

[1] La Gloriosa Aparicion, p. 53.

CHAPTER XII.

THE FRUITS.

THAT Guadalupe has produced rich fruits in New Spain is variously asserted and as variously proved. The people of the land attribute all the good they enjoy to the influence of their Holy Patroness: the Apparitions, the Shrine, the Devotion, they connect with whatever is worth revering or loving. Indeed, we have seen that the national sentiment proclaims the 12th of December the greatest of Mexican days. Nor, really, does there appear anything strong, pure, holy, happy, in the Republic, that grew up or was preserved without the blessing of Holy Mary of Guadalupe.

The spiritual fruits, however, are those which most concern us here; and to their abundance, as well as their close connection with the Tepeyac wonders, I have now to draw attention.

The results obtained in Christianising the Indians of New Spain have elicited the admiration even of prejudiced and unsympathetic writers. Millions of natives were instructed, and received the Baptism for which they clamored, in an astonishingly brief space of time. That the visible effects had some potent cause, other than those of which non-Mexican historians have commonly taken account, must appear evident to close readers.

Some authors attribute the countless conversions to the missionary zeal of the Spanish rulers; others to the religious docility of the native Americans. Though these reasons may be good ones, a slight examination seems to prove them only partial.

It must be admitted that the Court of Spain, as a matter both of conscience and policy, furthered the work of evangelisation. The constant governmental reminders to look first and always to the conversion of these peoples tended to create a good public opinion. It came to be universally admitted that no one had a right to interfere with the New World unless he helped to make it Christian. The principle was insisted on at home and in the colony. Its explicit enunciation came from the Holy See. In the so-called *Bull of Partition*—issued by Alexander VI., in 1493, to prevent collision between Spain and Portugal—it was "commanded in virtue of holy obedience" to provide immediately for the Christian training of all subject natives.[1]

The Spanish monarchs seem to have loyally endeavored to carry out the papal mandate. The rulers of the time, Isabella, Ferdinand, Charles, and Philip, manifestly ambitioned wealthy dominions; yet there is substantial evidence that neither for gold nor conquest were they willing to be deprived of the Sacraments and to lose their souls. Moreover, they had no hope of ruling the Indies without the missionaries. They knew, too, that, if derelict in their duty, they would never be let rest by

---

[1] "Ad terras firmas et insulas prædictas, viros probos et Deum timentes, doctos, peritos, et expertos ad instruendum incolas et habitatores præfatos in fide Catholica et bonis moribus imbuendum, destinare."

such resolute patrons of the natives as Ximenes and Las Casas. Zumárraga, of Guadalupan fame, was also an unflinching advocate. When a tyrannical official falsely asserted that he had the Emperor's permission to force laborers from Pánuco to the islands, the Bishop-Elect bravely wrote to the greatest monarch of the age: "If it be true that Your Majesty gave such a licence, go and do for it, in fear of God, most strict penance."[1]

Zumárraga, Las Casas, and Ximenes, are the three men who made personal liberty a fundamental point in New World government. They had the question so thoroughly discussed, and the human-divine right to one's self and one's property so unanswerably established, that the enfranchisement of every American was at most a question of time. The history of these real liberators is not yet sufficiently studied; but the fuller is the acquaintance with their lives and writings, the stronger grows the conviction that general projects of abolishing slavery might not have yet reached the stage of practical politics, were it not for the words and works of these three Spanish Bishops of four hundred years ago.[2]

In Mexico the effects of ecclesiastical philanthropy were felt at the very darkest hour of the conquest. They were, however, made manifest and strongly permanent only some years later. In 1537 Pope Paul III. authoritatively banned both slavery and spoliation. In his two Briefs of the 16th of June of that year, he treats as heresy the pretence that the natives were not men; he excommunicates all who, on that pretence,

---

[1] Letter to Charles V., 1529.
[2] Vide *Fiske's Disc. of Amer.*, II, p. 456 et seq.

deprive them of their liberty or of the dominion of their goods; he, finally, declares of no force or validity whatever had been thus wickedly accomplished.[1]

These papal letters, which the government respectfully published and seconded, were equivalent to a charter for the Mexicans. It was through their moral influence—together with the ceaseless advocacy of Las Casas and Zumárraga—that the *New Laws* were framed and promulgated by Charles V. in 1542. Of that famous enactment the most important passage is this: "We order and command that henceforth for no cause whatever, whether of war, rebellion, ransom, or in any other way, can any Indian be made a slave."[2]

Unfortunately, it was often difficult, at so great a distance from the seat of authority, to carry out the provisions of the best legislation. That legal rights were violently outraged we have seen in Zumárraga's troubles with Guzman and other crown officials. The prelate, however, had also to acknowledge the good will and valuable assistance of some civil administrators. He must have highly appreciated the general influence of Cortés; for, writing to Charles V. in 1529, he says, in reference to the daring leader's so often escaping assassination: "It appears a miracle, wrought that so much good might not be prevented." In the same connection he mentions an incident which is instructively characteristic. During the absence of Cortés in Guatemala, his subordinates and rivals had thrown Mexican affairs into fearful disorder. Of his return Zumárraga remarks: "Then as Don Hernando saw the maze which he had

---

[1] Breve Relacion, Disc. Prel.   [2] Fiske's *Discovery*, II., 474.

to face and disentangle, he retired to the monastery of St. Francis: there he confessed and communicated."[1] Truly, a Catholic conscience is something to depend on.

Though the missionaries' fundamental work was fairly finished when Velasco, the second viceroy, arrived in Mexico, yet his administration is said to have much furthered the evangelisation of the Indians. The mines had been a hindrance. In them labor was theoretically optional and comparatively well-paid. But as the work was considered a State necessity, it was often made a pretext for compulsion, and for the forced retention of the natives far from their dwellings. So Velasco, in 1550, restored more than a hundred thousand miners to their homes and families.

He seemed to be of the school of Ximenes who, thirty-four years earlier, had prescribed for the mines on the islands: that not more than a third of the actual laborers should be occupied in mining; that only neighboring men, over twenty and under fifty, should be hired for that work; and that women should never have to enter the mines. The custom of excluding women has been so tenaciously traditional in New Spain, that non-Mexican mine-owners of to-day, as well as their sympathising tourist friends, call it a *superstition*.

Ximenes's revenue regulations seem, in principle, very liberal. Two-thirds of all mine returns was decreed to the natives, and the other third to the State.[2] Probably these regulations were not honestly enforced when Velasco took up the government of Mexico; for, his recorded reply to the protests selfishly raised against him contains

---

[1] Icazbalceta's *Zumárraga*, Appen.   [2] Hefele's *Ximenes*, c. xxv.

these noble words: "The liberty of the Indians is worth more than all the mines of the world; and the imperial revenues can be no reason for trampling on divine and human laws."[1]

As the wonderful speed of conversion in New Spain is sometimes attributed to the habitually generous coöperation of the Court, so is it also to the innate disposition of the native Americans. That many of the Indians showed great docility of character is undoubted. But natural good qualities would not suffice to draw them to the faith and self-sacrifice of Christianity. What the Indians were is nowhere more simply and circumstantially stated than in the home correspondence of the first missionaries. In a joint letter of Zumárraga and the heads of missions there occurs this interesting passage:—

"This is a mild race, that does more through fear than through virtue. They should be protected, but not exalted. There is need of constraining the Spaniards to treat them well; in such a way, however, that they may not lose their reverence and fear of the Spaniards. They are workers when they have some one to command them; good cultivators when they expect to enjoy the fruit of their labor. They are so apt for trades that they learn them at sight; they seem rather to steal them the moment they see them than to learn them. They are diligent about cattle, but in other things a careless race.

"The elders are served in a wonderful manner, with reverence and fear. The people lie to a reasonable extent

---

[1] Cordova's *Mexico*, p. III, c. 3.

(*mienten razonablemente*); little, however, to one who treats them well—or not so much. Those evils they have with some good things; and it is a race that takes well to our Faith. They confess much, so that there is no need of questions. For the most part they yield to the vice of drunkenness, from which there is great need of restraining them. This the judges (*oidores*) are now seeking, through their good zeal for the honor of God. On this depends in great part the people's improvement and their salvation.

"The children of our houses already know much and instruct many. They sing plain chant and organ music competently."[1]

These details indicate that there was help, not unmixed with hindrance, in the character of the Indians. But the customs of the dominant tribes—the idolatry, polygamy, and ceremonial cannabalism—constituted the hugest of obstacles. Then, prejudice against the religion of the conquerors was naturally a strong opposing force. The horrid excesses of individual Europeans gave color to the opinion that Christians were wicked and heartless, worshippers of gold or of gods still viler. This impression counteracted the better influence of the government, and even of the missionaries. Something more was, therefore, required to induce these new peoples to take up a strange and difficult religion.

Of course the truth of Christianity and the grace of God are the fundamental reason of conversion: it is the beautiful goodness of Our Lord and of His doctrines that

[1] Letter to Spanish Court, March, 1531. Quoted in App. to Icazb.'s *Zumár.*

efficaciously attracts. But experience proves that God has His special way with all of us; and the Mexicans have recognised that He drew them to Catholicity by means of Holy Mary of Guadalupe. People and priests, native clergy and European missionaries, all testify to this: all affirm that Guadalupe was the attracting and the energising centre of Mexico's first faith and fervor. The historian Sanchez was saying nothing new when, in 1648, he wrote: "Mexico received the light of Heaven through the hands of Mary, the Virgin Mother of God: to her this country has ever acknowledged itself indebted for its Christianity."[1]

The same truth has been repeated in all forms, particularly by the chief pastors of the people. One of them, the eloquent Dr. Ibarra of Chilapa, lately reaffirmed it in very explicit terms. "It is true," he says, "that immediately after the conquest some apostolic men, some zealous missionaries, mild, gentle conquerors who were disposed to shed no blood but their own, ardently devoted themselves to the conversion of the Indians. However, these valiant men, because of their fewness, because of the difficulty of learning various languages, and of the vast extent of our territory, obtained, in spite of their heroic efforts, but few and limited results. But scarcely had the Most Holy Virgin of Guadalupe appeared, scarcely had she touched and sanctified our happy soil with her heavenly footsteps, and taken possession of this her inheritance, when the Catholic Faith spread, with the rapidity of light from the rising sun, through the wide extent and beyond the

---

[1] Imagen de Maria, cap. I.

bounds of the ancient empire of Mexico. Innumerable multitudes from every tribe, every district, every race, in this immense country; populous towns, whole nations; countless rational beings who were grossly superstitious, who were ruled by instincts of cruelty, oppressed by every form of violence, utterly degraded; returned upon themselves at the credible announcement of the admirably portentous Apparition of Holy Mary of Guadalupe; recognised their natural dignity; forgot their misfortunes; put off their instinctive ferocity; and, unable to resist such sweet and tender invitations, came in crowds to cast their grateful hearts at the feet of so loving a Mother, and to mingle their tears of emotion with the regenerating waters of Baptism. Most Holy Mary of Guadalupe it was who worked these prodigies of conversion to the faith, with the irresistible attractions of her graciousness and the ingenious inventions of her kind charity. All this she did for having been constituted by God the special Mother of the Mexicans. Hence can she say to us, with more reason than the Apostle St. Paul to the Corinthians: Though you had ten thousand preceptors and masters in the faith in Jesus Christ, I alone as your tender Mother, have engendered you and brought you forth."[1]

We have here, on excellent authority, the statement that the first heroic efforts of the missionaries were relatively poor in results. The work was not richly or permanently fruitful, until the Apparitions at Tepeyac threw the light of peace and union over the vanquished and their rulers, and gave the American natives to understand that they could be the special favorites of Heaven

[1] Guad. Serm., Oct. '95.

and the equals of any one on earth. The sudden change is marked by both civil and ecclesiastical historians. They indicate, quite independently, that the conversions before the Guadalupan event were few compared to those that almost immediately followed it.

Explanations, however, seem needed. From Zumárraga's report to the Toulouse Chapter of his Order, as well as from other contemporary sources, we learn that in the period between 1521 and 1531, that is in the first ten years of Spanish rule, there were baptised about a million of the natives.[1] If a fair proportion of these were ordinary adults, the success of the mission would manifestly be already great. But it seems that the Baptisms were, for the most part, restricted to the multitudinous orphans left by the war and sheltered in ecclesiastical establishments, to the dying, and to infants. The great Franciscan, Toribio de Benavente—whose religious poverty caused the Indians to give him the new name of *Motolinia*, or *the poor one*—declared that he found the grown natives for a considerable time very unwilling to become Christians. The reason was palpable: the men who could afford it had more wives than one. Hence, for them there could be neither Baptism nor blessing of marriage. The missionary, indeed, makes known that the Sacrament of Matrimony was very rarely administered before the year 1530, and almost solely in the case of young men who lived on the

---

[1] The number is controverted. The *Novi Orbis* text of the Bishop's letter has: *ducenta quinquaginta millia;* but the Gonzalez text has: *decies centum millia*. Similarly Isla's translation gives *250,000*, while Mendieta's gives *1,000,000*. Other authorities sustain the higher number.

monastic lands. But immediately after the Apparitions a great change was observed. The common people began to emulate continency and purity of life, and to cry out for Baptism. They had heard of the Mother of the true God, the *Most Clean Virgin*, who wished to favor them and be their Mother; so they crowded on the missionaries, demanding instruction and regeneration.

The physical labor of baptising was now the difficulty. The ceremonies had to be curtailed. Eye-witnesses aver that in a single day one priest sometimes baptised as many as six thousand persons. So astounding were the numbers that Father Toribio, when relating the facts in his *Indian History*, has to add: "Had I not witnessed it with my own eyes I should not venture to report it. I have to affirm that another priest and myself baptised in five days, at the convent of Quecholac, fourteen thousand two hundred and odd souls. We even imposed the Oil of Catechumens and the Holy Chrism on all of them—an undertaking of no little labor."[1]

The same excellent authority describes the eagerness, at this period, of all the natives to become Christians. When the friars passed along the highways or visited the villages the people hurried out to meet them. Whole families rushed up together. Some made signs that they wanted the water on their heads; others humbly asked the Sacrament; while others demanded it with great cries. They knelt around, supplicating the ministers of God to make them Christians. And when those who had been prepared were being baptised they sighed and wept so penitently and rapturously that they moved most

[1] Hist. Ind. Tr. 2. c. 3.

profoundly both the missionaries and the other catechumens.

"Then," adds *Motolinia*, with a touch of apostolic simplicity, "it was a thing to see, with what happiness and joy they took their little ones on their back and hurried home, unable to contain their felicity."[1]

The good Father had lamented that polygamy prevented conversion. No wonder that he rejoiced when, as he expressed it, the Lord put it into the hearts of the people to be satisfied with lawful matrimony. This was in the beginning of the Guadalupan epoch. The marriages then became a Christian wonder. They were conducted in a way that might seem to befit man's unfallen state rather than any condition incidental to the actual world. Mendieta, in his *Ecclesiastical History*, describes some of the scenes he witnessed. In the open air the Indian men and women came up in separate lines, following the Cross-bearer. As they passed the station of a first priest he imposed on all of them the Oil of Catechumens. Then with lighted tapers and chanted litanies they advanced to the holy Font, where another priest baptised them. Curving round on both sides the procession came again by the first priest, who now anointed with Chrism all these new Christians. Then the lines drew closer, and joining hands—each groom with his bride—they pronounced their marriage vows and received the Sacrament of Matrimony before the minister of God who had just poured on them the laver of regeneration. So with blessings and rejoicings they started on their new life, to be the worthy founders of the numerous Mexican Church.

[1] Ibid.

Mendieta mentions three thousand Indians thus baptised and married between the dawn and the late Mass of Christmas Day, in the year 1538.

The vastness of the numbers said to be converted, under the early inspiration of Guadalupe, might appear incredible, were not the authorities so good and so categoric. Father Alegre and other trustworthy authors are positive that Peter of Ghent baptised, with his own hand, more than a million of Indians. He was a Flemish Franciscan, and must have been recognised as a devout Guadalupan; for, in one of the oldest copies of the Picture, his figure was introduced in the background.

At the Easter of 1540, there were gathered into the single town of Tehuacan, for the Holy Week and Paschal solemnities, the tribes and chiefs of more than forty provinces. The people came, without urging or invitation, from a distance of fifty or sixty leagues; and so numerous were they that their languages indicated twelve different nationalities. It may hardly surprise us, therefore, to find Father Toribio—the revered *Motolinia* of the natives—calmly saying in his historical summaries: "To the best of my belief and in simple truth, there were baptised in those fifteen years (from 1524 on) above nine millions of Indian souls."[1]

Great as this number is it did not include the million or more baptisms administered by other missionaries besides the Franciscans. Hence, as one of the Mexican Bishops argued at the late Coronation, the ten years preceding the advent of Our Lady, with all the help of first missionary zeal and unblunted Spanish influence,

---

[1] Hist. Ind. Tr. 2. c. 3.

gave but one million of conversions; while an equal space of time following the Apparitions, though reactionary political forces were felt, gave fully ten millions. "In these facts," very pertinently asks Father Antícoli (from whose admirable Compendium several of the preceding details are taken), "who will not recognise the Spirit of God, moving so many millions to enter the kingdom of Christ? And when we consider that there occurred no portent or other supernatural event—at least none very manifest or extraordinary—to attract such multitudes, except the Apparition of the Virgin, we may say with much reason that the Vision of the Queen of Apostles called the Indians to the Faith." And the devout client of Holy Mary of Guadalupe cries out, with national fervor: "O Mother of the Mexicans! preserve this vine which thou thyself hast planted. *Respice et vide vineam istam quam plantavit dextera tua.*"[1]

Lest it should be thought that the hurried reception of Baptism was the whole work of conversion, it is well to note some significant facts. Within twenty years of Cortés's first meeting with Moctezuma, there were schools, churches, hospitals, and workshops, established for the natives, and much frequented by them. The thirtieth year of the conquest had hardly passed when there arose a great Mexican University. The papal and royal decrees are of the year 1552; and the new American seat of learning was made equal in all privileges with the famous University of Salamanca. Towns sprang into existence and episcopal sees were erected.

---

[1] Hist. Comp., p. 74.

Monasteries and convents were founded and built with astonishing rapidity; for the Religious Orders, being the first friends and teachers of the Indians, justly flourished on the grateful generosity of the whole land. The benefits they conferred on the people were great and greatly appreciated. Every monastic or missionary establishment was recognised as a centre of security and consolation and peaceful industry.

The Franciscans, who had come in 1523, displayed a truly seraphic zeal in defending and evangelising the new subjects of the Spanish monarchy. The Dominicans followed in 1526, and were quickly distinguished for their customary fervor and their apostolic eloquence. Learned Augustinians and Oratorians came soon after; and finally the Jesuit Fathers in 1572. These latter were not slow in characteristically signalising their presence by the splendid successes of their colleges. They chartered the second Mexican University, that of St. Ildefonso, in 1584.

About that time the children of the first Indian converts began to distinguish themselves as munificent patrons of learning; and one of their earliest foundations was St. Martin's Jesuit College.

In spite of individual acts of oppression or extortion —of which hypocritical bigotry talks more than of all the general good—the kingdom of New Spain was fast becoming a prosperous Christian community. Provincial Councils were already celebrated (in 1555, '65 and '85); and the strong arm of the Church was raised to shield every child of Spanish America. Mexico, overflowing with Catholic fervor, was sending missionaries to other lands. Before she was herself a century old in the Faith she could count her martyrs who died for God at home and abroad: witness St. Philip of Jesus and his companions martyred in Japan in 1597, and many missionaries in Florida and California during the first quarter of the seventeenth century.

Another Church as rapidly established, and at the same time as numerous, fruitful, and permanent, can hardly be shown by the modern apostolate. The building up of such a thoroughly Catholic nation, composed mainly of aboriginal Americans, is one of the greatest ecclesiastical wonders. And more admirable than the speedy conversion of the early natives has been the deep, lasting piety of the ordinary Mexicans. They are a people who have been exposed to the action of many agents of disintegration and deterioration; yet their Catholic devotion has remained most solid and most tender. Guadalupe is the explanation of such unexpectedly happy results.

Any circumstance that brings Christians into a peculiarly intimate relation with the God-Man is sure to give their religion a distinctive orthodoxy and spirituality; and nothing effects this faster than special love of the Lord's Mother and special dependence on her. She is still and always—we cannot repeat it too often—the infallible way to Him, and the shortest and pleasantest way. Once the Mexicans recognised that it was she who had come to establish alliance with them, they thought Christianity the most natural thing in the world and asceticism the best common sense. Hence were they and are they practical Catholics.

The well-informed Dr. Ibarra, whom I quoted earlier in this chapter, can say with reason: "The Mexican

Church, through the protection of the Most Holy Virgin of Guadalupe, is now as much in evidence as it was in its happiest days. Not for a moment has it interrupted its respectful, filial accord with the Chair of St. Peter, the pillar and ground of truth. Through its veins there still course those two powers of Order and Jurisdiction which carry life to the furthest extremities of the body, like the currents of invisible fluid that run round our globe and ceaselessly regenerate it. In the Church of Mexico there are still guardians of the sacred deposit of faith, as jealous as they are vigilant; and the mass of the simple faithful—that is to say, the whole Mexican people—docile to the voice of their pastors, march united and compact, through the difficulties that lie in their road, towards their heavenly country; as formerly the people of God advanced towards the land of promise, leaving stretched in the desert the carcasses of the blasphemers and the murmurers."[1]

---

[1] Guad. Serm., Oct. '95.

CHAPTER XIII.

THE FRUITS—(Continued).

THE speedy conversion and abiding faith of New Spain are the Guadalupan fruits mainly dwelt on by Mexican writers. There are, however, other spiritual fruits hardly less precious and, perhaps, of more immediate personal edification, to which it may be well to make some reference.

Devotion to Holy Mary of Guadalupe has moulded popular thought and action. It has superinduced on multitudes of individual souls characteristics of peculiarly beautiful Catholicity. The brightness and sweetness of the Tepeyac visions and promises passed into the lives of the neophytes, as did also their simplicity and strength. The special traits of those immediately connected with the Apparitions and the foundation of the Shrine seem to have been freely adopted by the people at large. High ideals became blessedly familiar. The Apparitional Mother could not be constantly before the eyes and minds of the faithful without some sacred tingeing of manners, and much conscious or unconscious imitation. Her humble ambassador and loved son was at once taken as an exemplar of Indian manhood. This fact alone is of immeasurable import; for, countless Mexican men have been and are being saved and sanctified by becoming, practically, other Juan Diegos.

Of Juan himself it is good and pleasant to think. About him there is a delicious air of simplest Catholicity. The figure in which he is commonly represented—a figure found by Boturini among the natives and universally regarded as true to life—is of singular attraction and expressiveness. The kneeling form, the eyes raised to the Apparition, the rapt attitude and countenance, strikingly recall the much-favored Indian and his beautiful history.

Happily there is a considerable amount known about this unpretentious servant of Our Lady; more happily still, it is all of purest edification. As he was baptised in 1524, the first year of the Franciscan missions, he was probably one of those who were prepared for the Faith before it came. His wife, Maria Lucia, was also one of the first to become a Christian; and their lawful marriage may be taken as indicating their worth even as pagans. Other things, indeed, go to show that they accepted the Gospel with rare whole-heartedness. Referring to the story, common among the Indians, that Juan and Lucia lived as brother and sister from the time they heard the missionaries praise chastity, Father Florencia remarks:—

"Here are two Indians—whom another might call barbarians—living for more than forty years in the midst of the vile customs of that gentilism in which unbridled sensuality ruled so despotically, and in which disorderly appetite was the law of action. Yet scarcely have they received the character of Christ in Baptism when they profess both the principles of the Christian Religion and the highest perfection of the Evangelical law; they lead the life of Angels on earth, and, in their weak flesh, aspire to the privileges of incorruptible spirits." [1]

Juan was forty-eight years of age at the time of his Baptism, and fifty-five when the Apparitions occurred. Two years before this latter great event his wife's death is marked: some place it two years after.

Though the narrative of the Tepeyac wonders is occupied with Our Lady's messenger rather incidentally than personally, yet it gives a charmingly perfect picture of him. The elderly man, we find, is accustomed to rise early and trudge six miles over the rough hills, to hear the Saturday Mass in honor of the Mother of God. That beautiful dawn of the morrow of the Immaculate Conception he is stopped on his way by heavenly music. The vision of Mary enraptures him, and he imagines he is in the promised Paradise, of which he has vague but noble ideas.

His unsophisticated candor makes him capable of obeying the Blessed Virgin and submitting to the Bishop, while presenting his own views to both of them. He thinks the Sovereign Lady, the Mother of the true God, should choose a more efficient ambassador than himself; and he sees that the Prelate's discounting his message is equivalent to rejecting it. Yet he obeys punctually.

The rebuffs at the palace and the discourtesy of the attendants are gently and bravely borne; they cannot turn him from his accepted embassy. But the duties of charity move him more than even visions and voices. His sick uncle he must help in body and soul; then he

---

[1] Estrella del Norte, p. 109.

will go back to listen to the Heavenly Lady. The naivete of his attempt to avoid being delayed by her, when he was running for the priest, is incomparably delightful. When, however, she assures him that all is well with his uncle, he unhesitatingly believes and asks only to be sent as she wills. Similarly he hurries to gather the roses where he was sure they could not grow; then he carries them off triumphantly, as a token of the Lady's right to command and a promise that her will should be accomplished.

A parallel to the rejoicing Indian bearing the fresh roses in the coarse *tilma* that was being made the medium of a great wonder, can hardly be found in ecclesiastical history, except in St. Elizabeth of Hungary, whose robeful of food for the poor was changed into sweet flowers, to mark Heaven's appreciation of the odors of charity.

Diego was grand when he insisted, with tears, on the sacred truth of his slighted message. He was grand, also, when in overjoyed simplicity he showed the sign of the miraculous roses. He was grandest when, in ecstatic wonder and love he gazed on the Picture whose Original he had already well described. There is not a trace of self-seeking or duplicity about this beautiful peasant. His course is limpid as the clear rivulet; and not even a hint of reproach is whispered against him. Father Sanchez, as witness at the *Information* of 1666, says that Juan Diego "left the fame of having lived with all strictness and virtue, so that it was not possible to attribute to him any defect." This is the remarkable point: that, having been thrown into such sudden prominence, into a position of highest delicacy, the simple neophyte did nothing that the most critical could call defective.

Several other witnesses in the same process make statements that indicate what an object of affectionate reverence and of instructive example the chosen Indian was to his ordinary fellow-countrymen. The second witness declared: "They always saw him occupied with affairs of the service of God Our Lord. He went most punctually to the *doctrine* and the divine offices, very frequently exercising himself in them. All the Indians of the time were heard to say that he was a holy man. They called him *the pilgrim*, because they always saw him going alone. Alone he went to the *doctrine* of the church of Tlatelulco; and after there appeared to him the Virgin of Guadalupe he abandoned his village, leaving his houses and fields to an uncle, as his wife was already dead. Then he went to live in a hut which was raised for him against the said Hermitage. Thither the natives of the said village (Quautitlan) went very frequently to see him, and to ask him to intercede for them with the Most Holy Virgin that she might give them good seasons for their *milpas*; for, all held him to be a holy man, since to him and no one else the Virgin appeared. Moreover, they always found him very contrite, doing many penances. This was public and well-known in the said village and its wards: and this he answers."

The fourth witness says: "They went to Juan Diego as to a man to whom such a thing had happened, to whom the Virgin spoke. They went to see him very often." And the fifth, speaking of his own relatives, says they went "with all the other Indian men and women to ask him to intercede with the Most Holy Virgin, as one so dear to her, that she might favor them."[1]

The Picture of her whom he had seen, manifestly became Juan's treasure. Where it was placed he lived. Having readily given up his little property, he spent seventeen years taking care of the Shrine. He swept and dusted and served there: the Indians add that he talked with the Holy Mother. All accounts dwell on his prayerful penance, as well as on the important fact that the Bishop allowed him to communicate three times a week. As we have seen, the natives regarded him as their official intercessor with the Mother of God, taking a precedent, as it were, from her act in using him as an intermediary in the affair of the temple. His simple humility rendered this extraordinary situation as safe as it was beautiful. He grew admirably ripe for Heaven.

The favored uncle Bernardino, about whom he was once so anxious, passed away calmly in 1544, blessed again, it is said, by a visit from Holy Mary of Guadalupe.

That to Juan Diego whom, in the Apparitions, she had called her "much loved son" and her "cherished little one" she consolingly manifested herself at the last hour, is a most general tradition and an altogether credible one. The holy man died at the Sanctuary, in 1548. He was buried in what is now the sacristy of the parish church; and on the wall of the baptistry—which corresponds to his former little hut—I have read, under his picture, the following simple inscription: "In

---

[1] Informaciones de 1666 y 1723.

this place Our Lady of Guadalupe appeared to an Indian called Juan Diego, who, for that reason, is interred in this church."

The name of Our Lady's faithful messenger is an honored one in Mexican homes and hearts. But better than the mere name, and more glorious to him in Heaven, is the wide-spread appreciation of his Catholic life and the very general imitation of his virtues. Reverent love of him is a power for good in his country. I have again and again seen devout Mexicans pray with the very attitude and expression of Juan before the Virgin. Among poor, fervent Indians the moral likeness to him is sometimes striking. Childlike, dignified, gladly mystic, they have often a personal intercourse with Heaven that lifts them altogether out of their paltry surroundings. They are blessed through the example and, I think, the intercession of Juan Diego. Than his there are few more beautiful or more fruitful characters to be found among the uncanonised saints of the Church. No wonder that Mexican parents have long expressed their best benediction by saying to their children: "May the Most Holy Virgin be to you as to Juan Diego:" or, "May God make you like Juan Diego."[1]

Great as is the good resulting among the men of Mexico from the thought of Juan Diego, still greater is the good effected among the women from the vision of Holy Mary of Guadalupe. From looking at her as she appeared in their midst, they have, it may be

---

[1] Ibid., 1°· Test.

reverently said, taken on a peculiar resemblance to her. Even in dress they modestly imitate her. If, to win to God the daughters of the still pagan land, she assumed something of their native garb and feature, it is certain that they have repaid the kind compliment by habitually forming and fashioning themselves on her virginal appearance. This may be partly unconscious, but it is very real.

Moreover, it has often been preached to them. "Let all women, whatever their rank," says the historian Florencia, adopting the words of St. Ambrose, "find in the Picture of this Sovereign Lady a figure of purity and a mirror of modesty: let them imitate her decorous reserve and the fitness of her most chaste attire. From this Picture, as from a reflecting crystal, there are reverberating not fewer tokens of honor and spotlessness than of light and splendor. Let them learn from it what they have to reproduce in their lives, what they have to correct in their dress, what they have to forego that they may give no scandal."[1]

The lesson has been well taken. The demeanor of the wives and daughters of the people is exquisite. One practice makes a deep impression on strangers: as the majority of the younger women have but nature's covering on their head, they pause when about to enter a church and raise their shawl or mantle to veil themselves humbly. There is in the act a grace of religious modesty that bespeaks faith and worship.

Nor is it, of course, in mere outward deportment that they tend to similarity with the Holy Mother. They know more is required: they let love of her shape their

---

[1] Estrel. del Nor., p. 166.

minds and hearts. To their Guadalupan devotion are clearly attributable the singular piety and purity for which they are universally distinguished.

This characteristic excellence of theirs is a subject not easily treated—at least not easily brought within the grasp of those who have never been in the churches or the families of the neighboring Republic. Superficial readers and tourists may be disposed to say that woman in Mexico counts socially for little; that she is either a domestic drudge or a person easily led wrong. In both estimates, ignorantly prejudiced as they must be, the truth is utterly missed. Nowhere else does female virtue receive or, perhaps, merit a more nearly worshipful reverence. The loving remembrance of the Virgin Mother of God, of Holy Mary of Guadalupe, both fashions the Mexican woman's life and regulates the bearing of her acquaintances in her regard. She is sacred and she knows it; and far higher is her position than that of the butterflies or viragoes of some more boastful civilizations. In this connection I may seem to exaggerate; so I prefer to quote. An observant writer, who had occasion to study closely these Guadalupan women, says of them—rather from a social than a religious standpoint:—

"The Mexican woman is the true priestess of the home. The home is her temple; there is her pedestal; there the tabernacle of the spotless pages of her history. The home of the great lady in Mexico has no boudoir—it has a sanctuary; to enter there you must bow the head and bend the knee. I shall never forget the impression made on me when I first entered a Mexican home; nor can I forget any of the first homes I entered. . . . There breathes in them an air of sweet moral warmth, of peaceful felicity, which, filtering into my heart, restored me to the life of the family, the life of sentiment, the life of the soul. Blessed be all honorable homes! Blessed a hundred times be the home of the Mexican woman! . . . As the Mexican woman is no coquette, everything in her home has an odor of sanctity. . . . Such is her chastity that only a woman could worthily celebrate it. . . . Her love is modest; . . . nothing profane enters into it; . . . she sanctifies it all. . . . The maternal affections she has admirably developed; she is the sublime type, the perfect ideal of the mother. . . . In other homes I have seen the cradle relegated to a back corner. In the home of the Mexican woman it is on a throne; it is put first in evidence, holding the place of honor; it is an altar before which the family, in the person of the mother, comes to worship. . . .

"The Mexican lady is eminently Catholic. There may be in that country many fanatical women, but there are no impious ones. The Mexican lady knows nothing of the malady of atheism. She is rigidly moral: ballroom coquetries, which the ladies of the fashionable world allow themselves in other countries, would in Mexico be condemned with the utmost severity. The Mexican lady has a morality which precepts alone did not give her; an instinctive, inborn morality, logical, vigorous, inflexible. No one can mislead her on moral points, though arguments the most brilliant, or the most captious be employed. For, sweet, bland, urbane as she is, she would rise majestically against the instigator of evil who should attempt to deceive her, and would say with all energy: You are mistaken; morality, like truth, is one and admits neither subtlety, nor paradox, nor distinction. . . .

"In the heart of the Mexican woman nestle all the virtues, most prominent among them being abnegation. She is insatiable of suffering. To keep it from her husband and children she absorbs all the sorrows that come her way, while her lips distil but honey and balm and essence and harmony. She is the star that illumines the obscure paths of misfortune; she is the shield of the weak, the consolation of the sad, the tender friend of the afflicted."[1]

Though this extract may sound high-flown and imaginative, experience bears out its substantial truth; and though it refers mainly to the wealthier classes it applies equally to the poorest wives and mothers in Mexico. Most generally they are admirable in all the qualities of the Woman and the Christian. It is quite plain, also, that their singular virtue is Guadalupan in character. The "instinctive morality" of which this writer speaks is largely the traditional and actual realisation of a Mexican woman's solidarity with her special Patroness, the Virgin Mother of the true God, Holy Mary of Guadalupe. To be, in public and private, fairly worthy of Our Lady, is like a natural, prime necessity.

Even the ready love of suffering is strangely and beautifully traceable to the Apparitions and the Picture. This, however, appertains to the whole people, men, women, and children. It has not at all escaped them that the only ornament Our Lady wears is a plain black Cross enclosed in a gold circlet. Then they notice

---

[1] De Flaquer . . . *El Tiempo*, 27 de Oct., '95.

that the supporting Angel has a similar brooch circlet, but without the Cross; and, in the theologically ascetic manner characteristic of the simplest faithful, they go on to discuss and infer the Holy Mother's connection with the graces of Redemption, so different from that of the highest heavenly Spirits. The immediate outcome of their speculations is an increased love of the Cross.

No doubt they imbibed devotion to the Sign of Redemption with their Spanish Catholicity. Wherever that has penetrated we meet at every step the title of the *Santa Cruz*, the *Vera Cruz*, the *Santa Vera Cruz*. But the Guadalupan revelations gave a special incentive to the devotion. "As the holy Picture appeared," writes Father Florencia, "to prepare and help on the redemption of these nations, the Mother of God, in order to move and attach them to the devotion of the Holy Cross, the instrument of our salvation, chose to deck and adorn herself with it: so that the Indians, seeing the esteem in which this Sovereign Lady held the Cross, might also love it. . . . And all know the piety of the natives of this Kingdom towards the Holy Cross, the solemnity and rejoicing with which they honor and celebrate it in the churches, in the chapels which they call *santocales*, in their own houses, and in all places. Who, indeed, would not be moved to the utmost devotion to the Holy Cross when he sees that the Queen of Heaven bears it on her breast as the richest jewel of her divine adornments? She thus teaches us Christians the value that we should set on this sign and standard of our Religion, on this noble device, this symbol of our holy profession."[1]

[1] Estr. del Nor., p. 164.

The Guadalupan Catholics learned early and well to love the Cross; hence comes their remarkable devotion to the Passion. The sufferings and death of Our Lord constitutes their strongest attraction; to bear something of what He bore is always at least a vague yearning of their lives. They must have representations of Him in His deepest anguish and shame. Very often they place prominently in their homes and in their churches figures of *the Lord in the Garden, the Lord at the Pillar, the Lord with the Reed,* or *the Lord on the Cross,* which shallower and more fastidious Christians cannot bear to behold. For them the art or presumed taste is little in comparison with the impressive lesson and the burning incentive to repentance and reparation. They never tire of looking on the Lord as the Man of Sorrows, or rather—as they would express it—as "God suffering." When they refer to the Passion it is generally as the "Passion of God"; hence its great fruitfulness in their devotions.

Indeed, the Mexicans may be singled out as a people who habitually lay peculiar stress on the fact that Christ is God. The very word 'God' without addition usually means, in the mouth of the common people, Our Lord rather than the Holy Trinity. And where the Sacred Humanity is much in evidence, as in the Life and the Ministry, they still commonly say "God did this," "God said this." Similarly, in reference to the Blessed Sacrament, they instinctively speak of Holy Communion as "receiving God," and of Exposition as "God unveiled" or "His Majesty manifested." Calling for the Viaticum is "sending for the *Amo*"—that is, for the Master of the House, the Father, the Lord.

A more beautiful thing in Christian life is rarely witnessed than the enthusiasm of a poor Mexican family about procuring a proper carriage to bring the *Amo*. The consequential joy of doing Him something like a personal service seems often to swallow up the sadness of the occasion. Of course the carriage is also for the Priest who bears the Blessed Sacrament, but he is lost to sight in the Majesty of his Master. And as the *Amo* approaches, all are on their knees, as are the people along the street and in the houses who have noticed that He is passing, and have whispered from one to another—"*El Santisimo!*"

This special attention to Our Lord's Person is to be noticed in connection with Guadalupe. It serves as a practical refutation of an ugly heresy; for, it proves the Catholic tenet and fact that devotion to Our Lady, far from obscuring the Divinity, serves most powerfully to throw into relief the Godhead of her Son. A right understanding of her awful elevation makes it evident that she is placed so near her Creator exactly that she may display Him and make Him more known to the race to which she herself belongs. Like other clients of hers the devout Guadalupans may seem to be occupied with her alone, when in reality they are but learning the clearest and straightest way to discern and tend towards God. We may remark, too, that it was as Mother of the true God she announced herself among them, and under that title they flocked to her. All honor given her was meaningless if not finally meant for Him; and to Him undoubtedly it was sent on, endlessly multiplied in degree and infinitely different in intention, simply because He was the true God.

One fact suffices to indicate how Guadalupan devotion draws to Our Lord. The faithful who run most to the Holy Mother and her Shrine are always looking for the Blessed Sacrament. In great numbers they crowd to receive It—frequently several thousands on the same morning at Guadalupe itself. Then Exposition is so much their delight that one rarely sees a solemn function announced without the addition—*su Majestad manifiesto todo el dia;* and the way in which they exult over its being for "the whole day" is redolent of childlike, gleeful devotion. For any passable reason—I might almost say, for any pious excuse—a day's Exposition is claimed; so that, at rather ordinary times, you may find it practised simultaneously in many neighboring churches, quite independently of the regular course of the Forty Hours. Besides, the Benedictions, Holy Hours, Vigils (*velaciones*), public Visits, are apparently ceaseless in Guadalupe and the City of Mexico. So that those who think most of the Holy Mother are farthest from forgetting the Divine Son.

Community of pious exercises and of happiness in them is an important characteristic of Mexican Catholicity. This also is to be eminently, though not exclusively, attributed to the good influence of Guadalupe. The people delight in praying, chanting, and making pilgrimages together. Many well-known sacred resorts help to develop this solidarity of religious feeling and practice. Its origin and maintenance, however, may be best claimed by Tepeyac and by the countless reproductions of the Shrine.

In hurrying to these holy places the children of Our Lady beam with gladness. They congratulate one another on their religious good luck; they prostrate themselves together; they pray, and communicate, and raise their thanksgivings in common. They are, I think, as contagiously blissful worshippers as any on earth. And the first consequence of their common "joy in believing" is united "strength in enduring." Guadalupan Catholics are not easily shaken; their virtue is proof against trial and allurement. For, together with the direct efficacy of merited grace, there is added to their force the steadfastness of knowing and feeling that so many spiritual friends openly sympathise with them. Faith is such a strong reality in Mexico that all—even the naturally violent and the naturally frivolous—are ready to acknowledge and proclaim that the love of Our Lord and His Mother is the best, noblest, happiest thing in life. There they honor saints living as well as dead.

The communication of spiritual gladness is most strikingly manifest when a number of the people explicitly band together for practices of piety. I have seen long processions and great crowds within and without the churches in uncontrollable enthusiasm. But I have oftener seen the kneeling groups of confraternity or sodality members in a calm, satisfied fervor, the sweetness of which was shining off their faces. In prayer, or in the reception of the Sacraments, the Indian Catholic takes a half-entranced attitude and expression. The Spanish Mexican may be more stately in bearing, but he is not less fervently demonstrative.

As might be expected, no place witnesses more of this happiness of piety than the favored Guadalupe. There, after a festive or special celebration, you may see many a person fairly intoxicated with the delights of holiness. Business men and students, matrons and schoolgirls, people of different race and of every condition, meet and rejoice in spiritual fellowship. And while they crowd out of the Basilica and around it, with their freely-displayed scapulars, badges, and multitudinous objects of piety, their countenances glow with that unearthly brilliancy which earnest worship so often imparts to the simple and the pure-hearted.

On those occasions the Children of Mary and the ladies of the special Guadalupan Congregations present a particularly admirable spectacle. The ineffable satisfaction depicted on the features of these devout women and girls, when they pray or communicate at the altar of the Holy Mother, has been time and again remarked. It moves and edifies many even of the cold or the indifferent. Characteristically beautiful, too, are the observations passed by Mexican spectators. They do not praise these devout worshippers: they praise Our Lady. No one else, they exultantly say, but Holy Mary of Guadalupe could excite such heavenly enthusiasm or produce such blessed results. Truly, a Catholic can hardly help loving these Mexican Catholics, so faithful is their love of the divinely appointed Mother of us all.

The study of Guadalupan influence in Mexico seems to bring out more points of religious excellence than are easily credited of any country or people. Generalisations of commendation, as of condemnation, are seldom corroborated by experience. In real life we are mostly middling. The more a man sees of the world the more he finds agglomerations of human beings very much alike everywhere: the good and bad mixed in rather slightly varying proportions. Narrow ignorance is generally the measure, as it is the foundation, of national boasting.

Something similar is true, at least generally, of the various parts of the Church: the faithful of one country are not very different from those of another. Of course there is less uniformity to be expected where the supernatural prominently intervenes; for, grace is God's free gift, and coöperation with it is not dependent on any set of circumstances. Some races have been extraordinarily blessed in the number and perfection of their Saints; and some peoples, through the providential fire of persecution, have had faith and purity amalgamated with their national and social life. Yet with all this, one may reasonably hesitate about accepting the high religious encomiums passed on any whole nation, and may fairly demand a test of their fitness.

In the case of Mexico, the test I would take is charity. Where charity is extraordinary, other extraordinary virtues need not surprise us. They may well be contained in it, as the less in the greater; for it is the fulfilment of the whole law. "My little children love one another. . . . Because this is the precept of the Lord; and if this only is done, it suffices." [1]

As far as human eyes can see, extraordinary charity is common among Mexican Catholics, charity as thorough as it is exquisite. No disturbance, upheaval, or persecution, has been able to loosen its traditional hold on society. Neither the villainous systematic pitting of one class against another, to which politics have been directed,

[1] Off. of St. John, Les. VI.

nor the cruelly tormenting propagandism of irreligion and heresy, which seems authoritatively encouraged to insult the faithful, has yet succeeded in destroying or seriously diminishing the sweetness of Christian intercourse and sympathy and help. Almsgiving is endless, and kind offices are universal. Hospitality is proverbial: it is maintained even under circumstances of provoking rudeness and vulgar prejudice on the part of certain visitors.

That the poor should be always with them, ordinary Mexicans consider as unregrettable as it is inevitable. They, of course, wish they had fewer mendicants, and fewer abuses under the guise of poverty; but they cling to the privilege of coming into personal contact with God's poor, and of courteously relieving for His sake the actually and visibly needy. Many coldly proper people, who tour through Mexico, are quick to inveigh against roadside begging—and, truly, they may find grounds of complaint. They should not, however, overlook the fact that where there are many who ask, there are habitually many who give. Something strikingly admirable, also, in Mexican almsgiving is the frequency with which the ordinary poor relieve those poorer than themselves. Indian peasants and other working people, who apparently might rather need help than have any to give, will not pass by the outstretched hand of the lame or the blind without contributing their mite and adding a word of kindness. All classes, absolutely without exception, retain and put in practice the instincts and principles of personal charity.

One most beautiful trait of Christianised human life I have frequently noticed. The usually decorous Mexican children evince a gushing, almost boisterous joy, when, on the Sunday or Holiday walk, the parents commission them to be the almoners. The manifest delight with which they convey the father's money to the poor, while often, at the mother's suggestion, joining to it their own toys or sweetmeats, is a vision to gladden the Angels of God. Such acts are as good as they are beautiful. They are not only an efficacious training in Catholic charity, but they are also an occasion of early experiencing the delight of a kind action, that delight whose savoury remembrance is ever after a reserve fund and reinforcement of virtue.

Daily almsgiving does not more distinguish Mexican Catholics than does their untiring industry in founding and supporting charitable institutions. They have and have always had asylums for the needy and the suffering of every description. Not even the ruthless plunder to which pretended liberalism has subjected the religious beneficence of the people, has been able to impede the currents of charity. Almost all observant visitors speak with admiration of the number and variety of the Hospitals and Refuges. And more admirable than their multiplication is their character, the air of mingled cheerfulness and sacredness that pervades them. The exquisite delicacy of charity is nowhere more striking.

If, in any Mexican town, you approach one of these temporary or ordinary abodes of the afflicted, you immediately notice how clean and bright and happy everything is made to look. The portal has its appropriate wall-paintings and inscriptions suggesting hopeful consolation; the courtyard has its flowers, fountains, birds; and whatever rules or regulations are displayed are redolent of tenderest humanity and religion. In the gateway of hospitals I have noticed the common-sense daily indication that beds were or were not vacant—an indication which saves inquirers much time and trouble. But, in addition, I have seen in some places the simply grand statement that recommendation of patients was not necessary and might rather be a hindrance: all required is that there be an unoccupied bed in the house and that the person presented seem to need it. No questions are asked; suffering humanity has recognised rights.

Mexican Orphanages, when compared to Hospitals, do not appear to some visitors or investigators proportionately numerous. The reason is well given by Sartorius, a late German commissioner on Emigration. Having lived in the country he knew its customs. "When parents happen to leave young children," he explains, "the godfather and godmother adopt them. Should they not do so, there immediately springs up between different families a rivalry for the privilege of sheltering the bereaved little creatures."[1]

Las criaturas—as, with most expressive tenderness, they commonly style children—are indeed valued in Mexico. Such fond, worshipful cherishing, without injurious petting, is of rare occurrence elsewhere. Lively faith makes baptized children sacredly dear: that they, like the early neophytes, are specially in the lap of the Holy Mother is fully understood. They are always first considered in the Mexican household; their pleasure and welfare are the determining factors in family views and undertakings. An apparent trifle may exemplify this fact.

[1] Cubas's *Mexico*, a. 3.

Among other trader's reproaches cast on the people at large, one often heard is based on the undue extent of toy-making and toy-purchasing. This minor branch of commerce has, admittedly, received exceptional attention; the necessaries of life are hardly more universally sold than are the mysterious mechanical treasures of childhood. But the impugned custom springs from admirable facts and principles. It simply means that children are many and much loved. And happy the nation of which that is true! The child-loving people is always highest in morality; it is, also, necessarily the great people of the future.

For the really Guadalupan refinement of affection in which Mexican parents show themselves so unsparing, they get a speedy return in the children's reverence and devotedness. The conduct of boys and girls, and even of grown men and women, in the presence of father or mother, is singularly ceremonious. Our possible first impression that it is exaggerated and not natural is quickly dispelled by the evidence of its graceful spontaneity and sincerity. Even formality becomes genial when filial piety inspires it; and in human intercourse few things are better or happier to behold than the eager gladness with which Mexican young people hasten up, in public or private, to greet the father and mother and kiss their hands. It is religion that makes such proceedings significant and possible.

The habitual relations of parents and children are a proof of the exquisiteness of Mexican charity; but a still surer demonstration of its supernatural thoroughness is found in the treatment of servants and dependents. All persons employed about the house are practically members of the family. It is not at all that the respective places are forgotten: they are punctiliously attended to. But in common interests, in every-day joys and sorrows, the domestics and their employers are as one; Christian sympathy blots out unnecessary distinctions. It is felt and honestly admitted that those who have to work for their living are as well children of God and clients of Holy Mary of Guadalupe as any one else. When Mexican families go out in holiday attire, as they often do with the whole household—parents, children, men-servants, and maid-servants,—the real equality manifested and maintained has about it a sort of Golden Age beauty which is nothing more than the comeliness of Catholicity.

Enough, I hope, has been said to indicate that the great Catholic community south of us possesses strikingly good characteristics, and that all it has best it gratefully connects with Our Lady's American title. The extent to which Mexican Catholics consciously enjoy Guadalupan fruits can hardly be conveyed to outsiders. We have already heard one of themselves say that the attempt to compute their indebtedness casts them on their knees to worship. Tepeyac has been to them a fountain of beneficent wonders, though to their pagan predecessors it was a place of cruellest horrors. Referring to the providential change from cannibalistic idolatry to Catholic piety, the erudite Clavigero says impressively: "To-day there is seen at the foot of the same hill a sanctuary dedicated to the true God, the most famous sanctuary of the whole New World. Thither the natives gather from the most distant parts to venerate the celebrated and truly miraculous Picture of Holy Mary of Guadalupe. Thus is a place of abominations transformed into a propitiatory; and these peoples are blessed with the abundant outpourings of the Lord's graces on the very spot that was bathed with the blood of so many of their ancestors."[1]

---

[1] Hist. Antig., Tr. 2. l. 6.

CHAPTER XIV.

THE PATRONAGE.

THE statement that Our Lady, under the title of Guadalupe, was proclaimed Patroness of New Spain signifies more than may at first appear. Declaring a patronage and decreeing a consecration are always solemn acts; but they can hardly mean as much for us as they did for completely Catholic communities. They have no longer the same social and national consequences. They are not, perhaps, taken so seriously, since their obligations are so much less onerous. But whether religiously or politically considered the Guadalupan patronage was of weighty import.

On this subject I have already touched, in connection with the Holy See's approval and the evidence of miracles. What is here to be said concerns the public bearing of New Spain and its people towards the Mother of God under her new American title. Their action throws light on the time and on my subject. Nor need it be to us of weaker edification to-day than it was a century-and-a-half ago to the admiring Catholic world.

What the people aimed at, in declaring Holy Mary of Guadalupe the Principal Patroness of their country, was to make themselves as specially hers as, they considered, she had made herself theirs. The *non fecit taliter omni nationi* was strong in their minds: they would correspond to it and gratefully belong to her as did no other nation. For two hundred years they had been thoroughly Guadalupan. The Holy Mother was their recognised Protectress; her name was borne by all who could; and the feast of her Apparitions was most joyfully celebrated. But where public official life was so explicitly Catholic, it was felt necessary to give Guadalupe more civil as well as ecclesiastical prominence. The idea of the national patronage had been always entertained, and various attempts were made to carry it into execution. The successful effort, however, was inspired—as often happens—only by stress of suffering. It was the pressure of plague, coupled with the hopelessness of smaller remedies, that drove the people on to accomplish what they had long meditated.

As in many other religious enterprises of those days, the civil authorities took the initiative. It was the Municipality of the city of Mexico that, in the beginning of 1737, urged the people and the clergy to proclaim finally and in worthy fashion the Virgin of Tepeyac their national Patroness. The measure was proposed immediately as the surest means of being delivered from the plague; but it was followed up as a thing fitting and almost obligatory.

The whole action of the Municipality gives one a high idea of the character of its members. They were evidently educated and religious laymen who approached this Guadalupan question as intelligently and seriously as the best statesmen might approach a fundamental question of government. They knew what the proclamation of a *principal patronage* entailed—for canon law, as well as theology, was then a part of every liberal education. They were aware that the patronal feast would have to be solemnised as double of first class, with obligatory abstention from servile work and obligatory assistance at Mass; that public business would have to cease and public dignitaries to assist in state at the Church ceremonies; that a liturgical octave should be fittingly celebrated, the subsidies being, of course, legally provided.

With the archiepiscopal and viceregal authorities the members of the Municipality had no reason to fear any difficulty; but they had the prospect of much labor in obtaining an approval of their act from Rome, and, perhaps, of complications with Madrid on the temporalities indirectly touched. Yet they went on steadily.

Having informally voted the patronage, and invited the Metropolitan Chapter to take action with them, they addressed themselves to Archbishop Vizarron, who was also Viceroy. Some sentences of their lengthy document will sufficiently display their purpose. "We," they say, "Felipe Cayetano de Medina y Sarabia y José Francisco de Aguirre y Espinosa, perpetual *Regidores* of this most noble city, and its Commissaries in the present affair, appear before Your Excellency in all judicial form and declare: That the Municipality has elected as most special Patroness the Sovereign Queen of the Angels, in her admirable Picture of Guadalupe which is venerated in her temple outside the walls of the city; . . . that it has determined to solemnise annually, with all possible devotion, the 12th of December, the day on which we celebrate her Apparition; . . . that we have been deputed to obtain that the obligation of a vow be imposed, as canonical procedure requires. . . . May it please Your Excellency to authorise us to vote and take the oath (without prejudice to the general oath which we shall advocate) with all the solemnity ordered by the Congregation of Sacred Rites in its decree of the 23rd of March, 1630." Expressing their confidence that Holy Mary of Guadalupe would still be their refuge—she "at the sole invocation of whose most sweet name pests and floods had ceased"—they continue: "To this is to be added the ardent, universal devotion with which all in general acclaim her, longing for the completion of the act proposed in this petition."[1]

Then the canons, induced by the magistrates, sent in the expression of their views. They argued the feasibility and fitness of the proclamation, and were explicit on vexed canonical questions. "Nor should any inconvenience be found," they say, "in putting on the public the burden of a feast day on which they must cease from labor; for there is no imposition in that which is voluntarily sought and anxiously desired, as is this solemnity of the 12th day of December by the common devotion of all the peoples of this America, *de todas las gentes de esta America.*"[2]

Though Vizarron, the Viceroy-Archbishop, was deeply desirous of seeing the patronage proclaimed, he seems to have acted with great judicial coolness. He passed the petitions on to his Promotor Fiscal, and awaited the legal opinion of that functionary. The opinion proved altogether favorable, declaring, among other commendations, "that the most noble city should be particularly

---

[1] Hist. Comp., p. 154. [2] Ibid., p. 156.

thanked for its Christian desire and fervent wish to procure the welfare of the republic by placing it under the sovereign and most powerful protection of Our Lady." [1]

The voting was thereupon authorised; and though according to the decree of Urban VIII. it would suffice to take the suffrages of the people through the chosen commissaries of the civil and ecclesiastical corporations, it was arranged, for greater formality, that every magistrate and canon should secretly cast his own individual vote.

The form of ballot used is worthy of notice. Each member of the Municipality was handed two folded billets, outwardly quite alike. One was blank, and would count as a negative vote; the other had written within: "I vote for Our Lady, the Most Holy Virgin, in her admirable miraculous Picture of Guadalupe, as Principal Patroness of this most noble City."

When the *Corregidor* who presided had made the scrutiny of the urn, he found that there were as many affirmative votes as there were magistrates present. The number is said to have been eleven. The unanimity was applauded; and, in Mexican books, the names of the voters are handed down as of benefactors to their country.

Soon after the Metropolitan Chapter was called to give its vote. Each capitular got a folded blank slip and another with the brief inscription: "I vote for Our Lady of Guadalupe as Patroness." Again the voting was unanimous, strongly confirming what had been done by the Municipality. The canons were twenty in number.

---

[1] Ibid., p. 158.

The next step was to summon to the Chapel of the palace the Commissaries of both bodies, to emit the prescribed oath of patronage. They came on the appointed day, the 27th of April, 1737. Then the ecclesiastics standing, with the right hand on the breast, the magistrates kneeling, with their hands between those of the Archbishop, swore in their name and the names of those they represented: To hold as Principal Patroness of Mexico and its territory Our Lady, the Holy Virgin Mary of Guadalupe; to keep and cause to be kept forever as a feast day the 12th of December, on which is celebrated her most wonderful and admirable Apparition. Among other things they bound themselves to have recourse to the Congregation of Rites for the confirmation of the Patronage and the Feast, and for the granting of a special Office. They also promised to labor for the extension of the Patronage to all New Spain, and for the governmental inscription of the 12th as a Court Holiday—that is, one on which the Viceroy, the Royal Audience, and the Tribunals, should be bound to assist in state at the Guadalupan services.

Though this ceremony in the Palace chapel was meant to be private, yet word had got out; and before the Archbishop had finished thanking God at the altar, the bells of the city were pealing and the artillery thundering as if a new sovereign were being acclaimed. It looked as if it were so. Even the members of the Royal Audience—from whom mock history would give us to expect nothing similar—wrote in admirable terms to the Archbishop as Viceroy. They reverently thank him for the furtherance given "to the constant vows and wishes of this City to declare by oath its Patroness and Protectress the Most Holy Virgin Mary under her admirable title and invocation of Guadalupe, her who is venerated in the temple outside the walls, where every one admires the incorruptibility of the weak palm fabric in the *ayate* on which the Sovereign Lady was pleased to imprint herself for the consolation of all, as has been successively and is still experienced."[1]

Now the *Corregidor*, learning that the solemn declaration was appointed for the 26th of May, issued an announcement ten days in advance, that the people and the city might be prepared. The enthusiastic excitement was boundless, as was the devout splendor of the celebration. Mexican words are the only ones of any use here. "It is easier," writes Father Antícoli, "to imagine than to describe suitably the enthusiasm that all Mexico displayed on this occasion; for when the people, who of themselves were so ready to show their affection for the Holy Mother of God, saw before their eyes the inspiring example of such high personages, and felt the fury of the plague diminishing, they put no longer any limits to their manifestations of love and gratitude to their heavenly Patroness. As one that has fallen sick away from home, forgets his pains, at the sight of his mother who unexpectedly comes to visit him, and joyfully clasps her in his arms, so Mexico forgot all ills, rose above all misfortunes, and set to work to honor her whose patronage was about to be vowed. In those three days (24th, 25th, and 26th of May, 1737) there was seen neither terrace nor roof without streamers, pendants, and banners of all sizes; the doorways, windows, turrets, were

---

[1] Ibid., p. 164.

decked with bright carpets, with pictures, and with rich hangings fancifully fringed. Flowers and sweet-smelling shrubs—some green, some dried and burnt with incense—formed as it were a cloud that reflected the sun in every tint and color. But what most attracted attention was the splendid frequency of the altars that stood in the doorways, windows, and balconies of the houses; for of the innumerable dwellings of Mexico there was not one without its festive decorations. In those days Mexico seemed less a city than a temple raised to the Mother of God who had appeared on the neighboring hill. On every pedestal, in every chapel, one only figure was seen —but multiplied as many times as there were altars—so many reflections as it were of her who had placed her throne, the seat of her power, on Tepeyac."[1]

The eloquent author goes on to describe how night was changed into day, with torches, illuminations, and fire-work castles. The salvos of artillery alternated with church chimes and orchestral strains; but the sweetest sounds came from the many families who prayed aloud before the altars. The great decorations, also, were reserved for the line of the procession. The wealth of flowers, wax lights, incense, and tapestry, that marked the way was a thing of wonder. Niches and altars were thickly scattered, and the loved form of Holy Mary of Guadalupe was everywhere visible. The different guilds raised magnificent constructions and displayed costly representations of Our Lady, one being a pure silver statue of the Immaculate Conception. At certain points flowers alone were seen; ground, walls,

---

[1] Ibid., p. 167.

pillars, arches, were wholly hidden in them. On the great plaza the artillery was drawn up, with many standards and trophies. The surrounding public edifices vied one with another in tasteful magnificence of decoration, the corporation building and the palace displaying special gorgeousness of adornment.

Though we might think that splendor could be carried no farther, yet the Cathedral is said to have thrown all else into the shade. It is, even unadorned, a magnificent structure within as well as without; but when rejoicing Mexicans deck it—as they alone know how—it is incomparably grand.

It has borne its part in justifying Mexico's claim to be called the *Rome of the Americas*. Its foundation was as early as 1573—when the timbers of the *Mayflower* were still in the green wood; and its dedication dates from 1667. Millions were expended on it. Being the church of the successors of Zumárraga, who always regarded themselves as the special guardians of the Guadalupan Picture and traditions, it has witnessed many great manifestations of devotion to the Holy Patroness.

On that momentous occasion in 1737 it was like another Guadalupe. The temporary altar erected for the ceremonies of the day was glittering in silver, in lights, in flowers, and pearls. It was overhung by lofty, rich canopies, and it bore up a reproduction in roses of the hill of Tepeyac surmounted by a shining rainbow: there in the midst stood a figure of Our Lady, just as she appeared to Juan Diego.

The procession which took place on the evening of the 25th was as solemn and imposing as the whole civil and ecclesiastical resources of the Metropolis, together with the enthusiastic concurrence of the entire population, could in any way make it. The moving exultance of the Indians was one of its most admirable features. They regard Holy Mary of Guadalupe as belonging particularly to them; so when they see her publicly and strikingly honored their joy becomes uncontrollable. That afternoon they rushed from point to point to get a look at the *Holy Mother* borne aloft in triumph on the shoulders of priests, while magistrates and nobles thronged around to get each their turn in carrying the canopy. They danced and sang in their gladness, repeating the old Guadalupan chant: The Virgin is one of us, the Indians! our Clean Holy Mother! the Virgin is one of us!

A pretty device of theirs was much applauded. They had placed on the flat roofs, by the route of the procession, life-size figures of Juan Diego, holding up the *tilma* as he did when hurrying in to the bishop with the token of the flowers. And as the priests were passing, the *tilmas*, by some clever mechanical contrivance, were suddenly unfolded and showered roses on Our Lady, while displaying each of them her full Guadalupan figure.

The night was spent around the Cathedral and on the illuminated plaza. The people prayed and sang and rejoiced. Multitudes marched out on pilgrimage to Guadalupe, where the Shrine was kept open to receive them. There they knelt, looking at the Picture that to their simple, fervent love was like the presence of her who was next morning to be officially declared their Patroness.

16

The act for which such preparations had been made was fittingly accomplished at the Pontifical Mass, on Sunday the 26th of May, the feast of St. Philip Neri. After the Gospel the edict was read, the oath of patronage was publicly registered, and fervent thanksgiving went up from many devout hearts.

This Guadalupan measure of 1737—a measure whose civil and religious details suggest many reflections on present-day Christian society—was not in itself complete. This patronal vow bound only the City of Mexico and its immediate territory; but, as we have seen, it included the promise to get the adhesion of all New Spain. This was at once undertaken. The provincial cities were invited to do as the Capital had done; and, with a fervor that seemed to grow as it went, they all placed themselves by oath under the Patronage of Holy Mary of Guadalupe. The widening circles took in towns and villages, until there was hardly a hamlet in the land that had not celebrated its regularly representative consecration.

Even this did not satisfy the national desire. The Patronage should be vowed in the name of the whole country and the whole people at the very place of the Apparitions, in the commemorative Basilica, before the miraculous Picture. But so solemn and universally binding an act could not be attempted without all legal guarantees and formalities. Every corporate body in the kingdom had to send commissaries, or else to delegate its powers, so that the general patronage might be validly constituted and the corresponding obligations undoubtedly incurred. The proceedings took time. The difficulty of communication, then naturally great, was a cause of much delay. The need of hurry was, also, less felt when each community had declared the Patronage for itself and was carrying out its individual provisions. Then, too, some isolated cases of captious opposition were probably a slight clog—though they but served to enhance the moral unanimity, and to intensify the wish for a grand, unassailable, national declaration.

All was finally in order before the December of 1746, and on the 4th of that month the aged Viceroy-Archbishop received the oath of the country's delegates. A splendid cortege of all the officials and nobles of the city accompanied the Commissaries to the palace of the Prelate. The presence of Vizarron—a truly great Spaniard, who seems to have been equally admirable as Viceroy and as Archbishop—increased the enthusiasm of the distinguished assembly. The childlike piety of the venerable man was charmingly edifying. He began to tell the Commissaries "that he was unable to express his eagerness to see quickly accomplished this undertaking of the National Patronage; that now, seeing fulfilled his most ardent desire, he felt the greatest interior joy; that he had always professed a most tender devotion to the Virgin who was about to be recognised and declared by oath the Patroness of their country, but that now he felt drawn more than ever before to place himself under the protection of Mary, as a child presses to the heart of its mother. They had the proof before them, he continued; for there were disposed throughout his palace more than forty Guadalupan pictures; and he added, with graceful humor, that no such picture could enter there and go out again, for every one was either bought or begged or lovingly seized upon. The Commissaries wondered as they contemplated the tender piety of the holy old man who was radiant with joy."[1]

Before this venerable Metropolitan and representative of the Spanish Crown the delegates swore, in the name of Mexico and all its States, to regard and hold and serve as Principal Patroness "the Most Holy Virgin Mary, Our Lady, in her portentous Picture and title of Guadalupe." The same oath was repeated, with extraordinary solemnity and rejoicing, when the promulgation of the nation's decree was made at Guadalupe, on the Feast itself, the 12th of December, 1746.

It must interest American Catholics to note that a patronage similar to that established in Mexico was declared for this country just a century later. The Baltimore Council of 1846 chose Our Lady, under the title of the Immaculate Conception, as Patroness of the United States. The first decree says: "The Fathers, with eager desire, with acclamation and unanimous accord, have chosen the Blessed Virgin Mary, Conceived without Sin, as Patroness of the States of Federal America; imposing, however, no obligation to hear Mass and abstain from servile works on the feast itself of Blessed Mary's Conception."[2] That the Baltimore Fathers were influenced in 1846 by what was done in New Spain in 1746, may not be provable. The patronages, however,

---

[1] Hist. Comp., p. 187.

[2] At the suggestion of the Propaganda the Patronal Feast of the United States was made a day of precept by the Second Plenary Council of Baltimore. This new decree was confirmed by Pius IX. in 1868.

were similar; on certain points they were identical. Holy Mary of Guadalupe is Our Lady of the Immaculate Conception; for the Apparitions were of that mystery, of which, too, the miraculous Picture, given in 1531, is undoubtedly one of the earliest and best representations. As we have seen, this was recognised on all hands: we may even add that it was liturgically declared. For when, so early as 1668, Clement IX. was petitioned to make the 12th of December a special Guadalupan feast, he answered that, as the Picture was of the Immaculate Conception and the day was within the Octave, celebrating the Immaculate Conception was sufficiently celebrating Guadalupe. He also issued a Brief to that effect;[1] but his decree was nobly supplemented or replaced by the larger legislation of Benedict XIV.

In all that the people of New Spain had hitherto done for the Guadalupan patronage they were careful to make reservation of the rights of the Holy See. They promised to get their elections and decrees confirmed by papal authority, and to solicit from the Congregation of Rites the privilege of a proper Mass and Office. No time was lost in undertaking these further measures. The embassy to the Holy See of the Jesuit, Father Lopez, who presented to Benedict XIV. Cabrera's beautiful copy of the Picture, had as main object the securing of Rome's approval.

Very ably the envoy conducted his business. But at the moment success seemed assured it was rendered highly problematical by what might be called a tech-

---

[1] Estr. del Nor., p. 175.

nical difficulty. The Congregation of Rites, though fully satisfied with the actual Guadalupan evidences and demands, inclined to the decision that no distinctive liturgy should for the moment be sanctioned. The reason was that in the archives of the Congregation no specific documents were found to show that the cause had, at an earlier period, been formally introduced at Rome. Father Lopez knew that the documents of 1663 and 1667 should be in the Eternal City; but where to find them was his trouble. His most diligent researches proved fruitless. The documents he found were good for other purposes—as, for example, the decree of the Vatican Chapter, obtained by Boturini in 1740, authorising the coronation of the Picture; or the earlier decrees of Benedict XIII. and Clement XII. concerning the Collegiate.

Since the archives did not furnish what he wanted he had recourse to the libraries; but with as little success. In the great library of his confreres at the Roman College he found marked on the catalogue an Italian book that would suffice. Its title was: " Historical Relation of the admirable Apparition of the Host Holy Virgin Mother of God, under the title of Our Lady of Guadalupe, which occurred in Mexico, in the year 1531. Its author, Anastasio Nicoselli; dedicated to the R. P. M. F. Raymundo Capisucchi, Master of the Sacred Palace; printed in the Italian tongue, at Rome, in the year 1681."

Nicoselli was a Roman Prelate; and it was known that in writing his Guadalupan work he had used and even transcribed the Mexican Documents sent to the Holy See in the seventeenth century. This, therefore, was the very book Father Lopez wanted in order to show juridically that the demand now presented to the Congregation of Rites had been formally made long before.

Unfortunately, though the title was on the catalogue the work itself was nowhere to be found in the library. The envoy's disappointment was great. His embassy, like those that preceded it, seemed about to be a failure, though it had been so auspiciously inaugurated in the very presence of the Sovereign Pontiff. To augment the Father's anguish his allotted time in Rome was hurrying to a close.

But unexpected help came. One Saturday morning, as the distressed Guadalupan passed along the streets, he was aroused from his sad reflections by the cry: "Old books! old books!" To satisfy the vender who pursued him, he glanced at the offered volumes, and what was his delighted astonishment to recognise in one of them Nicoselli's precious Relation. With it and the other documents in hand he easily removed all objections. The Congregation of Rites approved the special Office and Mass, and the Holy Father, on the 25th of May, 1754, issued the Brief of which there is question in the second chapter.

While their envoy was still in Madrid, providing for the free execution of the pontifical decrees he was bringing home, the Roman edition of the new Office reached the Mexicans and caused great joy. Preparations were immediately made to receive fittingly the successful ambassador. The week's journey from the Capital to Vera Cruz did not deter a splendid national deputation from going so far to meet the humble Jesuit. He was led in triumph to Guadalupe where the Archbishop, the Chapters, the Courts, the Magistrates, and the general faithful, were awaiting his arrival.

Entering the Sanctuary and advancing to the altar of the Holy Patroness, Lopez took the pontifical Brief from his neck, where it hung by gold cords, and placed it in the hands of Archbishop Rubio, Vizarron's successor. Little knowledge of Mexico is required to understand that the rejoicings were hearty and heartily manifested. The reading of the long-desired Roman approbation excited immense enthusiasm. The exultance grew and grew beyond limits when it was found that all the best things they had ever heard or said of Guadalupe were readdressed to them by Benedict XIV. himself; that the great Pontiff not only sanctioned the special Office and Mass but imposed them on all priests and choir religious; that he similarly imposed the Feast of precept with its octave; that, finally, with Apostolic Authority, he decreed, declared, and commanded (*statuimus, declaramus, jubemus*) that the Mother of God, named of Guadalupe, should be recognised, invoked, and venerated, as Principal Patroness and Protectress of New Spain.

The extent of this New Spain, for which the Patronage of Holy Mary of Guadalupe was decreed as well by pontifical as by local authority, is a matter of concern for American Catholics. More than half of the territory which bore that title in 1754 is now comprised in the United States. The Floridas, East and West, were Spanish then and even until 1819; so was the old Louisiana—what forms now the central States west of the Mississippi—from 1762 to 1803, though not in the very year the Patronage was declared. These possessions, however, seem to have been ecclesiastically governed rather from Havanna than from Mexico; but in the privilege of the Guadalupan Office and Mass, which was extended to all the Spanish dominions, they naturally shared. The parts of the actual United States that were certainly included in the Guadalupan decrees are: Texas, New Mexico, Arizona, Utah, Nevada, and California.

It is worthy of remark, also, that these lands—with the doubtful exception of Texas—had not yet come under the jurisdiction of Baltimore when the United States Patronage was declared. When that was explicitly assumed by them, in place of their Guadalupan patronage, may not be easily determinable.

Happily, the Mother of God was chosen Patroness in 1846 as well as in 1746; and subsequent legislation makes, perhaps, clear that the very similar titles of *Guadalupe* and the *Immaculate Conception* are now coextensive with the corresponding national boundaries. Nevertheless, it seems undesirable that Our Lady's special American appellation should lose its hold on any territory it ever blessed. To be Guadalupan was a spiritual happiness for persons and places; better spread the name than let it drop. Not, indeed, that there is any danger of its dying out; for in the south-western States—especially in the Archdiocese of Santa Fe—there are scores of churches and missions of which Holy Mary of Guadalupe is still recognised as either the Titular or the Patroness.

From a Catholic standpoint there is no escaping the conclusion that the Tepeyac events placed the whole Western world in new particular relations with Our

Lady. Her best American children feel this and wish it more generally understood. A thrill, as at the touch of a great thought, ran through the distinguished assemblage which the 1895 ceremonies brought together in Mexico, when an Archbishop from the United States suggested that measures should be taken to have Holy Mary of Guadalupe declared Patroness of all America.

CHAPTER XV.

THE CORONATION.

CROWNING images of Our Lord and His Mother is a simply beautiful method of expressing Catholic fealty and love. In some form it must have been practised from the earliest Christian times—whether the crowns were of gold or of flowers; for the thought of His manifold royalty by nature, and of her royalty in the Divine maternity, is inseparable from belief in the Incarnation.

As a well-defined liturgical function the coronation of sacred figures is most noticeable in the last three centuries. Since Alexander Sforza left, in 1636, some of his property to the Chapter of St. Peter's for the express purpose of furnishing crowns for the more remarkable representations of Our Lady, the ceremony has acquired a recognised ritual. Certain conditions are necessary, and, apparently, an explicit sanction. The statues or pictures crowned by that first of Chapters must be famous for *antiquity, miracles,* and *public veneration.* The prescribed ceremonial has to be properly carried out; and a painting of the figure crowned is then to be sent to Rome. The canons' sacristy at St. Peter's is the treasury of these interesting copies.

The Popes also have frequently crowned images of the Mother and Child, or of the Immaculate Conception. They have done it with their own hands, or by order—delegates doing it in their name. Sometimes they themselves furnished the crowns; sometimes they seem to have determined the destination of those furnished by the Most Venerable Chapter.

We have seen that the coronation of Holy Mary of Guadalupe was conceded by the Vatican Canons, at the instance of the zealous Boturini, in 1740; and that governmental interference prevented the accomplishment of the pious undertaking. If the prevention was an evil, good came of it. The delay was long, but the final success was worth all the anxious expectation. A century and a half was not too long to wait for the event witnessed in 1895, an event that has made an epoch in Mexican, perhaps in American Catholic, history.

What might have been but a devout ceremony was made a great national act of faith. The Bishop of Colima expressed a fact when he said: "The Coronation is the solemn plebiscite of the religious and social dominion of Most Holy Mary in Mexico."[1]

All the Guadalupan traditions and memories were gathered up and reasserted, reconsecrated. Hundreds of years of trust and gratitude were magnificently voiced at once. So many generations had tried to honor the Mother of God, to rejoice worthily in her special favor, to display fidelity to her gracious covenant; and now these Mexicans of the nineteenth century eagerly seized the occasion to crown all past efforts by crowning their Heavenly Queen, Queen by right as well as in deed.

[1] Guad. Serm., Oct. 7, '95.

Nor was the project one of mere passing enthusiasm or superficial religiosity. Its solid good is seen in its depth of faith. It was Guadalupe's fundamental connection with the Catholicity of the nation that was to be acknowledged, extolled, perpetuated. In the Bishop of Tabasco's powerful effort to present to the public the true significance of the Coronation, we find enunciated and developed the two following propositions: " Mexico owes to her great Patroness the gift of Faith and the conservation of so precious a treasure. In the Coronation of the sacred Picture she immortalises, before future generations, her immense gratitude."[1] This, the Mexicans felt, was a correct expression of their views and intentions: their straining after an ideal so lofty had many very admirable results.

When they began to speak about the projected Coronation, they seemed to exaggerate. If, however, we look closely we shall find that acts passed beyond words, that more was accomplished than even was proposed. This is often true of Mexican religious affairs: when there is exaggeration it is more in action than in speech. Empty pretence and hypocritical display are practically unknown among that Catholic people; but let a good undertaking be started in their midst, and, ordinary as it may be, there is no saying what proportions it will finally assume. This very Coronation is a striking example.

At a college table, in the year 1886, it was suggested that the time was come to see about crowning Holy Mary of Guadalupe. The proposal came from the lamented Archbishop Labastida; but the idea was so immediately

---

[1] Guad. Serm., Oct. 9, '95.

appropriated that many seemed to have it at the same time. Then, though the matter was not noised abroad, appeals and petitions for the Coronation began to pour in on the ecclesiastical authorities. As the project ripened fast, recourse was soon had to the Holy See. In a letter received on the 12th of March, 1887, Leo XIII. not only allowed but ordered that the American Virgin be solemnly crowned. It was then proposed to have the ceremony on the last day of that year, on occasion of the Holy Father's sacerdotal jubilee. When, however, the necessary preparations were being considered, it was thought fitting to improve the surroundings of the Picture. A new altar for Our Lady was suggested, so that on the day of her coronation she might have an entirely suitable throne and canopy. But a new High Altar in the Collegiate should be the best that modern art could furnish; and that, it seemed, would demand changes in the choir and apse. Next, the sanctuary constructions projected should have a new crypt to support them, and by this great modification others would be entailed.

The question finally resolved itself into making hardly any change at all or making a vast one; and the Guadalupans, who are not accustomed to take the smaller alternative in religious affairs, decreed and executed the complete, gorgeous renewal of the Basilica, of which mention is made in an earlier chapter.

The work proposed looked, in Mexico's circumstances, gigantic—some said, visionary. A providential man was needed for the undertaking; and, truly, he was found in the present Guadalupan Abbot, Bishop Antonio Plancarte y Labastida. A typically devoted ecclesiastic, he had for twenty years been lavishing his varied resources on Mexican education and religion. His getting charge of the work required to honor fittingly the Holy Patroness was a guarantee of its success. He issued a form of catechism in which the simplest faithful could learn what the Coronation meant, why it should be undertaken, and how it was to be accomplished. The moral and material support of pastors as well as people was quickly secured; the work went on; and, though the strain must have been great, the heroic efforts of seven years had finally their happy triumph.

An excellent effect of the waiting and the protracted struggle was that much edifying enlightenment was incidentally thrown in the people's way. Scripture references to crowns and crowning were rehearsed; all the reasons which serve to prove that the Mother of God is Queen of Heaven and earth were learnedly expounded; her special claims to sovereignty in the New World were most lovingly detailed and chanted.

Abortive opposition only strengthened hearts and hands. The vulgar attacks of officious outsiders, and the bitter jibes of degenerate countrymen, forced from even the less fervent of the people an outburst of enthusiastic affection.

The moral consequences were great. You cannot have a whole nation passing from mouth to mouth the definite propositions: We have now to honor the Mother of God; and this is how she is honored: We have now to please our Holy Mother; and this is how she is pleased —without a strongly practical expansion of devout sentiment. It is not like vague social self-righteousness, that makes unctuous professions, but strives for nothing higher than respectable comfort. The most or the least intelligent Mexican, who determined to have his share in crowning Holy Mary of Guadalupe, determined also to make some fitting improvement in his own life and conduct.

Then a splendid exercise as well as example of virtue was found in the generosity evoked. All giving, and giving, apparently, without a trace of earthy motive! The mites of the poor counted much; so did the abundant gifts of the rich. No society could fail to be influenced for good by the sight of a dozen of its leading ladies praying for the privilege of having their gold and diamond ornaments wrought into a diadem for the Virgin Mother of God. Their offer was accepted; and the imperial crown of Guadalupe will long cast its lustre on their names.

The Crown itself is a treasury of instruction and a monitor of Catholic piety. It is symbolic—resting firmly on the dioceses and archdioceses with their medallions and escutcheons, running up in Tepeyac roses and starry brilliants, and terminating in a diamond Cross. The Angel of the Apparitions is well represented in the six figures of archangel that form a round, holding between them, two and two, the six archiepiscopal shields. The flowers recall Juan Diego; the heraldic eagle on the globe is national; and the sign of faith and redemption crowns all. The design is Mexican; the execution—as the best was sought—is Parisian. The work cost thirty thousand dollars.

Some concomitants of this great Crown are interesting. A silver fac-simile of it, beautifully wrought by Mexican artists and intended for every-day use in the Sanctuary, was presented by twelve young girls who were orphaned of their mother. They wished thus to express their special dependence on the Mother of God. Similarly the Bishop and people of Chilapa wanted to emphasise the fact that they had already made themselves, individually, the subjects of the Guadalupan Queen; so they brought her a golden sceptre and a golden rose.

With the nearer possibility of the much-desired ceremony the people's expectant fervor naturally increased. All the early part of the year 1895 was marked by immediate preparation. Devout Guadalupans were eager, anticipating great things. Glimpses of the new Collegiate grandeurs, sketches of the matchless splendor of the Crown, notices of vast pilgrimages and most distinguished visitors—all heightened the popular joy, and hope, and desire. So many were coming from every part of the Republic that the citizens felt their country would be fully represented. Moreover, bishops and priests were announced from the United States and Canada, from Central and South America; so that the whole Continent seemed about to acclaim Holy Mary of Guadalupe. This made her children happy.

Here, again, we cannot help remarking that the most admirable thing about these Mexican religious proceedings—and the pleasantest for Catholics to dwell on—is the faithful love always displayed towards our Mother in Heaven. To her the people of that land are loyal; and because her miraculous Picture represents her very immediately, and is a special pledge of her love, they surround it with all tenderest reverence. The thought that it was about to be restored to its Shrine, now gorgeously embellished, that it was to be magnificently enthroned and crowned, was a source of most pious rejoicing.

They had regretted to see it taken down from its place and removed out of the Basilica to the small adjoining church—though the necessity was evident. Most affecting, indeed, in its simplicity, is the account of what occurred in 1888, when that translation had to be effected. On a mere surmise of what was intended, the people, with tapers in their hands, crowded into the Collegiate. They knelt, looking up at the Picture; and, as if they thought it would be less visible or less well placed for some time, they sighed and wept. Their emotion was intensified when they perceived the old Abbot kneeling alone in a corner, with his eyes raised to Our Lady, while two great streams of tears rolled down his face. Some aged members of the Chapter were around, similarly affected.

As the translation did not occur as soon as expected, the people dispersed; but they watched the hour and returned with their tapers. Then as the great frame was first noticed to start from its place, there burst from the multitude an *ay!* of compassion or fear, and much sobbing was heard. They accompanied the veiled Picture out of the Basilica, through the few yards of street and into the old church of the Capuchin Nuns. When they saw it neatly placed there, and had had the satisfaction of singing a *Salve* and leaving their lighted tapers, they went away somewhat consoled.[1]

During all the time the Picture remained in that temporary location, the throng was there. The devotion was, perhaps, as great as it could be anywhere; but

---

[1] Album de la Coron., p. 112.

the people looked and spoke as if they felt it pathetic to have the Holy Mother kept out of her own house. The day they saw her back they wildly exulted. In their rejoicing they counted up how long she had been outside the Basilica, and, curiously enough, they found it was just seven years, seven months, and seven days—from the 23rd of February, 1888, to the 30th of September, 1895.

With the restoration of the Picture to the restored Basilica the festivities really began. Every day of October was made sacredly glad. But the day of days was Saturday, the 12th, the appointed day of the Coronation. The Matins and Lauds at the Shrine the evening before, the illumination of the *Villa* and the Capital, the pious, good-humored crowding, gave a foretaste of the joyous celebration.

The early hours of the morning offered strangely admirable sights. The whole city seemed moving out to the Collegiate. Every means of conveyance was in demand; while many, by choice or necessity, went on foot. That some made it part of the day's devotion to walk out was evidenced by the fact that well-to-do families were seen moving along in groups of eight to a dozen, the men with uncovered heads, and all reciting prayers in great recollectedness.

The day had, at Guadalupe, all the splendid solemnity that could be given it by the assistance of forty bishops, of hundreds of priests, and of literally countless thousands of the faithful. The simple press reports of the proceedings are eloquent, even in their disjointedness. Nor do the stiff formalities of the Notary's acts exclude all that was inspiring and moving. We find it recorded that, at the hour of None, the small fraction of the immense concourse that could find room in the spacious Basilica had been admitted. The Prelates and Priests were in their places; and the ceremony began. When the Archbishop of Mexico, as celebrant, had taken his seat, the Abbot of the Collegiate advanced with the Crown and placed it in his hands. The Archbishop then delivered it to the Canons, receiving their oath "to retain it and keep it over the august head of the Picture of Holy Mary of Guadalupe." The acts of this delivery having been read, as well as the Brief of His Holiness ordering the Coronation, the Crown was blessed and carried round in solemn procession. Pontifical Mass was, next, celebrated, after which the Most Reverend Celebrant entoned the *Regina Cœli* and proceeded to the Coronation. He was acting as delegate of Leo XIII. in whose name the act was performed; and the distinction of assisting him was granted to Archbishop Arciga of Michoacan, as one of the three prelates who had specially promoted the Coronation: the great age of the other, the venerable Archbishop of Guadalajara, prevented his being present.

Amidst the quivering stillness of eager expectancy the two Archbishops ascended to the platform. Then they reverently raised the Crown to its place, saying: "As by our hands you are crowned on earth so may we merit to be crowned by Christ with honor and glory in Heaven."

When "the assisting prelates, the regular and the secular clergy, and the faithful who filled the Basilica, saw the Crown imposed, they three times burst unanimously into *vivas!* to the Holy Patroness, joining to these demonstrations prolonged and thundering applause." The cry resounded on all sides: *Viva la Reina de los Mexicanos!*

Viva la Virgen de Guadalupe! The crowds outside caught up the acclaim and spread it through the *Villa;* and soon all the bells "were ringing out to the world, with joyous echo, that there had just been felicitously accomplished the most auspicious event that Catholicism has registered in America."

Within the Sanctuary those moments were grand. "In all present there was a veritable explosion of gladness, of exultation, of enthusiasm. Men and women wept for joy, and the scene became sublime. All felt themselves possessed by the faith of the Christian, while their souls filled with undefinable sweetnesses."[1] Certain points in the proceedings particularly affected the assistance. The eagerness with which one Archbishop was seen to kiss the Picture before crowning it, and the shining tears on the face of the other as he descended from the platform, were moving traits. Then when the Prelates on ceremony came to lay down their crosiers and mitres before the crowned Virgin, and all the other Archbishops and Bishops spontaneously advanced to do her similar homage, it was felt that Holy Mary of Guadalupe was indeed made Queen of Catholic Mexico. A choice category of her subjects was, also, characteristically represented. Twenty eight Indians, from the neighboring village of Juan Diego, one for each diocese in the Republic, held a conspicuous position, and picturesquely expressed the loving fidelity of the native race to their cherished Sovereign.

Feeling ran high in the vast assembly. The tearful emotion of so many men and women, the irrepressible *vivas!* in the sacred place, the sense of being in the midst

---

[1] El Tiempo, Oct. 12, 24, etc., '95.

of electrified, ecstatic souls, made enthusiasm strongly contagious, and deeply affected even the coolest strangers.

The presence of so many foreign ecclesiastics might have been somewhat of a restraint on the ordinarily childlike expansiveness of Guadalupan devotion; but the more thoughtful of the people drew from the circumstance a fresh motive for exultant gladness. The assistance of representative Bishops from north and south made it look to them as if their Holy Patroness was really being crowned Queen of the Western World. That this their great neighboring Church should have sent ten or more Archbishops and Bishops was particularly suggestive.[1]

The orator of the day, the truly eloquent Bishop of Yucatan—whom sickness unhappily kept absent, but whose great sermon was read at the evening exercises—had a felicitous inspiration when he said: "In crowning Our Lady we follow the example of the Tutelar Angel of America, of him who bears on his shoulders the Apparitional Image of Guadalupe; we follow the example of all the other Angels of the Churches and Nations of the New World." And as he felt that the Mother of God, "in choosing the Mexicans as her people, constituted herself Empress and Patroness of all America," he could well cry out: "O happy America! O fortunate West Indies! O blessed Mexico! you the Queen of Heaven chose and sanctified. Not only has she done to you as she did to no other nation, visiting you with such love, such predilection, such maternal tenderness, but in the

---

[1] Mexican papers mention: the Archbishops of New York, Cincinnati, New Orleans, and Santa Fe; and the Bishops of Natchez, Columbus, Ogdensburg, Nashville, Dallas, Springfield and Galveston; with the Vicars Apostolic of Indian Territory, Brownsville, and Arizona.

rich gift of her Picture, of this miraculous image of Guadalupe, she has left you the testimony that your vocation is her work. O all ye nations of America! cast your crowns at the feet of your Queen and Patroness, as in Heaven the four and twenty Elders do at the foot of the throne of the Divine Lamb, her Son." [1]

Lest it should appear that the sentiments of the rejoicing Guadalupans, or the words that officially expressed them, were more lofty than deep, I must further quote this masterly Coronation Sermon:—

"But which and of what kind," asks the Right Reverend Orator, "must be the filial crown that we offer to our Most Holy Mother of Guadalupe? Shall it be of refulgent stars? Shall it be of precious stones? or of fine gold? or of beauteous flowers? Oh! understand well: the filial crown for our Mother must not be composed of stars or pearls or gold or flowers, but of ourselves. This is the wish, this the desire, this the glory, of our admirable Mother. . . . I conjure you, therefore, beloved brethren, in the felicity of the great day we celebrate, that you be good and loyal sons of our Most Holy Mother, the Virgin Mary of Guadalupe; true and worthy sons by the purity of your Catholic Faith, by the spotlessness of your lives and habits: remaining ever firm in the unity and perfection signified by the twelve stars that shine on the immaculate brow of Mary. . . . Oh yes! august Lady and Mother, full of filial love and profoundest gratitude, we come to crown thee, and of our hearts and souls we make thy diadem. We know that if we did not crown thee as Queen and Mother, we

---

[1] Coron. Serm., Oct. 12, '95.

should be, not only unworthy vassals and ungrateful children, but also creatures rebellious to their Lord; for in crowning thee we crown and glorify as last end our sovereign and most merciful God, since it is He that created and exalted thee for His own honor and for the splendor of all His truly admirable works. . . . O Sovereign Lady of America, Queen of Angels and Mother of men, Empress of the New World, Standard and Protectress of Mexico, Virgin of Guadalupe, in crowning thee with to-day's ritual solemnity we recognise who thou art, what is thy worth and what thy significancy; as thou truly art we acknowledge and acclaim thee, to thee we swear allegiance. Most absolutely art thou bound up and identified with the high mysteries of our Faith, with the maxims of the Gospel, with the regeneration of humanity, with the liberty and civilization of the world. By the singular favor of your descent and Apparition on this hill of Tepeyac which you thus changed into the Cenacle of the New World, and by the pledge you left us in your miraculous Picture, you have become the basis and the capital, the pedestal and the crown, of our history and nation, of our Church, of our culture, of our Independence, and of all our hopes in time and eternity."[1]

It was not alone in the *Villa* and the City of Mexico that the day was fervently celebrated. All through the beautiful valley and up into the encircling hills, in every parish and every shrine, participatory devotions were held. Still more, at distances that prevented many from going to Guadalupe, were the special services individually elaborate. Beyond the mountains, down the shelv-

---
[1] Ib., ad fin.

ing country to the Gulf and to the Pacific, far south in the palmy villages and away north in the dustier mining districts, wherever is found a venerable church or the newest adobe chapel, the united people solemnised the Coronation of their Queen.

The Catholic press of the time is filled with enthusiastic reports, every township seeming to think that nothing could surpass its own demonstration. In a sense they were all inimitable, so exquisitely did each give local expression to the Guadalupan fervor.

Great preparations were made for the appointed day. In some cities each of nine churches had in succession a day's Exposition of the Blessed Sacrament, all of them or the principal one having it on the twelfth. The order followed on the feast seems generally to have included a Communion Mass early, and a solemn Office in time to finish at the exact hour of the Coronation in the Collegiate. Dials had been made and distributed, to indicate for the whole Republic the very instant of the great national act at the Capital. A form of prayer had, also, been spread broadcast—through the zeal, I believe, of the Bishop of Querétero. The leaflets said: "At the hour of the Coronation all the faithful, whether they be in the churches, in their houses, or in the streets, will salute the Sovereign Lady, saying: Hail, August Queen of the Mexicans! Most Holy Mary of Guadalupe, hail! Pray for thy Nation, that it may obtain what thou, our Mother, thinkest most fit to ask; and bless thy children who from here below salute thee. Hail! *Ave Maria.*"

As the provincial reports are most numerous and in many points similar, I choose a fairly representative

specimen. It comes from San Louis Potosí. Though
the devotion of the Potosans has been long renowned,
it glows with unaccustomed splendor in the warmth of
their present Bishop's princely piety—princely, that is,
in the St. Louis fashion. Having mentioned some of
the preparations, and recorded the highly significant fact
that more than ten thousand Communions had been
received that morning in St. Louis and its suburbs,
the reporter continues:—

"Never have we seen at the Holy Sacrifice such crowds
of people or such proofs of devotion. With the har-
monies of the orchestra and the chants of the choir, there
were mingled the sobs of the multitude prostrate at the
feet of the Mother of God. Hardly could men, women,
or children, restrain their weeping. . . . Mass ended at
a quarter to ten, according to the meridian of Mexico.
The celebrant exchanged the chasuble for the pluvial,
and, together with the deacons, awaited the coming of
the supreme moment. At 52 minutes and 39 seconds
past nine the priests, advancing to the middle of the
altar, entoned the *Te Deum*. The small bells began to
ring. Then the chimes and great bells of the shrine
announced to the city that that was the instant at which
the Metropolitan of Mexico was raising the Crown of
gold over the miraculous Picture. Full pealing from
all the churches in the vicinity immediately followed;
and the thundering rattle of tens of thousands of rockets
resounded in the air.

"In those moments all who were in the churches, or
at home, or in the streets, stood still where they were, as
if at the same instant a mysterious current traversed
every frame; and nothing was seen but the movement of

the lips as the angelic salutation sprung from the heart to stir them, or the tears that furrowed the cheeks—ay, even those that, perhaps, from childhood had not been wet with such vivifying dew.

"When the *Te Deum* was finished, the gentlemen who form the Junta in charge of worship in the sanctuary, and other distinguished persons, took up the sacred picture and organised a procession round the interior of the church, while the Litany of Loretto was being sung. A thing to see was the way in which all the tearful eyes remained immovably fixed on the sacred picture."[1]

The fervor at San Louis Potosí, though manifestly great, was not singular: hundreds of other places rivalled it. The greatness of the number of Communions seems to have been a very general feature, many of the reports stating that "multitudes," and "vast multitudes," and "countless multitudes," were seen at the Sacred Table.

The practical sweetness of Mexican charity was evidenced in the various Coronation Banquets given to the poor. Crowds of them were feasted—as many as three hundred in some of the Colleges.

The public rejoicings in the afternoon and evening were universal. Wherever any gathering of poeple was possible—in remote Indian hamlets and out on the ranchos, as well as in towns and cities—decorations were displayed and sounds of gladness prevailed. There were bonfires in the fields, and fireworks (of the Mexican artistic kind) in every village. In fact the decorative and illuminative materials of the country must have been all used up; for the reports from several districts

[1] El Estandarte, Oct. 17, '95.

mention that no more colored stuffs could be had to make banners and streamers, no more Chinese lanterns, toy-balloons, fireworks, etc. Most remarkable of all was that music should be found to run short in Mexico; yet from different places it was announced that no more bands or orchestras could be got, even for hire: all were engaged by the public or by individual families. In that musical land those who have occasion to deck their dwellings, or raise altars or trophies on their own grounds, generally have conveniently located some instrumentalists whose duty is to attune the household and the visitors to the spirit of the celebration.

The festivities of the Coronation were, naturally, much tinged by patriotism. To be Guadalupan is to be truly Mexican. The Dolores *grito* of Independence and the flag of the patriots are always religiously remembered. Hence on this greatest of Guadalupan days the national colors were to be seen everywhere.

Present political peculiarities entered but little into the celebration; yet they may be mentioned, as they furnished the slight contrasts and shadows that made the general glad unanimity more striking. Petty officials—mainly in Zacatecas and Aguascalientes—wishing to conciliate the anti-religious, rather than democratic, liberalism which, at present, is supposed to have most to give in Mexico, tried here and there to coerce the Guadalupan fervor. Unfavorable municipal regulations were strained to harsh and even illegal severity. The ringing of bells was ridiculously prevented. Policemen stood on guard in the belfries, or took away the bell-ropes. Boys who managed to toll the bells were taken prisoners; and when, at the sight of the youthful captives, the enthusiasm of some women caused them to cry out: "Viva Maria Santisima de Guadalupe!" they, too, were put under arrest. Then gentlemen, who had to expostulate with the police for treating these ladies and children with brutal roughness, were in their turn seized on.

The president of a Municipal Council, who had gaily adorned his house—a thing which no law forbade—and who refused to remove the decorations at the behest of a little mushroom tyrant, was imprisoned for forty-eight hours and fined twenty-five dollars.

These petty persecutions, however, were but local and ephemeral. The Catholic sufferers came out of them with a new halo on their brows and new fervor in their hearts. Serious trouble might, indeed, have been apprehended from some of the utterly brutal vexations inflicted on unoffending citizens. At one important place the people were marching processionally outside the church. To do this with religious emblems is considered illegal. But these people carried only the statue of Hidalgo, the Liberator, the Father of their Independence. However, the perspicacity of an ignorant gendarme discovered that the well-known banner held aloft in the hand of the statue, having on it the Guadalupan figure, was sufficiently religious to break the law. He ordered it removed. The people must have smiled as they reminded the representative of authority that the Guadalupan flag was national, and, moreover, that there and then it could not be removed, as it formed part of the plaster statue. Nothing deterred, the champion of legality rushed in and plucked so violently at the banner that he tore off the whole arm from the venerated figure.

In similar circumstances almost any other people would have torn the wretch limb from limb. But the Mexicans—Pueblans they were—merely expressed their pain at the *impolite, unauthorised* proceeding, and then continued the procession with their maimed statue.

Ordinarily they are not a people to keep quiet under insult; but on days of great Guadalupan gladness they seem to put violence away at a distance. Nevertheless, reflection on that Pueblan incident, and on a few others like it, makes one wonder how perfect peace was preserved. Great graces were apparently given to make the day, even outwardly and in detail, a marvellously religious success.

This Mexican Coronation of Our Lord's Mother is, without doubt, most variously instructive and edifying. Merely to know that, in the dull end of the nineteenth century, there is near us in rich abundance the old-time chivalry of devotion and enthusiasm of spiritual ideals, is enlightening and helpful. Of earlier Guadalupan demonstrations we might be inclined to say that their fervor belonged to more Catholic generations and with them was passed away. But here, before our eyes, is the ardor of childlike piety domineering a new, ambitiously progressive Republic.

Such a national celebration gives happy testimony of the present state of religion and augurs well for future fidelity. It was, therefore, no surprise to hear the Chief Pastors of the people deliberately affirm that, in the religious annals of the land, only the days of the Apparitions in 1531, and the day of the final declaration of the Patronage in 1756, could be compared to the day of the Coronation in 1895.

CHAPTER XVI.

CONCLUSION.

THE strength of the Church in the New World is seldom realised. On this side of the Atlantic the number of Catholics, all counted, fairly equals the whole population of the United States. Of such a multitude of believers the moral force would be immense, did they but feel how many and how fundamentally united they are. When they come to have more fraternal intercourse, more outward communication in matters distinctively religious, more participation in particular pious privileges, a bloom of Christianity may be expected here as fair, perhaps, as any that ever adorned the Old World.

Even North America by itself is a great stronghold of the Faith. Between Panama and Alaska there are more than thirty millions of the children of the Church. That they, again, do not know one another more generally, and are not more conscious of their close spiritual solidarity, is certainly to be regretted. But time must, naturally, tend to remedy that defect; and present circumstances seem to promise speedy fruits of appreciative acquaintance and devout sympathy. The mutual interest more and more manifested between the Spanish-speaking Catholics and the English-speaking—these latter roughly covering this country and Canada—is a ground of happy anticipations. And, undoubtedly, if the two great—and, numerically, about equal—Churches above and below the Rio Grande, rejoiced and sorrowed and strove together, religion would make giant strides in this most progressive of the Earth's divisions.

Whatever, therefore, helps to draw God's people, north and south, into more effective union is of sacred importance. Guadalupe has often, especially in recent times, been felt to be a strong tie: some think it destined to be the golden link. The devotion connected with the place and with its history is preëminently American and Catholic. Its cultivation will bear fruit.

Mere curiosity about Mexican traditions and practices may be an occasion of great good to the Catholics of Canada and the United States. We learn much by occupying ourselves with our southern neighbors. In the first place we shake off many injurious prejudices; for we can hardly fail to perceive how outrageously lying are the commoner Anglo-Saxon accounts of Latin peoples and colonisations. And surely our acquisition of truer views is desirable. It is bad enough that stolid bigotry should have rendered grossly misleading the American histories that Catholics have had to use; but it is indefinitely worse that the educated faithful—sometimes, their educators—should continue to retail most baseless falsehoods about a great part of our earliest and our actual brethren in this Western Hemisphere.

One of the best tests of a man's Catholic scholarship might, at present, be found in his ability to give and demand fair play when there is question of the nations that colonised America under—partially or primarily—the inspiration of faith and the direction of the Church. To say they were not the Church is to state a plain truth; but to say so, in order to be free to leave them to the mercy of their maligners, is to shirk a religious duty.

As a matter of history these colonists were, in great part, sincere and even zealous Catholics. Their real religion must, on the whole, have influenced their treatment of their fellow-creatures. To admit that it did not is as false in principle as it is in fact. It is because the Spanish, Portuguese, and French colonists were Catholic that the native races could survive and flourish under their rule. Abuses there were, of course; but every abuse —a point most worthy of note—was loudly denounced by the countrymen and coreligionists of the wrong-doers. Remedies also were immediate and effective, as they always have been where the Church had influence. Elsewhere the natives were exterminated, and hardly a voice was raised in protest. Indeed we can but conjecture sadly the extent of the enormities perpetrated, by the palpable fatality of the results.

As ability to defend the colonisers who made the propagation of the Faith part of their enterprise, is a mark of Catholic scholarship, so is fairness to these same colonisers an indication of thoroughness in any American historian. This is being slowly recognised. The Bancrofts were a long advance—one on the other, and both on Prescott and Robertson—in impartiality and trustworthiness; yet they are left far behind by the more penetrating and broader-viewed John Fiske. Not even he, however, has dug down to the solid truth on all points.

Acquaintance with Guadalupan Mexico has, from this external or historical stand-point, a peculiarly good effect.

It helps us to rectify our opinions on "the Spaniards in America"—a category of people whom anti-Catholic or half-Catholic education renders many ludicrously incapable of comprehending. That Mexico to-day contains twelve millions of Catholics is not, surely, in spite of Spain, nor without her help. If the thought occurs to us that they should be still more numerous, we have to remember that, as in the Old World in earlier centuries, war and pestilence made vast reductions in population; and that, moreover, Mexico has now but half the territorial extent it had in Spanish times. Mile by mile the country is as thickly populated as the United States, though immigration has been comparatively insignificant; and non-Catholics hardly boast of being one in a thousand, even reckoning, with the imported sects, the secret societies and the scattered savages.

Particularly to be remarked is the prevalence of the native race. Statistics and appearances indicate that nine millions of the people have Indian blood in their veins,—half of these, probably, no other blood. They too, these natives, have held and hold positions of eminence in every walk of life, civil, military, and ecclesiastical. Where shall we look for similar final results in European colonisation?

The Christian work of the coloniser is to preserve and elevate the uncivilized native. To come and take his place, bringing with us more or less of our old civilization, may or may not be beneficial to us, but it is certain ruin to him. In New Spain the Indians survived and became American Catholics. That fact is a compendium of history.

Introduction to the children of Holy Mary of Guadalupe may have for us other precious results. It opens up to our view very attractive visions of neighboring Catholic life. It edifies and may, in some points, suggest imitation.

It will, perhaps, be said that the Catholics of the United States need not look beyond themselves for subjects of edification; or, rather, that others might well copy from their example. In this there is truth. Nowhere more than here does the calm fidelity of the children of the Church, in the midst of headlong worldliness, unanswerably argue the common-sense reality of religion. Practical belief here is tested and sifted sincerity.

The secure business-footing on which are placed most extensive, freely contributed Church finances, is also peculiarly distinctive of this country. Nor is the support of the ministers of God more amply and admirably provided for in any other part of the world. As in the practicalness of sincere Catholic lives, so in the economy of religious temporalities, the faithful of the United States may be offered as an example to all their brethren.

But there are high characteristics of Christianity which they in turn will gladly recognise in others. The simple piety of complete abandonment to the motions of grace, the quick tendency to what resembles heroic virtue, the mystic indifference to paltry surroundings, and the daily aspiration to asceticism and holiness—these things seem less common here than in some older Catholic communities. In fact the folly of the Cross is comparatively rare among English-speaking peoples; while, it cannot be denied, it enters largely into the temper of the Saints.

The Mexicans appear to have it—with, possibly, some human folly intermixed—; and to see them moved by it is useful to us, even though their particular practices should not serve for imitation.

They have always been ready to sacrifice material interests to spiritual. Some think they were, at times, too ready to neglect the temporal under pretence of the eternal, and that indolence often took advantage of piety. However this may be, their sentiment of contempt for merely worldly advantage was prominently evidenced; and neither the exaggeration nor, perhaps, the simulation of this spirit could fail to recall the lessons of the Cross.

Again, the tender naivete of many of their pious customs may be advantageously considered, though not necessarily adopted, by more matter-of-fact Christians. There is a childlike simplicity of affection in their relations with God and with the Blessed. They venture on reverent familiarities with Heaven. Our Lord and His Angels and Saints are approached in daringly fond ways; but, as we might expect, it is Our Lady, *the Holy Mother*, that is specially worshipped with the ingenuousness and the ingenuity of filial intimacy. Her name is given with great frequency; and boys, as well as girls, must have it either in first or second place. And as *Mary* or *Guadalupe* cannot be given to all, they find means of reduplicating the sweet appellation. Devout terms connected with the Virgin Mother and her shrines are taken as names. Hence is it that in Mexican lists we meet so frequently—*Concepcion, Engracia, Salud, Dolores, Asuncia, Carmen, Pilar, Rosario, Soledad, Luz, Nieves, Loreto, Refugio, Paz*, etc., etc.

Multiplied feasts of Our Lady are celebrated under peculiarly beautiful titles that, though found in the commonest Mexican calendars, are hardly mentioned elsewhere—except, perhaps, in one or other religious directory. Thus we meet—'Our Lady of Light,' 'of Peace,' 'of Consolation'; 'Our Lady of Grace,' 'of Pity,' 'of Refuge'; 'Our Lady of the Angels,' 'of Bethlehem,' 'of the Unprotected.' There are feasts of her 'humility,' of her 'joys,' of her 'Prodigies'; and of herself as 'Queen of All Saints,' as 'Mother of the Divine Pastor,' as 'Mother of Beautiful Love.'

Of course all the commoner feasts, earlier and later, are celebrated; and some have characteristic observances. I have noticed particularly beautiful practices in connection with the Assumption. On the fifteen days preceding there are, in the churches, exercises called *Gradas* (steps) in preparation for the solemnity. On the 13th, *El Tránsito* (the passing-away) of Holy Mary is regretfully commemorated. A figure of the Divine Mother is laid-out near the sanctuary. The bed is surrounded with flowers and, in some churches, with rows of apples to recall the words of the Canticle. The people come in to watch and pray—perhaps, to weep; and when the children, who have to be told what this strange proceeding means, hear that Holy Mary is dead, they begin to raise an uproar that can be quieted only by assuring them that though she died she is alive—as they will see two days later.

Then, on the 15th the church is brightly festive. Music and incense are in the air, as the people hurry in and kneel around a crystal casket which is almost hidden in flowers. Every one has been piling them on it and about it; and as the simple worshippers bend down and peer in they can see that it contains only lilies and sweet-smelling herbs. Then, thinking where she is, they join in the songs.

I have seen Indian men and women kneel around one of these Assumption caskets, and look reverently into it and kiss it or the ground near it, and glow with happiness as they whispered to their little ones what it all meant. I also saw different persons gather up the rose-leaves from the floor and carry them away as something sacred. They themselves may, indeed, have brought those very roses there; but they consider that the use made of them renders them now a precious memorial.

It is good for us of colder regions to see the pious ardor of these Mexican practices, though we may have no call to imitate them, nor the grace to do so profitably. They are a lesson and a testimony. It is possible that one of these southern Assumption celebrations evokes more simple love of Our Lord's Mother—and consequently of Him—than could be found in a year's Christianity in some northern parishes.

It is not alone for affectionateness that these Guadalupan Catholics are remarkable. Their knowledge of sacred things is also wonderful. Apparently uneducated peasants are quite familiar with special devotions to the *In-dwelling Spirit*, to *Divine Providence*, to what they call *Los Divinos Desagravios* (satisfactions). They occupy themselves with things that many other Catholics scarcely think of. Among their peculiar practices may be noticed their *Caminata (way) de Santo Tobias*, their novenas of *Santo Tadeo, San Pafnucio, San Expedito*, etc., etc.

To make religion inseparable from their daily lives they have a heavenly patron for every trade and profession. In stores and shops an appropriate statue or picture is prominently placed, and lights are kept burning before it. Indeed one of the most characteristic features of a Mexican town at night is the twinkling of the "Saints' lamps." They shine on every side, especially in the poor one-room dwellings along the streets; and the sacred representation they illuminate makes the home and the workshop look holy. It is oftenest the incomparably delicious figure of Holy Mary of Guadalupe.

These peasants seem, also, to read, or get their children to read, books of piety that certainly are not common. I was once accosted by an elderly Indian woman who had just made a purchase in a bookstore behind the Cathedral of the City of Mexico. She held towards me a new book and asked whether it was *el verdadero* (the right one). I glanced at it and told her it was the *Life of the Good Thief*. "That's it," she replied joyfully, "that's it." Not knowing what she meant to do with the work, I ventured to say: "You don't read?" "No," she said, "but *las criaturas* (the children) do." "Why do you specially want the *Life of the Good Thief?*" I curiously continued. She paused, and then with an expression that reminded me of the comicality of certain other peasants when they see through an objection to their catechism answer, she replied: "What seems to me is that we're all somehow *thieves;* and we'd want to be *good* ones before we die."

The unusual acquaintance of Mexican Catholics with religious affairs may come partly from the custom of publishing over the whole city or locality all the devotions that are taking place. Every church porch is placarded with what is going on in every other church—for if there be any rivalry between parishes it seems to be only in charity, fervor, and fraternity. The frequency of printed announcements is extraordinary, especially in a country where printing might be supposed to be expensive and rather limited. Not only are notices posted up by church authorities, but also, with permission, by individual Catholics. Mortuary announcements are, of course, nothing very extraordinary; others, however, are. A practice which manifests the hot, surging life of Catholicity, is the initiating, privately and individually, special devout, supererogatory celebrations. It is a usual thing to see announced that certain persons want an exceptional solemn office in honor of Our Lord, or His Mother, or His Mysteries; and that the expenses (in music, flowers, lights, personal service, etc.) will be gladly borne by them. They, therefore, request all the devout souls who can to assist and join with them in pious intention.

This kind of generosity is frequent; and it sometimes takes peculiar forms. The luxury of a week's Spiritual Retreat—board and lodging included—is occasionally offered by good people to those who may need but cannot afford it. Procuring Missions for poor districts is done on a larger scale.

Another side of this charitable generosity may look to us naiveté itself, though in Mexico it hardly calls for comment. It is generosity in demand, in asking prayers and pious concurrence. You may meet at a church door the printed, earnest request from 'a person,' 'one of the faithful'—no acquaintance, no one having any special claims—to hear the *thirty-three Masses of St. Gregory* for an intention, or to offer *fifteen Communions* for a particular object, or repair to an appointed church and altar for *a series of devotions* in common.

You will, probably, think it difficult to satisfy such demands; but you cannot help admiring the confidence of charity that makes them possible and practical. The frequenters of these churches are constantly in the meshes of some heavenly net. Whether they resign themselves or resist they feel intimately the meaning of Christian brotherhood and of the Communion of the Saints on earth.

If I dwell on these minor traits of Catholic life in the land of Holy Mary of Guadalupe, it is because I think them of opportune edification. Among the English-speaking faithful the fine flour of devotion risks being lost. As a rule we are too much in contact with heretical pretences of Christianity, with successful sanctimonious worldliness, to be ready to respond to every touch and breath of supernatural piety. Catholics whose temporal and natural advantages may appear much less, are often, through uncontaminated simplicity of inherited faith, far more sensitive to the delicate impressions of grace. In poor Mexico spiritual instincts are tinglingly active that farther north seem still dormant or at least undeveloped.

The indirect advantages arising from acquaintance with Guadalupan history and life would be sufficient to induce us to occupy ourselves with it. But other reasons are yet more powerful. The fact that such things happened on this continent, and the fact that there is here such a miraculous Picture, such a wonder-working devotion, are matters that challenge the attention of every American Catholic. The facts themselves cannot reasonably be called in question. Knowing the Church's action in the matter and considering its import, we have to conclude that mistake about Guadalupe is practically impossible. The Mother of God appeared there, and gave the Picture, and obtained—still obtains—blessings and miracles for her devout worshippers.

The absence and exclusion of doubt concerning the Apparitions and their effects—an absence and exclusion warranted by the Church's confirmatory acceptance of the tradition—is what authoritative Mexicans must have in view when they speak, as does Father Antícoli, S. J., of our having *infallible certainty* of the Guadalupan Miracle;[1] or as does the late Bishop Vargas, of our holding it on the *infallible teaching* of the Church.[2] What these learned Guadalupans firmly grasp is the fact that Church legislation presupposes a foundation of truth.

To all of us the Tepeyac account must recommend itself when we call to mind the evidence in its favor, and the rigorous sifting of that evidence both in Mexico and at Rome. Moreover, it excellently bears all the usual tests: uniformity of records, piety of authors, universal veneration, miracles, and visible fruitfulness. Nor does it suffer at all when compared with other special revelations. Comparisons are, indeed, unnecessary—might be misleading, or injurious. The Mexicans do not indulge in them, at least not jealously. But travelled strangers who become acquainted with Guadalupe are, naturally,

---

[1] Magist. de la Iglesia, p. 74.   [2] Supra, p. 5.

inclined to compare; and their references are always highly eulogistic. Centuries back it was stated by those who had been at Loretto that, once they left the Holy House, no other place gave them so intimately, as did Guadalupe, the same feeling of nearness to the Mother of God. Italians, as well as Spaniards, readily put the American Shrine on a par with their own most cherished sanctuaries. Others have expressed similar appreciations.

When a French-Canadian prelate, who preached at Guadalupe during the Coronation festivities, deliberately classed the Shrine of the Picture as first among Our Lady's sanctuaries in the New World, he but said what all must admit. Nor does it startle us greatly to hear one of Christian Reid's characters cry out that the Guadalupan story is more beautiful even than that of Lourdes—much as that is to say; for, undoubtedly, the Indian Narrative is a flawless gem of modern Catholic tradition.

It is well to notice that neither in the history of the Miracle nor in the practice of the Devotion is their anything that offers even the appearance of extravagance. There is, of course, the supernatural and the wonderful; but there is nothing that the most moderate-minded can object to, as being unnecessarily strange or at all meaningless. Peculiar phenomena, at which crabbed sense may be tempted to demur in other special revelations, are strikingly absent from the Tepeyac visions and messages. The Miracle is there, certainly, and its bold, unvarying announcement; but all is admirable in simplicity, sincerity, and gracefulness. It really looks as if Guadalupe were made to suit the devotion of continued ages and of cosmopolitan peoples.

That American Catholics will gain much by an intelligent and affectionate cherishing of Our Lady's American title, there can be no reason to doubt. To honor her under any special title is to open for ourselves a rich source of grace; and the more the title is connected with our individual circumstances the more fruitful is it in our devotions. It is like an appointed way, a part of our convenant—as experience can hardly have failed to convince us. Nor should it escape our observation that if origin, length of time, nobility of record, can impart and interpret titular characteristics, then Our Lady's title of Guadalupe is both sacredly and distinctively American.

Moreover, here and now such a devotion is remedial as well as nourishing. It counteracts materialistic tendencies. The very Picture, with its heavenly modesty and delicacy, can be made an efficient bulwark against aggressive worldliness. Its sweet lineaments, kept constantly before the eyes and faithfully transferred to the mind, are capable of attracting to noble purity of character and life. It helps to love the Immaculate Virgin—what then may it not do?

While leading to precious intimacy with Heaven, the Guadalupan beliefs and practices excite admiring gratitude and chivalrous devotedness. Their utter separation from earthly pomp or pretence allies them closely to very simple faith. The devotion makes men interior without their knowing it, and draws them quickly to Divine union. That this should be its effect we need not wonder; for it is proved to be a devotion most pleasing to the hidden one whose beauty was all within—to the New Eve, the only unspotted daughter of our race, without whom there is, providentially, neither beginning, nor continuance, nor consummation, of our union with God.

To honor Our Lord's Mother under the title she chose for herself in this New World, is therefore good for us individually; and while, in any degree, we so honor her we may happily be hastening the day when, for the good of multitudes, Holy Mary of Guadalupe will be universally hailed as Our Lady of America.

INDEX.

ABAD, Father, S. J., poet, 132.
Abuses, in colonization, denounced by Catholics, 273.
Acuña, Vicar, miracle at Mass of, 179
Aguiar, Archbishop, 141.
Alarcon, Archbishop, on Guadalupan tradition, 13; letter of, 51; represented in Shrine, 150; crowning the Picture, 260.
Alegre, Father, historian, 203.
Alexander VI., legislates for New World, 192.
Alexander VII., sanctions introduction of Guadalupan cause, 17; favorable to, 21.
Altimirano, on Guadalupe, 65.
Alva, Fernando de, papers of, 77.
Ambrose, St., 215.
America, happy, loved of Mary, 4; glory and crest of, 4; coat of arms of, 5; honored and blessed at Tepeyac, 13; birth of, to light of the Gospel, 69; gift to Church of, 132; remedy for ills of, 190; first seat of learning of, 204; protected by Church, 205; asking Guadalupan Patronage, 235; Patroness of, 250; most auspicious event in history of, 261; Church in, 271; empire of Mary, 262, 264.
American, devotion, 1, 15, 272; Marvel, 4; Bouquet, 5; histories, misleading, 272; historians, 273; title of Our Lady, distinctively, 284.
Americans, first Guadalupans, 4; most special mother of, 5; native, grasped mystery of Incarnation, 66; Spanish, wrote much on Guadalupe, 82; Our Lady's love of, 190; native, qualities of, 196.
Amo, El, of Mexicans, 220, 221.
Andalusian, an, miraculous deliverance of, 186.
Angel, in Picture, 131.
Angels, apparition of, 182, 183; their longing to wait on Mary and gaze on God, 184; tutelar, of New World, 262.
Anglo-Saxons malign Latins, 272.
Annals, Tlaxcalan, bear witness, 78; historian Sanchez in accord with, 93.
Antícoli, Father, S. J., an authority, v; vigorous pen of, 11; on Guadalupan conversions, 204; on Patronage, 238; on certainty of Guadalupan facts, 282.
Apostolic, Authority, exercise of, in favor of Guadalupe, 20, 248; Process, Guadalupan, 93, 95.
Apparitions, Guadalupan, certain, 1, 282; as regarded by Catholics, 2, 3; in themselves, 15; Guadalupan, not to be controverted, 26; ecclesiastically undeniable, 30; stopped oppression of Indians, 64, 67; details of five, 99–112; proved by miracles, 173.
Arizona, under Guadalupan Patronage, 249.
Assumption, how celebrated in Mexico, 277, 278.
Atotonilco, standard of, 71.

INDEX.

Augustine, St., 115.
Augustinians, in Mexico, 205.
Authors, Mexican, v; Guadalupan, refute all objections, 7; various but unanimous, 93.
Averardi, Archbishop, present Pro-delegate, encourages Guadalupan devotion, 42.
Ayate, of Juan Diego, 117, 118, 119.
Azcapotzalco, canticle of chief of, 80.

BALLOTS, cast for Guadalupan Patronage, 236.
Baltimore, decrees of, on patronage, 244; jurisdiction of, 249.
Banner, of Guadalupe, 10, 268, 269.
Baptism, of natives, 191, 199, 200, 201, 202, 203, 204.
Bartolache, Dr., 10.
Basilica, Lateran, at Guadalupe, 143.
Becerra Tanco, Father, an authority, v; narrative of, 77; Guadalupan historian, 96, 97; on preservation of Picture, 121; on copying it, 128; on name—Guadalupe, 130; on miracles, 154.
Belzunce, Bishop, 163.
Benedict XIV., a Guadalupan authority, vi; approval of, 16; honor of glorifying American Virgin reserved to, 21; liturgical acts of, 22; venerates copy of Picture, 23; impressed by Guadalupan story, 24; Brief of, on Patronage, Office and Feast, 25; sealed New World Sanctuary, 28; quoted remarkable words on Picture, 115; made Shrine a Lateran Basilica, 143.
Benedict XIII., created Collegiate Chapter, 17; granted indulgences for *Feast of the Apparitions*, 28.

Bernard, St., 189.
Book of Sensation, 35.
Boturini, documents of, 77; manuscripts and labors of, 81, 82.
Bouquet, American, 5.
Breviary, lessons of, 37.
Brief, of Benedict XIV., 25; a Guadalupan charter, 26; probatory force of, 27, 28, 29; of Paul III., against oppression of Indians, 193.
Bull, or Brief?, 25; of Partition, 192.
Bustamente, blustering of, 154.

CABRERA, *American Marvel* of, 4; picture by, presented to Benedict XIV., 22; observations of, on Picture, 117; commission report and book of, 120, 123; calls Picture an *Immaculate Conception*, 131; works of, at Well Chapel, 144.
California, under Guadalupan Patronage, 249.
Campos, Dr., quoted, 5.
Canada, represented at Coronation, 257; Catholics of, 272; prelate from, on Guadalupe, 283.
Candles, miraculously lit by Picture, 179.
Canonical Hours, those bound to, must recite Guadalupan Office, 25.
Canonization, of miraculous images, opposed, 21; of Guadalupan title, 29.
Carmona y Valle, Dr., medical testimony of, 166.
Carrillo y Perez, *American Bouquet* of, 5; note of, on Indian Narrative, 100; on Picture, 115.
Carvajal, Don Antonio, escape of, 175.
Castilla, D , silver-leg cure of, 181.
Castillo, historian, 12.
Cathedral, of City of Mexico, 240.
Cemetery, at Guadalupe, 145.

INDEX. 289

Certainty, of Guadalupan facts, 1, 282.
Charity, in Mexico, 225-230.
Charles V., letters to, 84, 194; rebuked by Zumárraga, 193; *New Laws* of, 194.
Charter, of Guadalupe, 26; of Mexicans, 194.
Chilapa, synod of, 57; Bishop and people of, to their Queen, 257.
Children, treatment of, in Mexico, 228, 229.
Children's Pilgrimage, 87, 157.
Chivalry, Guadalupan, 6; of faith, 67; of devotion, 270, 284.
Church, pointing the way, vi; submission to, vi; definitions of, demanded by quibblers, 7; does not define in matters of private revelation, 26; judgment of, on Guadalupe, 30; daily life of, best guide, 58; sanction of, historical evidence, 74; strength of, in Western World, 271; share of, in colonisation, 272; legislation of, supposes foundation of truth, 282.
Church-building, significance of, 133; in Mexico, 134; no hindrance to industry, 136.
Clavigero, historian, on Picture, 114; on transformed Tepeyac, 231.
Clement IX, granted Guadalupan jubilee, 17; friendly to cause, 21; on Guadalupe and Immaculate Conception, 245.
Colima, Bishop of, on Coronation, 254.
College, of Sts. Peter and Paul, 80.
Colloquy, of Juan Diego with Our Lady, 103.
Colonisation, Catholic, 272, 273; where best, 274.
Colors, in Picture, 115, 118, 121, 124.
Communion, of Guadalupan Mass, 41.

Communions, of Juan Diego, 213; numerous at Guadalupe, 222; at Coronation, 266, 267; many asked, 281.
Comparisons, favorable, to Guadalupe, 282, 283.
Concord of Bishops, Guadalupan fruit praised by Leo XIII., 36.
Confraternities, early, at Shrine, 16.
Congregations, Guadalupan, 17.
Continent, this, visited by, Mother of God, 1; Church of, 4; Apparitions and Picture for whole of, 4; acclaiming its Queen, 257, 262; great facts on, to notice, 280, 281.
Convent, at Guadalupe, 141; miracle at St. Catherine's, 164.
Conversion, of natives, 191, 196, 198; fundamental reason of, 197; God's way of, 198; before and after Apparitions, 200, 203.
Coronation of Picture, ordered by Leo XIII., 36; evoked Bishops' love of the Holy Mother, 47, 48; letters concerning, 51; in 1740 already conceded, 81; meaning of, 251; epoch-making event, 252; moral effects, of, 255; celebration of, 259-269; a lesson, 270.
Cortes, 62, 194, 195.
Councils, first Mexican, 90, 205.
Critics, of Mexico, 136.
Cross, worn by Our Lady, 218; love of in Mexico, 219; folly of, 275.
Crown, of Holy Mary of Guadalupe, 256; to be filial, 263.

DALGAIRNS, Father, quoted, 18, 165.
Dávalos, Archbishop, 159.
Dávila, historian, 23.
Dedication of Shrine, 138, 140, 142.
Devotion, Guadalupan, character of, 6; recommended by Leo

XIII., 36, 41; practised by all classes, 57, 58; reformed society, 89; drew the whole land, 92; spirit and exemplars of, 150; not miracle-seeking, 152; miraculously preached, 182; moulding character, 208; drawing to the Cross, 219; to Our Lord's Person, 221, 222; communicative, 223; practical, 255; instructive for Americans, 275; for all English-speaking Catholics, 281; free from extravagance, 283; remedial, 284.

Diaz, Bernal, bears witness, 91, 154.

Dicitur, in papal documents and Guadalupan Office, 26, 27.

Dominicans in Mexico, 205.

Donations. for Shrine, 140, 141, 142, 148; generous, of five prelates, 149.

Durango, Archbishop of, 149.

ECCLESIASTICAL standing of Guadalupe, vi; life and Guadalupe, 54.

Effect, of opposition, increased devotion, 12.

Elizabeth, St., and Juan Diego, 211.

England, last Catholic Queen of, 22.

English speaking Catholics, and Spanish-speaking, 271; not remarkable for folly of the Cross, 275; lose fine flour of devotion, 281.

Enriques, Viceroy, interference of, 91.

Episcopate of Mexico, corroborating tradition, 1; answering objections, 35; relations of, with Holy Mary of Guadalupe, 43; formula of belief of, 45; piety and zeal of, 47, 53; dignity and formality, 51; exercising authority in favor of Guadalupe, 55; characteristic generosity of, 149.

European, excesses, 197; colonisation, 274.

Evangelicals, in, Mexico, 11.

Exposition of Blessed Sacrament, frequency of, 222.

Exquisitio Historica, 35.

Extermination of natives, where the Church was not, 273.

Extravagance, no appearance of, at Guadalupe, 283.

Extremadura, statue, unlike Picture, 130.

FAITH, rests on Revelation, 2; may be exercised on private revelations, 2; what is not of, 6; attacks on Mexican people's, 8; connection of, in Mexico, with Guadalupe, 36, 37; protestation of, in *Miracle*, 55; evidence of, in Church-building, 134; overruling in New Spain, 135; strong reality in Mexico, 223; exercised in Coronation, 253. 261, 263; sincerity of, in United States, 275; inherited, uncontaminated, 281; in Guadalupan practices, 284.

Feast, Guadalupan, indulgences for, 17; liturgically raised, 20; to be made obligatory, 21; decreed by Benedict XIV, 25, 29, 248; vowed by nation, 234.

Feasts of Our Lady, in Mexico, 277.

Flood, deliverance from, 157.

Florencia, Father, S. J., an authority, v; belief of, 12; on Indian customs, 79; on Picture, 115, 215; on Guadalupan *Via Sacra*, 146; on miracles, 155, 181; on Juan Diego and Maria Lucia, 209; on the love of the Cross, 219.

Franciscans in Mexico, 205.

Fuenclara, Viceroy, arrested Boturini, 81.

INDEX. 291

GARCÍA de Mendoza, had Guadalupan Acts, 88.
García Montaño, saved at sea, 177.
Ghent, Peter of, baptizing Indians, 203.
Gil Blas, on Guadalupe, 61.
Glory, Conception in Grace and, 130.
Gospel, of Guadalupan Mass, 40.
Gradual, of Guadalupan Mass, 40.
Granado, silver-head cure of, 180.
Gregory, St., thirty-three Masses of, 281.
Guadalajara, Archbishop of, 48; his translation of Leo XIII.'s verses, 49; his part in Coronation, 260.
Guadalupe (Gwa-da-loó-pay), too little noticed by English-speaking Catholics, 31; a title of Our Lady, 4; called "American Bouquet," 5; now asserting its claims, 5; well head of Mexican piety, 11; combination against, 11; name insisted on by Benedict XIV, 27; what it is to Mexico, 59; Order of, 70; bulwark of faith and freedom, 72; place naturally injurious to paintings, 124; name explained, 129, 130; town of, 145; support of Catholics, 206; centre of happy piety, 223; suited to all, 283.
Guadalupan solemnity in Rome, 168.
Guarantee, Roman, held by Guadalupe, 19.
Guiridí y Alcocer, treatise of, 5.
Gusman, persecuting Zumárraga, 86.

HERESY, refutation of, 221; encouraged, 226; mimicking Christianity, 281.
Hidalgo, Father, standard of, 64; true Mexican, 70; inscription on banner of, 71; in Coronation, 269.

Hierarchy, and Guadalupe, 43; virtues of, 53; Guadalupan correspondence of, with Holy See, 95.
Hill Chapel, 144.
Historical grounds of devotion, 73.
History, so-called, 7; Guadalupan, quoted by Benedict XIV, 29; relation of, to special revelations, 74; only complete, 75; mock, 237; advances in American, 273; compendium of, 274; Guadalupan, tested, 282; free from extravagance, 283.
Holy Mary of Guadalupe, in Catholic life and liturgy, 1; domain of, 5; Roman Chapel, 17; chosen Patroness, 22; title of Mother of God, 25; indulgenced invocation of, 42; viceroys consecrated to, 45; bishops devout to, 54; whole people in relation with, 59; description of *Gil Blas* writer, 63; loved by every Mexican, 64, 65; in her Picture, 116, 129, 130; throne for, 140; attracting the pious, in life and death, 145; happy who serve her, 182; forming women of Mexico, 214-218; refuge of nation, 235; belonging to the Indians, 139, 241; hold of, on United States, 249; to be declared Patroness of all America, 250.
Holy Office, reprehends opposition to Guadalupe, 14.
Holy See, sanctioning Guadalupan usages, 1; believes tradition, 16, 19; attitude of, towards new devotions, 18; providing for New World, 192.
Hospitals, abound in Mexico, 227.

IBARRA, Dr., quoted, 53, 198, 206.
Ibarra, painter, and other masters, 121; on copying Picture, 128.
Ildefonso, St., University of, 205.

Immaculate Conception, 130, 131; unique memorial of, 186; Apparitions, of that mystery, 245.
Incarnation, saving power of, 66; grasped by natives, 66; consequences of believing, 251.
Independence, and faith, safe, 49; Labarum of, 64; struggle for, 70; *grito* of, 268.
Indians, called irrational, 63; first Guadalupan writers, 75; records of, 79; testimony of, in Apostolic Process, 94, 212; a source of their civilization, 138; at translation of Picture, 142; promised aid at Guadalupe, 151; marvelous escape of one, 180; not unworthy of credit, 183; delivered from power of demons, 186, 189; conversion of, 191; characteristics of, 196; eagerness for Baptism of, 201; model of, 208; love of, for Our Lady, 241; at Coronation, 261; flourished under Catholic rule, 273, 274; knowledge and reading of, 278, 279.
Indulgences, Guadalupan, 17, 25, 28; granted by present Prodelegate, 42; for Protestation of Faith in *Miracle*, 57; probative force of, 58.
Information, Canonical, 12.
Italian, at Guadalupe, 81.
Italians, jealous for Loretto, 21.
Italy, Guadalupan Office extended to, 18.
Iturbide, Emperor, 70.

JACINTA, Sister, miraculous cure of 164.
Jesuits, characteristics of, v; suppression of, 80; expulsion of, 169; as historians, 189; as teachers, 205.
John, St., 225.
John Damascene, St., 182.
Juan Andrés, Indian testimony of, 172.

Juan Bernardino, sickness of, 107; cure of, 109, 112; death of, 213.
Juan Diego, favored Indian, 34; mentioned in Breviary lessons, 38; cloak or *tilma* of, 55; called —son, by Our Lady, 63; representing America, 69; will of relative of, 78; circumstances of, 98; in the revelations, 99–111; commemorated in Shrine, 150; model of Mexican men, 208; character and mission of, 209–214; represented at coronation, 261.
Jurisdiction, in Patronage, 249.
Juridical Acts, Guadalupan, 87, 88, 93.
Juridical Process, on Guadalupan miracle in Rome, 170.

KNOWLEDGE, of sacred things, among Mexican peasants, 278, 279.

LABASTIDA, Archbishop, in exile, 46; commemorated in Shrine, 150; suggested Coronation, 283.
Lamp, falling on worshipper's head, 178.
Lamps, Saints', in Mexico, 279.
Las Casas, 61; denunciations of, 67; patron of Indians, 193.
Lasso de la Vega, Father, 76.
Laws, New, against slavery, 194.
Leo XIII., Guadalupan authority, vi; surpassing predecessors, 16; Guadalupan acts of, 18, 33; characteristics of, 31; an audience with, 32; letter of, 35, 254; dear to Mexicans, 41, 42; Guadalupan verses of, 48, 148; services of, commemorated in Shrine, 150.
Leon, Gomez de, testimony of, 89.
Liberators, real, of Western World, 193, 196.
Liberalism, present Mexican, 268.
Libraries, Mexican, examined, 7.

INDEX. 293

Linares, Archbishop of, quoted, 69.
Lopez, Father, S. J., envoy to Rome, 22, 245, 248.
Lorenzana, Cardinal, statement of, 78; Guadalupan preaching of, 88.
Loretto, Lourdes, and Guadalupe, 74, 283.
Louis, St., 6, 266.

MADONNAS, of great painters, different from Picture, 116; miraculous, 125, 168; American, in Rome, 169.
Manning, Cardinal, quoted, 15.
Manso, Archbishop, 159.
Manuscripts, native, fate of, 80, 82.
Maps, Indian, record *Miracle*, 75, 79; perpetuated tradition, 88.
Maria, Lucia, 90, 209.
Marseilles, plague of, 163.
Martin, St., College of, founded by Indians, 205.
Martyrs, Mexican, 206.
Matrimony, among native Christians, 200, 202.
Maximilian, and Order of Guadalupe, 70.
Mendieta, on conversion and marriage of Indians, 202.
Mexico, republic of, contains Tepeyac, 4; not whole Guadalupan domain, 5; Church of, faithful and numerous, 58; fighting for religion, 71; visibly Catholic, 134, 135; in festival, 61, 142; municipality of City of, 233; population of, 274; spiritual instincts of, 281.
Mexicans, true, Guadalupan, 59, 268; generosity and zeal of, 140, 141, 147, 148, 256; all, give to Guadalupe, 149, 224; take miracles as matter of course, 152; lastingly and universally Catholic, 206, 207; definite in belief, 220; united in pious practices, 222; charity of, 225–230; magnanimity of, 253; loyalty of, to Our Lady, 257; given to folly of the Cross, 276; characteristic practices, 277–281.
Mezquia, Father, testimony of, 83.
Mier, Dr., retracted sermon of, 10.
Mining Laws, in Spanish America, 195.
Miracles, modern, 6; Guadalupan, 88; mentioned by historian of Cortes, 91, 154; evidence of, in Picture, 118; first at Tepeyac, 139, 149, 157; to be expected at Guadalupe, 151; why not oftener recorded, 153; called "innumerable," 154; mentioned in Office, 155; various, 157-190; Guadalupan, in Rome, 166, 169; none unworthy, 167; conclusions concerning, 173; moral, 189.
Miraculous pictures, not exempt from ravages of time, 125.
Missionaries, necessary, 192; letter of, 196; first efforts of, 199; fruitful labors of, 204; soon sent out by Mexico, 205.
Moctezuma, family of, 76; time following, 204.
Monta, Catalina de, cured at well, 179.
Montufar, Archbishop, arraigned by refractory preacher, 9; had Information taken, 88; preaching and decrees of, 89, 90; improved the Shrine, 139.
Montufar, J. J., on Immaculate Conception, 130.
Morelos, Father, decrees of, 71.
Mother of God, appeared on this continent, 1, 282; visiting poor wayfarers, 15; Mother of the Mexicans, 23, 140; called Holy Mary of Guadalupe, 25; new title for, in liturgy, 28; love of, in Mexican faith and morality,

44; wearing Mexico's crown, 49; Mother of the Indians, 63; native Catholics cling to, 72; wishes of, in Apparitions, 100; synonymous with *Guadalupe*, 130; effective prayer to, 156; Our Lady of America, 249, 285.

Motive, of Guadalupan devotion, demonstrated, 18.

Motolinia, the poor one, 200.

Moya y Contreras, Archbishop, 90.

Muñoz, memorial of, 9; advocate of Pistoian revolters, 10.

Museum, Mexican, parchments of 82.

Music, abounds in Mexico, 268; marvellous, at Guadalupe, 184.

NAME, *Guadalupe*, to first-born daughters, 64; origin of, 112, 129; sweet and powerful, 235; pious reduplications of, 277.

Napoleon, in Spain, 71.

Narrative, Indian, 98; a flawless gem, 283.

Nation, Mexican, and Guadalupe, 59; born at Tepeyac, 64; noble origin of, 65; existence and independence of, due to Guadalupe, 68, 70, 72; blessed at Tepeyac, 191; sworn Patronage of, 244; piously enthusiastic, 270.

Nevada, under Guadalupan Patronage, 249.

Newman, Cardinal, on certain miracles, 167.

New Mexico, under Guadalupan Patronage, 249.

New Spain, Office accorded to, 17; Guadalupan demands of, 20, 21; Patroness and Protectress of, 25; ecclesiastical wealth of, 135; troubled history of, 45; miracles in, 155; blessed through Guadalupe, 191; quickly Christianised, 205; attitude of, before Our Lady, 232; extent of, 248.

New World, temple of, 5; sanctuary and patronage of, 28; in Guadalupan Office, 39; best material treasure of, 132; evangelized by Rome and Spain, 192; in special relations with the Mother of God, 249; strength of Church in, 271; Our Lady's chosen Title in 285.

Nicholas, St., church of, in Rome, 18, 169.

Nicoselli, Roman Prelate, on Guadalupe, 246.

Non-Catholics, few in Mexico, 274; unreasoning, 167.

Non fecit taliter, considered **arrogant**, 21; appropriated to Mexico by Benedict XIV., 23; influencing New Spain, 233.

Novenas, Mexican, 142, 265, 278.

Nuns, Capuchin, at Guadalupe, 144; church of, 258.

OAXACA, Bishop of, authenticating a miracle, 160.

Offertory, of Guadalupan Mass. 41.

Office, special, accorded, 17; sixth lesson summary of, 33; new lessons, 37; references of, to America, 40, 41; imposed by Benedict XIV., 248.

Opponents of Guadalupe, 7; not Catholics, 8, 26; unsuccessful, 11, 12; severely reprehended by Rome, 14.

Opposition, little and tainted, 8, 9; indirectly useful, 12, 13; recent, bitter, 34, 35, 255.

Oratorians, in Mexico, 205.

Orphanages, comparatively little needed in Mexico, 228.

Ortega, Archbishop-Viceroy, begging for Guadalupe, 146, 41.

INDEX. 295

PAINTERS, commission of, 118; declaration of, on Picture, 119, 120.
Painting, different kinds in Picture, 121.
Paintings, in Well Chapel, 144; in Shrine, 149.
Patrick, St., and Zumárraga, 85.
Patronage, Guadalupan, sworn for all North America? 5; actual oath, 237, 244; erected under Benedict XIV., 17, 25; supplication for, 22; over Kingdoms or Provinces, 29; vow of, stops plague, 162; meant much, 232; advocated by civil authorities, 233; celebration of, 238-242; as decreed by Benedict XIV., 248.
Pavon, Sacristan, cure of child of, 179.
Pensil Americano, v.
Peralta, testimony of, 92, 154.
Philip II., correspondence with, 90.
Picture, facts concerning, certain, 1, 282; the "American Marvel," 4; "illuminates this hemisphere," 5; miracles through, 12; influence of, in stopping plague, 21; copy of, to Benedict XIV., 22; marvellous as it professes, 33; ordered crowned by Leo XIII., 36; "made famous in its very origin," 41; everywhere in Mexico, 59; labarum of independence, 64, 71; seen to be undecaying, 73; celebrated in Indian chants, 80; formation of, 110; apparition and veneration of, 111; name of, given by Our Lady, 112; what Mexicans say of, 114; expressions used by Benedict XIV., 115; manifests supernatural origin, 116; 'canvas' of, described, 117; colors, 118; scientific examinations of, 119, 123; rough treatment and accidents, 126; copying, 127; description of, 128, 131, 132; name accounted for, 129; of Immaculate Conception, 130, 245; treasure of Western World, 132; extreme reverence for, 141; enshrining and translation, 142; always centre of attraction, 147: brought into suffering city, 159; miracle through copy of, 165; another copy proved miraculous in Rome, 171; rays from, light altar candles, 179; reflects all womanly virtues, 215; showing the Cross, 218; special guardians of, 240; tenderness of Mexican affection for, 257, 258; actually here, 281; influence of, 284.
Pius VI., extending Guadalupan privileges, 18; miracles in reign of, 171.
Pius IX., had Roman chapel dedicated to Holy Mary of Guadalupe, 18, 168.
Plague, ravages of, stopped by devotion to Picture, 21, 157, 161, 233.
Plancarte, Bishop, Abbot, 150, 254.
Plebiscite, of Mexico, 252.
Pocito, church, 144; miracles, 172, 173, 180.
Poor, the treatment of, in Mexico, 226.
Popes, on Guadalupe, 16, 19, 31.
Possession, demoniacal, prevented, 186, 188.
Preacher, refractory, 9.
Prejudices, shaken off, 272.
Preparation, of canvas, 118.
Preservation of Picture, 122, 124, 238.
Press, Mexican, examined, 7; anonymous communications to, 11; favorable to Guadalupe, 60; first in Western World, 84; reports of Coronation, 259, 260, 266.

INDEX.

Pretext, for dropping practice of religion, 11.
Printing, Zumárraga's, 84; in Mexican religious affairs, 280.
Privilege, of Guadalupan Office, in Spanish dominions and Italy, 17; in Florida and Louisiana, 249.
Prodigies of Mary, 168.
Profile, in copying Picture, 128.
Protesta de Fe, 55.
Protestant Associations, efforts of, 72.
Puebla, Bishop Vargas of, quoted, 3, 68, 282; miracle in, 164.

QUEEN, Our Lady, in the divine maternity, 251; of Mexico, in right and deed, 252; claims to sovereignty, 255; of Western World, 257, 262, 264.
Querétero, Bishop of, his gift, 149; zeal of, 265.
Quintero, Father, his sister's cure, 160.

REBOA, Father, testifying to Guadalupan miracle in Rome, 169.
Recuperation, of plundered Church, 11.
Refuges, abound in Mexico, 227.
Reid, Christian, an opinion of, 283.
Religion, supernatural, exclusive, 6.
Religious Orders, first friends of natives, 205.
Retreats and missions, as alms, 280.
Revelation, to Prophets and Apostles, 2; treasure of the Church, 15.
Revelations, special, significance of, 4; object of, 6; Church's view of, 15.
Reynolds, portraits by, retouched, 125.

Ricards, Bishop, quoted, 19.
Rio Grande, Church above and below the, 272.
Rites, Congregation of, its Guadalupan Acts, 24, 247; reviewing Guadalupan history, 34; new decrees of, 35.
Rodrigo de la Cruz, saved by *su paisana*, 178.
Rome, aroused by opposition to American devotion, 14; and Guadalupe, 16; favorable, 18; treatment of whole question by, 20; Guadalupan miracle there, 166; of the Americas, 240.
Rosary, causeway to Guadalupe, 146.
Roses, miraculous, 34, 109, 110, 111.
Royal Audience, Guadalupan, 237.

SAIL Memorial, 144.
Saints' Lamps, in Mexico, 279.
Salazars, their testimony, 89.
Salvatierra, Viceroy, donation of, 140.
Sanchez, Father, book of, 93; on the Picture, 115, 117; on Immaculate Conception, 130; on miracles, 155.
San Louis Potosí, Bishop of, his gift to Guadalupe, 149; his piety, 266.
Santa Anna, President, and Guadalupe, 70.
Santa Cruz, college of, 76.
Sarmiento y Heredia, Dr., quoted, 69, 190.
Sartorio, Dr., quoted, 13.
Sartorius, German Commissioner, 228.
Satan, baffled by Picture, 186.
Sceptre and Rose, from Chilapa, 257.
Scholarship, test of, 272, 273.
Scientists, on Picture, 119, 123; on Roman miracle, 170.

Secret Societies, efforts of, 72.
Sermon, for Coronation, 53, 262, 263, 264.
Servants, treatment of, in Mexico, 229.
Sforza, Alexander, furnishing crowns for Our Lady, 251.
Shrine, referred to by Leo XIII., 36; vigils and retreats there, 45; claimed by each diocese, 46; legal recognitions of, 70; Indian celebrations at, 79; called *Holy House*, 91, 145; demanded by the Mother of God, 101; place of, 111; history, 136-150; Citadel and Cenacle, 139; Collegiate and Lateran Basilica, 143; recent renovation of, 147, 254; benefactors commemorated, 150; Mexican recourse to, 153; most famous of Western World, 230, 283.
Sign, demanded, 105; given, 110, 111.
Sigüenza y Góngora, D., testimony of, 77; manuscript collection of, 80.
Silence, negative argument, 9; stock in trade of objectors, 11.
Sinoesio, Mrs., miraculous escape of, 155.
Slavery, banned by Holy See, 193.
Solidarity, of Mexican women with Holy Mary of Guadalupe, 218; of American Catholics, 271; of Mexican pious people, 280.
Somaglia, Cardinal, decree of, 169, 171.
Sonora, letter of Bishop of, to Our Lady, 50.
Spain, cause of, taken up by Mexico, 71; helping evangelization, 192, 274.
Spaniards, going to Shrine, 12; faith of, 67; in America, 274.
Spanish, dominions and office, 17; mining regulations, 195; monarchs, anxious to be saved, 192; bishops, liberators of Western World, 193.
Special devotions, appointed way, 284.
Synod, of Chilapa, a statute of, 57, 58.

TABASCO. Bishop of, on Coronation, 253.
Tallepietra, Father, testifies in Rome, 170.
Tehuacan, Indian Easter there, 203.
Tepeyac, American, 4; splendors of Virgin of, 6; pilgrimage to, desired by Benedict XIV., 24; home of Mexican nation, 64; star of, 65; signification of, 98; Shrines to Virgin of, 136, 137; buildings on and around, 144; place of marvels, 154; America's refuge, 190; beneficent transformation of, 230; seat of Holy Mary's power, 239.
Tescoco, descendant of Kings of, 77.
Texas, and Patronage, 249.
Thomas, St., 2.
Tiempo, El, Catholic daily paper, v.
Tlatelolco, Church of, 98, 107, 108.
Tlaxcalan, annals, 78.
Tobias, St., Way of, 278.
Tolpetlac, village, 98, 102.
Toribio, Father, on conversions, 200, 203.
Tornel, Deputy, Guadalupan work of, 93.
Torquemada, historian, 12.
Torre, Dr. de la, testimony of, 88.
Tradition, best guide, 7; true sense of, 75.
Transito, El, of the Blessed Virgin, 181, 277.
Tullantzinco, Guadalupan memorial at, 176.

TWELFTH-day, celebration of, 46; of December, greatest Mexican feast, 61, 191; in 1531, 107; in Mexican vow, 234, 235; court holiday, 237.

UNITED States, patronage of, 244; Guadalupan territory in, 248, 249; prelates of, at Coronation, 262; comparative population of, 274; Catholics of, may give and take example, 275, 281; profit by Guadalupe, 284.
University, of Mexico, manuscripts of, 79; suppression of, 80; early foundation of, 204; second Mexican, 205.
Urban VIII., decrees of, 29, 236.
Uribe, Dr., testimony of, 79.
Utah, under Guadalupan patronage, 249.

VALDERAMA, Father, cure of, 151, 181.
Valeriano, historian of Guadalupe, 76.
Vatican Council, Guadalupan feast, during, 168.
Velasco, Viceroy, friend of miners, 195; noble words of, 196.
Vera, Bishop, an authority, v; quoted, 6, 26; vigorous pen of, 11; name—Guadalupe explained by, 130.
Verdugo Licentiate, on Guadalupe, 68.
Veronica's *Holy Face*, reminder of, 129.
Veytia, Sister Mariana, 144.
Viceroys, at Shrine, 45.
Villanueva, Vicar, verified miracles, 181.

Visions, acts of Omnipotence, 15.
Visitation, connection of Guadalupe with mystery, 40.
Vizarron, Archbishop-Viceroy, and Patronage, 234, 235, 243.

WELL, at Guadalupe, 110; Church of the, 144; cures there, 172.
Wills, corroborative of tradition, 78.
Women, not admitted to mines, 195; of Mexico, 214-218; at the Shrine, 224; giving Crowns to Our Lady, 256.
Wonders, American, 3; in our religion, 15; at Tepeyac, fruitful, 191.

XIMENES, protector of Indians, 193; mining enactments of, 195.

YUCATAN, letter of Bishop of, 52; his generosity, 149; Coronation sermon, 262.

ZACATECAS, gift of Bishop of, 149.
Zumárraga, of holy memory, 34; mentioned in Breviary lessons, 38; illtreated by enemies of natives, 67; lost Guadalupan letter of, 83; position in Mexico, 84; benefactor of Western World, 85; charges against, 87; with Juan Diego, 102; inaugurating Shrine, 138; commemorated there, 150; advocate of Indians, 193; on Cortez, 194; on missions, 200.

www.ingramcontent.com/pod-product-compliance
Lightning Source LLC
Chambersburg PA
CBHW031902220426
43663CB00006B/731